*Lorraine H*

# A RAISIN I

## AND

# THE SIGN IN SIDNEY BRUSTEIN'S WINDOW

Lorraine Hansberry touched the taproots of American life, as only a very few playwrights ever can, in *A Raisin in the Sun*, the play that made her in 1959, at twenty-nine, the youngest American, the fifth woman, and the first black playwright to win the Best Play of the Year Award of the New York Drama Critics. In *Raisin*, wrote James Baldwin, "never before in the entire history of the American theater had so much of the truth of black people's lives been seen on the stage." Published and produced worldwide in over thirty languages and in thousands of productions nationally, the play "changed American theater forever" and became an American classic, as *The New York Times* summarized recently. In 1961, Hansberry's film adaptation of the play won a Cannes Festival Award and was nominated Best Screenplay; in the 1970s it was adapted into a Tony Award–winning musical; and in the 1980s a major resurgence began with revivals at a dozen regional theaters and the 1989 *American Playhouse* production for television of the complete play, unabridged for the first time. In the 1990s, the same acclaimed reception of Hansberry's classic play continues.

On January 12, 1965, during the run of her second play, *The Sign in Sidney Brustein's Window*, cancer claimed Lorraine Hansberry. She was thirty-four. "Her creative literary ability and her profound grasp of the deep social issues confronting the world today," predicted Martin Luther King, Jr., on her death, "will remain an inspiration to generations yet unborn." These words have proved prophetic as more and more of her work has become known.

*To Be Young, Gifted and Black*, a portrait of Hansberry in her own words, was the longest-running off-Broadway drama of 1969; it has been staged in every state of the Union, recorded, filmed, televised, and expanded into the widely read "informal autobiography" of the same title (not to be confused with the play), while the title itself (from her last speech) has entered the language.

*Les Blancs* (The Whites), her drama of revolution in Africa, presented posthumously on Broadway, received the votes of six critics for Best American Play of 1970 and, since its acclaimed revival at the Arena Stage in Washington, D.C. in 1988—followed by a production at Boston's Huntington Theatre—began a resurgence of other productions into the 1990s.

In her plays Hansberry illuminated the extraordinary lives and aspirations of "ordinary" people—black and white, American, African, and European—confronting the most fundamental challenges and choices of the century. Her published works include the abovementioned plays, *To Be Young, Gifted and Black: Lorraine Hansberry in Her Own Words*; *Les Blancs: The Last Collected Plays* (including *The Drinking Gourd* and *What Use Are Flowers?*); and *The Movement*, a photohistory of the Civil Rights struggle. Excerpts from her speeches and interviews are recorded in the Caedmon album *Lorraine Hansberry Speaks Out: Art and the Black Revolution*.

# A RAISIN IN THE SUN

## AND

# THE SIGN IN SIDNEY BRUSTEIN'S WINDOW

■

## LORRAINE HANSBERRY

Robert Nemiroff, editor
With a New Foreword by
Jewell Handy Gresham Nemiroff,
a Note by Robert Nemiroff, and
Critical Essays by Amiri Baraka and Frank Rich

VINTAGE BOOKS
A DIVISION OF RANDOM HOUSE, INC.
NEW YORK

Library of Congress Cataloging-in-Publication Data
Hansberry, Lorraine, 1930–1965.
[Raisin in the sun]
A raisin in the sun, and ; The sign in Sidney Brustein's window /
by Lorraine Hansberry ; Robert Nemiroff, editor ; with notes by Robert Nemiroff and critical essays by Amiri Baraka and Frank Rich ; with a new foreword by Jewell Gresham Nemiroff. — 1st Vintage Books ed.
p.   cm.
ISBN 0-679-75531-4
1. Afro-American families—Illinois—Chicago—Drama. 2. Jewish men—New York (N.Y.)—Drama. I. Nemiroff, Robert. II. Hansberry, Lorraine, 1930–1965. Sign in Sidney Brustein's window. III. Title.
IV. Title: Sign in Sidney Brustein's window.
812' .54—dc20     95-8917
CIP

*Manufactured in the United States of America*

23rd Printing

# CONTENTS

# FOREWORD TO THE VINTAGE EDITION

by Jewell Handy Gresham Nemiroff

When Lorraine Hansberry died in 1965 at the age of thirty-four, she left behind an undated journal entry subsequently widely quoted in prefatory material to various publications of her works: "*If anything happens—before 'tis done—may I trust that all commas and periods will be placed and someone will complete my thoughts.*"

The playwright must have known that in the person of the literary executor to whom she entrusted her life's work—her former husband and creative collaborator—someone was already in place to begin the process.

Robert Nemiroff died in 1991. He survived Lorraine Hansberry by twenty-six and a half years, during which period (except for completion and production of his own play, *Postmark Zero*, on which he was working at the time of her death) there was never a single moment when he was not meticulously editing or seeking to publish or produce one or another creation from the impressive body of work this artist produced in her brief lifetime.

He was well aware that a playwright with a single critically acclaimed play—and one other playing on Broadway to mixed reviews at the time of her death—was hardly likely to be remembered unless it could be made known that the range, depth, and breadth of the artist encompassed far more than the promise reflected in the two works seen by the public. That the artist's first play made her, at twenty-nine, the youngest American, the fifth woman, and the first African American to win the coveted "Best American Play" award from the New York Drama Critics Circle made little difference even in a Broadway season that included new plays by Tennessee Williams and Archibald MacLeish, and a revival of a Eugene O'Neill work.

Robert Nemiroff knew very well that his was the important task of making certain—in the face of the loss of Lorraine Hansberry—that the American stage did not also lose the rich lore of the African American experience and the profound vision of the young Chicago-born playwright.

Bob Nemiroff's contribution to the Hansberry legacy now represents a part of dramatic and literary history. His illuminating introductions to the writer's dramas, essays, fiction, speeches, and poetry for the reading public and the careful notes he provided for the acting versions of her dramas are invaluable; his critical analyses and explorations with scholars, critics, students, and others, insightful and fascinating.

For the twenty-fifth anniversary of *A Raisin in the Sun* (produced by the Roundabout Theatre in New York City, followed by a run at the Kennedy Center in Washington, D.C. and the PBS *American Playhouse* television production), Nemiroff restored scenes and lines cut for various reasons, including economic considerations, when the play was originally produced. The expanded twenty-fifth-anniversary edition was published in 1987.

In this new Vintage edition (1995) of *A Raisin in the Sun* and *The Sign in Sidney Brustein's Window*, Robert Nemiroff's Notes, like all of his prologues to Hansberry's works, continue to provide contextual history.

The additional critical essays prefacing *A Raisin in the Sun* are "An Appreciation: *A Raisin in the Sun*, the 25th Anniversary" by Frank Rich, former longtime drama critic of *The New York Times* (presently *Times* editorial columnist) and Amiri Baraka, the fiery African American poet, playwright, and critic, whose own prolific contributions to African American and American drama and letters during the activism of the 1960s were foreshadowed by Hansberry in her 1959 play.

Baraka, one of the leading figures in the Black Arts Movement of the 1960s, for a time characterized *A Raisin in the Sun* as "bourgeois" drama. Nemiroff found it particularly gratifying that the historical moment came when some of the same radical voices were raised in affirmation of the play and author.

Frank Rich was the first major critic to begin to consistently refer to *A Raisin in the Sun* as an American classic. On the twenty-fifth-anniversary production, *The Washington Post* followed by placing the play in "the inner circle, along with *Death of a Salesman, Long Day's Journey into Night* and *The Glass Menagerie.*"

In the current era, it can be clearly seen that—aside from the individual mastery of their form by the playwrights—one aspect that all these plays have in common is the conflict between American families and the society in which they live. Within this context, all three plays are about the shape and substance of American dreams.

While Eugene O'Neill's autobiographical masterpiece *Long Day's Journey into Night* is more nightmare than dream, this drama of one family's agonizing descent into intolerable darkness reaches to the level of classical tragedy: powerful, lyrical, and illuminating the anguish of the human condition.

Hansberry herself compared her protagonist, the younger Walter Lee Younger, to Arthur Miller's Willy Loman in *Death of a Salesman.* The tragedy of Willy Loman, as Miller makes clear, is that, on behalf of his sons, he stumbled on the seductiveness of the American dream for material possessions and popularity and lost his footing. It was a mistake that Hansberry's great mother figure, Lena Younger, could not permit her children to make in the interest of their survival.

Of the three plays, *The Glass Menagerie* is almost the flip side of the coin of *A Raisin in the Sun.* Here the mother, Amanda Wingfield, lost in memories of a "never, never land of mythic grandeur," as the late Georgian writer Lillian Smith described such a plight, can do little to help her fragile daughter or her poetic son because she is a pathetic victim of illusions of the past.

Williams' portrayal of the crippled, fragile Laura yearning for one brief moment that the dreams of her mother for her—arising out of the visit of her brother's friend, a "gentlemen caller"—might come true is one of the most tender portraits of a vulnerable spirit in drama. The gentleman caller will come—and go, permanently—and so will

Laura's brother-poet, and so will the dreams of all the family members.

In *A Raisin in the Sun*, Hansberry could not permit either herself or her major characters to fall victim to any illusions about the old "verities" of the human heart, as William Faulkner calls them: pride and dignity, fortitude, compassion, and perseverance. We understand what Lena Younger must represent for her children, even as we also understand that the Walter Lee Youngers of the society cannot—will not—indefinitely suffer their material dreams to be deferred.

The twenty-fifth-anniversary edition of Hansberry's great play, with its restored passages, makes clear that the stalwart mother figure, Lena Younger, understands as well. She makes no compromises either with history or valid dreams; hence her insistence that her son take care not to betray either.

For her second play, *The Sign in Sidney Brustein's Window*, Hansberry left the working-class African American experience of *A Raisin in the Sun* to write about people like those she knew in New York's Greenwich Village, a setting she described in her opening note as "the preferred habitat of many who fancy revolt or, at least, detachment from the social order that surrounds us."

The play opened, to mixed reviews, on October 15, 1964, at Broadway's Longacre Theatre. Three months later, on the day of Lorraine Hansberry's death, the curtain came down in tribute to her. The play did not reopen. In his essay, "The 101 'Final' Performances of *Sidney Brustein*," Bob Nemiroff illuminates an extraordinary moment in the history of the American stage when Hansberry's colleagues of the professional stage and screen became aware that the playwright was dying and rallied to help save the play as if through it, they could save her. One major tribute to Hansberry from a fellow artist during this period came from an Englishman, novelist John Braine, author of *A Room at the Top*, among other works. Braine came to New York during the run of *Brustein* and, familiar with *A Raisin in the Sun*, decided to see the new Hansberry play. His response to it, published as a personal communication in the *Village Voice* is titled, "An Appreciation: *Sidney Brustein*—a 'Great Play'—No Other Word Is Possible." The following is a representative passage:

> It is drama of such clarity that one may return to it again and again, and, I expect, emerge as deeply moved—and each time the more illumined . . . there are no characters that can be dismissed or defined on the basis of personal relationships alone. Each is larger than expectation has permitted either them or us. . . . All are real. Miss Hansberry, I am convinced, doesn't know how to create a character . . . who isn't gloriously diverse, illuminatingly contradictory, heart-breakingly alive. . . . *The Sign in Sidney Brustein's Window* is a great play. The word "great" is, I know, grotesquely misused, but no other adjective is possible.

Since the original production, *Brustein* has had one additional Broadway staging, a musicalized version that did not work. Though the play is regularly performed by amateur and small professional theaters, this play has not yet come fully into its own. I suspect that significant life still awaits it.

Meanwhile, in the new Vintage edition of the play— accompanying the expanded, twenty-fifth-anniversary version of *A Raisin in the Sun*—*Brustein*, like its companion, will reach ever-expanding audiences as both plays continue to be read and performed on stage.

Lorraine Hansberry no longer stands alone in portraying the African American experience on the professional American stage. She has been followed by distinguished playwrights, none more so than August Wilson, the Pulitzer Prize–winning artist whose epic works currently come forth, one after another, to widen horizons and delight us.

But *A Raisin in the Sun* remains a work that is as powerfully relevant today as when it was written. It continues to be among the most performed works in the American theatrical repertory.

As Eugene O'Neill stands as the Father of the modern

American drama, Hansberry stands as the Mother of modern African American drama. Strange, however, to call her "mother" of a vast body of cultural experience. She, whose photographs show so young a woman, vibrant with life, who—like the figures on Keats's Grecian urn—remains with us, eternally young.

But the vision and wisdom—and the hope—reflected in her brief life and first work lives on. As Frank Rich observed, "[*A Raisin in the Sun*] changed the American theater forever."

For this, we are supremely indebted to Hansberry. And to Robert Nemiroff, who knew all along what others of us had yet to learn.

February, 1995

# NOTES ON THIS NEW EDITION

by Robert Nemiroff

This new edition *of A Raisin in the Sun* and *The Sign in Sidney Brustein's Window* restores to *Raisin* a number of scenes and lines staged for the first time in the new revivals of the play—passages that had been cut in the original production, but which Lorraine Hansberry later felt were important to the play.

"The events of every passing year add resonance to *A Raisin in the Sun*. It is as if history is conspiring to make the play a classic." So wrote one of the four *New York Times* critics who successively, in the last three years, has used the term "classic" in reviewing new productions. The unprecedented resurgence of the work that began in its twenty-fifth anniversary year and continues with no end in sight (ten revivals at major regional theaters at this writing, and a pending national tour) occasions this new edition.

Produced in 1959, the play presaged the revolution in black and women's consciousness—and the revolutionary ferment in Africa—that exploded in the years following the playwright's death in 1965 to ineradicably alter the social fabric and consciousness of the nation and the world. As so many have commented lately, it did so in a manner and to an extent that few could have foreseen, and the years have made plain just how pertinent some of the excised passages were. A number speak directly to issues and concerns unfamiliar to many at the time but inescapable now: value systems of the black family and the conflict between generations; concepts of African American beauty, identity, hairstyle; class differences between the Youngers and the Murchisons; the relationships of husband and wife, black men and women; and, in the final scene between Beneatha and Asagai, the larger statement of the play—and the ongoing struggle it portends. Other passages—for example, the bedtime scene between Walter and Travis (entirely cut in the original) and the scene with Mrs. Johnson—speak to the motivations and goals of the characters and put into sharper relief the underlying issues—and consequences of the action.

Not one of those cuts, it should be emphasized, was made to dilute or censor the play or to "soften" its statement, for everyone in that herculean, now-legendary band that brought *Raisin* to Broadway—and most specifically the producer, Philip Rose, and director, Lloyd Richards—*believed* in the importance of that statement with a degree of commitment that would have countenanced nothing of the kind. How and why, then, did the cuts come about?

The scene in which Beneatha unveils her natural haircut is an interesting example. In 1959, when the play was presented, the rich variety of Afro styles introduced in the mid-sixties had not yet arrived: the very few black women who wore their hair unstraightened cut it very short. When the hair of Diana Sands (who created the role) was cropped in this fashion, however, a few days before the opening, it was not properly contoured to suit her: her particular facial structure required a fuller Afro, of the sort she in fact adopted in later years. Result? Rather than vitiate the playwright's point—the beauty of black hair—the scene was dropped.

Some cuts were similarly the result of happenstance or unpredictables of the kind that occur in any production: difficulties with a scene, the "processes" of actors, the dynamics of staging, etc. But most were related to the length of the play: running time. Time in the context of bringing to Broadway the first play by a black (young and unknown) woman, to be directed, moreover, by another unknown black "first," in a theater where black audiences virtually did not exist—and where, in the entire history of the American stage, there had never been a serious *commercially successful* black drama!

So unlikely did the prospects seem in that day, in fact, to all but Phil Rose and the company, that much as some expressed admiration for the play, Rose's eighteen-month effort to find a co-producer to help complete the financing was turned down by virtually every established name in the business. He was joined at the last by another newcomer, David Cogan, but even with the money in hand, not a single theater owner on the Great White Way would *rent* to the new production! So that when the play left New York for tryouts—with a six-hundred-dollar advance in New Haven and no theater to come back to—had the script and performance been any less ready, and the response of critics and audiences any less unreserved than they proved to be, *A Raisin in the Sun* would never have reached Broadway.

Under these circumstances the pressures were enormous (if unspoken and rarely even acknowledged in the excitement of the work) *not* to press fate unduly with unnecessary risks. And the most obvious of these was the running time. It is one thing to present a four-and-a-half-hour drama by Eugene O'Neill on Broadway—but a *first* play (even ignoring the special features of this one) in the neighborhood of even *three*??? By common concensus, the need to keep the show as tight and streamlined as possible was manifest. Some things—philosophical flights, nuances the general audience might not understand, shadings, embellishments—would have to be sacrificed.

At the time the cuts were made (there were also some very good ones that focused and strengthened the drama), it was assumed by all that they would in no way significantly affect or alter the statement of the play, for there is nothing in the omitted lines that is not implicit elsewhere, and throughout, *A Raisin in the Sun*. But to think this was to reckon without two factors the future would bring into play. The first was the swiftness and depth of the revolution in consciousness that was coming and the consequent, perhaps inevitable, tendency of some people to assume, because the "world" had changed, that *any* "successful" work which preceded the change must embody the values they had outgrown. And the second was the nature of the American audience.

James Baldwin has written that "Americans suffer from an ignorance that is not only colossal, but sacred." He is referring to that apparently endless capacity we have nurtured through long years to deceive ourselves where race is concerned: the baggage of myth and preconception we carry with us that enables northerners, for example, to shield themselves from the extent and virulence of segregation in the North, so that each time an "incident" of violence so egregious that they cannot look past it occurs they are "shocked" anew, as if it had never happened before or as if the problem were largely passé. (In 1975, when the cast of *Raisin*, the musical, became involved in defense of a family whose home in Queens, New York City, had been fire-bombed, we learned of a 1972 City Commissioner of Human Rights Report, citing "eleven cases *in the last eighteen months* in which minority-owned homes had been set afire or vandalized, a church had been bombed, and a school bus had been attacked"—in New York City!)

But Baldwin is referring also to the human capacity, where a work of art is involved, to substitute, for what the writer has written, what in our hearts we *wish* to believe. (As Hansberry put it in response to one reviewer's enthusiastic if particularly misguided praise of her play: ". . . it did not disturb the writer in the least that there is no such implication in the entire three acts. He did not need it in the play; he had it in his head."[1]

Such problems did not, needless to say, stop America from embracing *A Raisin in the Sun*. But it did interfere drastically, for a generation, with the way the play was interpreted and assessed—and, in hindsight, it made all the more regrettable the abridgment (though without it would we even know the play today?). In a remarkable rumination on Hansberry's death, Ossie Davis (who succeeded Sidney Poitier in the role of Walter Lee) put it this way:

The play deserved all this—the playwright deserved all this, and more. Beyond question! But I have a feeling that for all she got, Lorraine Hansberry never got all she deserved in regard to *A Raisin in the Sun*—that she got success, but

[1] "Willie Loman, Walter Younger, and He Who Must Live," *Village Voice*, August 12, 1959.

that in her success she was cheated, both as a writer and as a Negro.

One of the biggest selling points about *Raisin*—filling the grapevine, riding the word-of-mouth, laying the foundation for its wide, wide acceptance—was how much the Younger family was just like any other American family. Some people were ecstatic to find that "it didn't really have to be about Negroes at all!" It was, rather, a walking, talking, living demonstration of our mythic conviction that, underneath, all of us Americans, *color-ain't-got-nothing-to-do-with-it*, are pretty much alike. People are just people, whoever they are; and all they want is a chance to be like other people. This uncritical assumption, sentimentally held by the audience, powerfully fixed in the character of the powerful mother with whom everybody could identify, immediately and completely, made any other questions about the Youngers, and what living in the slums of Southside Chicago had done to them, not only irrelevant and impertinent, but also disloyal . . . because everybody who walked into the theater saw in Lena Younger . . . his own great American Mama. And that was decisive.[1]

In effect, as Davis went on to develop, white America "kidnapped" Mama, stole her away and used her fantasized image to avoid what was uniquely *African* American in the play. And what it was saying.

Thus, in many reviews (and later academic studies), the Younger family—maintained by two female domestics and a chauffeur, son of a laborer dead of a lifetime of hard labor—was transformed into an acceptably "middle class" family. The decision to move became a desire to "integrate" (rather than, as Mama says simply, "to find the nicest house for the least amount of money for my family. . . . Them houses they put up for colored in them areas way out always seem to cost twice as much"). Mama herself—about whose "acceptance" of her "place" in the society there is not a word in the play, and who, in quest of her family's survival over the soul— and body-crushing conditions of the ghetto, is prepared to defy housing-

[1] "The Significance of Lorraine Hansberry," *Freedomways*, Summer 1985.

pattern taboos, threats, bombs, and God knows what else —became the safely "conservative" matriarch, upholder of the social order and proof that if one only perseveres with faith, everything will come out right in the end, and the system ain't so bad after all. (All this, presumably, because, true to character, she speaks and thinks in the *language* of her generation, shares their dream of a better life and, like millions of her counterparts, takes her Christianity to heart.)

And perhaps most ironical of all to the playwright, who had herself as a child been almost killed in such a real-life story,[1] the climax of the play became, pure and simple, a "happy ending"—despite the fact that it leaves the Youngers on the brink of what will surely be, in their new home, at *best* a nightmare of uncertainty. ("If he thinks that's a happy ending," said Hansberry in an interview, "I invite him to come live in one of the communities where the Youngers are going!"[2]) Which is not even to mention the fact that that little house in a blue-collar neighborhood —hardly suburbia, as some have imagined—is hardly the answer to the deeper needs and inequities of race and class and sex that Walter and Beneatha have articulated.

When Lorraine Hansberry read the reviews—delighted by the accolades, grateful for the recognition, but also deeply troubled—she decided in short order to put back many of the materials excised. She did that in the 1959 Random House edition, but faced with the actuality of a prize-winning play, she hesitated about some others which, for reasons now beside the point, had not in rehearsal come alive. She later felt, however, that the full last scene between Beneatha and Asagai[3] and Walter's bedtime scene with Travis (originally conceived as a separate scene, but

---

[1] *To Be Young, Gifted and Black*, New York: New American Library, p. 51.

[2] "Make New Sounds: Studs Terkel Interviews Lorraine Hansberry," *American Theatre*, November 1984.

[3] At the suggestion of director Harold Scott in the rehearsals for the New York production, I have substituted for a few transitional lines in this scene the lines from another draft about money and "dreams . . . that must depend on the death of a man."

now as the climax of the scene with Mama) should be restored at the first opportunity, and this was done in the 1966 New American Library edition of *A Raisin in the Sun* and *The Sign in Sidney Brustein's Window*. As anyone who has seen the recent productions will attest, they are among the most powerful (and most applauded) moments in the play.

Because the visit of Mrs. Johnson adds the costs of another character to the cast (not an inconsequential consideration at most theaters) and ten more minutes to the play, it has not been used in most revivals. But in those where it has been tried it has worked to great—and hilarious—effect. It is included here in any case, because it speaks to fundamental issues of the play, makes plain the realities that await the Youngers at the curtain, and, above all, makes clear what, in the eyes of the author, Lena Younger—in her typicality within the black experience—does and does *not* represent.

What is for me personally, as a witness to the foregoing events, most gratifying about the current revival is that today, some twenty-eight years after Lorraine Hansberry, thinking back with disbelief a few nights after the opening of *Raisin*, typed out these words—

> . . . I had turned the last page out of the typewriter and pressed all the sheets neatly together in a pile, and gone and stretched out face down on the living room floor. I had finished a play; a play I had no reason to think or not think would ever be done; a play that I was sure no one would quite understand. . . .[1]

—her play is not only being done, but that more than she had ever thought possible—and more clearly than it ever has been before—it is being understood. The two pieces by Frank Rich and Amiri Baraka that I have selected, from among the many that might have been chosen for this volume, are—from quite different worlds and perspectives—examples of that.

Finally, a word about the stage directions and inter-

[1] *To Be Young, Gifted and Black*, p. 120.

pretive descriptions: These are the author's original directions combined, where meaningful to the reader, with the
specifics of Lloyd Richards' classic original staging (in-
corporated by Hansberry into the first acting edition) and
with, in some instances where they enhance understanding
of situation and character, those of later directors—most
notably Harold Scott, whose successive revivals culminat-
ing in the inspired Roundabout Theatre production for
the Kennedy Center, have given the revised text, in my
view, its fullest realization to-date.

In 1970 Julius Lester, in a groundbreaking essay on
Hansberry for the *Village Voice*, put his finger on the heart
of *The Sign in Sidney Brustein's Window*:

> The play was produced a year and a half before white
> liberal intellectuals were to be confronted by the spectre of
> black power. *Sign* was a conscious warning. Lorraine Hans-
> berry was speaking to those white intellectuals of her own
> generation and telling them to prepare for what was to
> come . . . she cared enough about her white intellectual
> counterparts . . . to beg them to prepare to pick up the
> gauntlet and return to the field. . . . On another level, how-
> ever, the play is a warning to those of us who are now
> young as Sidney once was and who will be growing older.
> . . . Where will we be ten, fifteen years from now, with our
> books, our records, and our dreams? Where will we be if
> (or when) the bubble bursts? . . . All of us will, in one way
> or another, have to walk the painful road walked by Sidney
> Brustein and I hope that at the end of it, we can say, as
> Sidney does, that he is "a fool . . . who believes. . . ." Her
> idealism is a kind that we don't have anymore . . . and if
> that is true, then chaos and barbarism stretch before us
> into infinity.[1]

In the twenty-two years since Sidney's Sign came down
from its "window" on Broadway, Lester is neither the first
nor the last to express such a viewpoint. The play has been

[1] "Young, Gifted and Black: the Politics of Caring," *Village Voice*,
May 28, 1970.

variously called, in critical studies, histories of the theater and by reviewers, "a form of poetry [that] illuminates whole segments of life" (*Saturday Review*, 1966), "a mirror to the life of the human race" (*Playbill*, 1968), "a key play in the history of modern American drama . . . both in its subtly complex writing, and its philosophical premises" (Emory Lewis, *Stages: The Fifty-Year Childhood of the American Theatre*, 1969), and "one of the most sensitive and fully developed portraits of a Jew in contemporary drama" (Ellen Schiff, *From Stereotype to Metaphor: The Jew in Contemporary Drama*, 1982). It has been reprinted in *Best American Plays*, staged all over America in productions of varying quality, and in 1972 there was an abortive (woefully underfinanced) effort to return it to Broadway in a new semi-musicalized version that did not work.[1] Every year there are another twenty or so productions at small or university theaters, and every time, it would seem, the play engenders in some of the participants and some in the audience—I have met or received letters from literally hundreds—the same passion and intensity of commitment that marked its original "101 'final' performances" on Broadway. If anything, the play is more potent, more pertinent and moving in its painful affirmation of humanity, and its challenge to our times and to what we do with our lives, than on the day it was written.

This edition follows the author's original conception of Act Three, Scene One, and incorporates passages from that scene not used on Broadway or included in the Random House edition. But because the author was too ill at the time of its staging to complete the final honing (and in one area restructuring) she envisioned after seeing the full work on its feet, it is, in this unabridged form, a play not without flaws. These have been addressed in several recent experimental productions, reflecting my last discussions about the play with Hansberry, the knowledge gained from various productions through the years, and especially the insights of director Alan Schneider, who at the time of his tragic death in London was contemplating a major revival. The results are reflected in the new

Samuel French acting edition for the stage.

At this writing, I have reason to anticipate that the kind of truly major production by a director and company of the stature required to bring the play's full dimensions to life will shortly occur—and that, therefore, the larger history of *Sidney Brustein* as a play—and as a challenge to our age—is only beginning. We shall see.

Croton-on-Hudson, N.Y.<br>January, 1987

# ACKNOWLEDGMENTS

In his Acknowledgments, in the published version (1987) of the expanded twenty-fifth-anniversary revival of *A Raisin in the Sun*, Robert Nemiroff said that the individuals and institutions responsible were too numerous to record. On his behalf now, eight years later, I thank all those who still go unrecorded and all who have played a role in keeping the legacy of Lorraine Hansberry alive in the years since her death.

My special thanks to those of the Roundabout Theatre in New York, and the production that followed at Kennedy Center, who joined in the full length restoration of Hansberry's classic play. And to Harold Scott, the director, whose brilliance and skills shed new light in a new era, and the new generation of actors who gave so generously of themselves in their performances. Delroy Lindo and Olivia Cole, Danny Glover and Esther Rolle, Starletta DuPois, Kim Yancey, Vondee Curtis Hall, Joseph Roberts, Lou Ferguson, and Stephen Henderson.

Special acknowledgment of actor John Fiedler, who appeared in the original Broadway production and, as a labor of love, repeated the role of Karl Lindner in the twenty-fifth-anniversary revival.

My gratitude to the steadfast ones through the years: Dr. Burton D'Lugoff, physician and closest of friends—creatively, professionally, and personally—to Bob and Lorraine, and to me; Estelle Frank and Sol and Faye Medoff, without whose support, the important work of the Hansberry estate could not as readily have gotten underway; all members of the Nemiroff family and mine; Samuel Liff of the William Morris Agency; Alan Bomser, my lawyer; Seymour Baldash, accountant and friend; and Dr. Margaret Wilkerson, Hansberry's biographer, who continues to bring her keen critical judgment to bear for me as she did for Bob.

Finally, a special tribute to my late husband, Robert Nemiroff, by whose side I was privileged, for twenty-four and

xxvi ACKNOWLEDGMENTS

a half years, to observe and participate in the passionate dedication of one gifted human being to the legacy of another. And
to his associate, the late Charlotte Zaltzberg, who worked so
faithfully alongside him in the second Broadway production of
*The Sign in Sidney Brustein's Window*, later becoming coau-
thor of the book for the Tony Award–winning musical, *Raisin*.

To them, and to all those who love art and life and believe in
the potential of the human spirit, I am profoundly grateful.

Jewell Handy Gresham Nemiroff          Croton-on-Hudson,
                                                New York
                                        February, 1995

# A RAISIN IN THE SUN

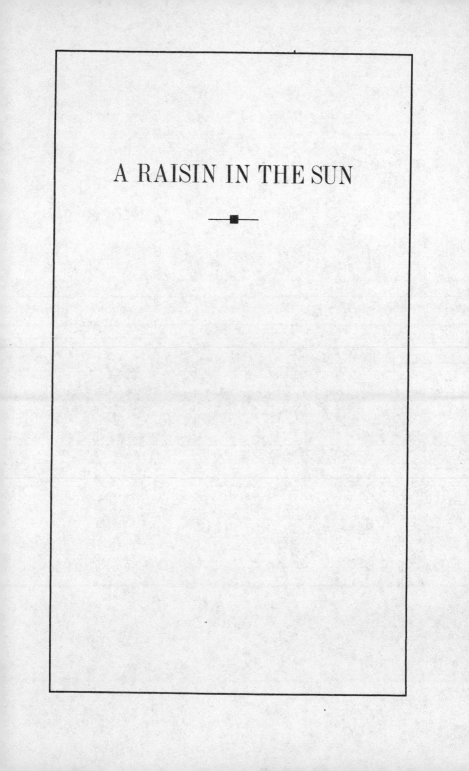

To Mama:
*in gratitude for the dream*

What happens to a dream deferred?
Does it dry up
Like a raisin in the sun?
Or fester like a sore—
And then run?
Does it stink like rotten meat?
Or crust and sugar over—
Like a syrupy sweet?

Maybe it just sags
Like a heavy load.

*Or does it explode?*

—Langston Hughes

# A RAISIN IN THE SUN
## The 25TH Anniversary

by Frank Rich

Chicago—It was 25 years ago that a 28-year-old black woman from this city changed American theater forever with her first produced play. The woman was Lorraine Hansberry, and the play, of course, was *A Raisin in the Sun.*

Taking her title from Langston Hughes's poem "Harlem," Miss Hansberry forced both blacks and whites to reexamine the deferred dreams of black America. She asked blacks to reconsider how those dreams might be defined; she demanded that whites not impede the fulfillment of those dreams for one more second. And she posed all her concerns in a work that portrayed a black family with a greater realism and complexity than had ever been previously seen on an American stage. A writer of unlimited compassion, Miss Hansberry believed that all people must be measured, as she put it, by both their "hills and valleys."

Miss Hansberry, who died of cancer at the age of 34 in 1965, wrote *Raisin* well before the marches on Washington, the assassination of the Reverend Dr. Martin Luther King, Jr., and the inner-city explosions. Yet, with remarkable prescience, she saw history whole: Her play encompasses everything from the rise of black nationalism in the United States and Africa to the advent of black militancy to the specific dimensions of the black woman's liberation movement. And she always saw the present and future in the light of the past—clear back to the slavery of the Old

7

South and the new slavery that followed for black workers who migrated to the industrial ghettos of the North.

Miss Hansberry works within the confines of what might be called a kitchen-sink drama, set in a cramped, tri-generational household on the South Side in the 1950s. At the plot level, *Raisin* is about how the Younger family will spend a ten-thousand-dollar insurance payment it has received after its patriarch's death—and about whether the family will move into a now-affordable new home in a hostile, lily-white neighborhood. But Miss Hansberry's real drama is the battle for the soul and identity of Walter Lee Younger, the family's son.

Walter, 35, is a chauffeur who wants to get rich by opening a liquor store. Without quite realizing it, he oppresses his wife, Ruth, a domestic, and mocks the ambitions of his 20-year-old sister, Beneatha, a fledgling activist and medical student. "I got me a dream," says Walter early in the play—but his dream is not to be confused with Dr. King's. What he wants is "things," and, as he tells his horrified mother, Lena, he no longer regards money merely as a passport to freedom but as the essence of life.

In this sense, Walter is not just a black victim of white racism but also a victim of a materialistic American dream that can enslave men or women of any race. Seeing *Raisin* again, one is struck by how much Miss Hansberry's protagonist resembles those of other Chicago writers, from Dreiser's Sister Carrie to David Mamet's proletarian schemer in *American Buffalo*. What makes *Raisin* so moving is that Walter finally does rise above his misplaced values to find a new dignity and moral courage—and that he does so with the support of his contentious but always loving family. . . .

—*The New York Times*
October 5, 1983

*A Critical Reevaluation:*

# A RAISIN IN THE SUN's
# Enduring Passion

by Amiri Baraka

In the wake of its twenty-fifth anniversary, Lorraine Hansberry's great play *A Raisin in the Sun* is enjoying a revival of a most encouraging kind. Complete with restorations to the text of scenes and passages removed from the first production, the work is currently being given a new direction and interpretation that reveal even more clearly the play's profoundly imposing stature, continuing relevance, and pointed social analysis. At major regional theaters in city after city *Raisin* has played to packed houses and, as on the night I saw it, standing ovations. It has broken or approached long-standing box office records and has been properly hailed as "a classic," while the *Washington Post* has called it succinctly: "one of the handful of great American dramas . . . in the inner circle, along with *Death of a Salesman, Long Day's Journey into Night,* and *The Glass Menagerie.*"

For a playwright who knows, too well, the vagaries and realities of American theater, this assessment is gratifying. But of even greater significance is the fact that *A Raisin in the Sun* is being viewed by masses of people, black and white, in the light of a new day.

For *Raisin* typifies American society in a way that reflects more accurately the real lives of the black U.S. majority than any work that ever received commercial exposure before it, and few if any since. It has the life that only classics can maintain. Any useful re-appreciation

9

of it cannot be limited, therefore, to the passages restored
or the new values discovered, important though these are:
it is the play itself, as a dramatic (and sociopolitical)
whole, that demands our confirmation of its grandeur.

When *Raisin* first appeared in 1959, the Civil Rights
Movement was in its earlier stages. And as a document
reflecting the *essence* of those struggles, the play is un-
excelled. For many of us it was—and remains—the
quintessential civil rights drama. But any attempt to con-
fine the play to an era, a mind-set, an issue ("Housing")
or set of topical concerns was, as we now see, a mistake.
The truth is that Hansberry's dramatic skills have yet to be
properly appreciated—and not just by those guardians of
the status quo who pass themselves off as dramatic critics.
For black theater artists and would-be theorists especially,
this is ironic because the play is probably the most widely
appreciated—particularly by African Americans—black
drama that we have.

*Raisin* lives in large measure because black people have
kept it alive. And because Hansberry has done *more* than
document, which is the most limited form of realism. She
is a *critical realist*, in a way that Langston Hughes, Richard
Wright, and Margaret Walker are. That is, she *analyzes*
and *assesses* reality and shapes her statement as an aesthe-
tically powerful and politically advanced work of art. Her
statement cannot be separated from the characters she
creates to embody, in their totality, the life she observes:
it becomes, in short, the living material of the work, part
of its breathing body, integral and alive.

George Thompson in *Poetry and Marxism* points out
that drama is the most expressive artistic form to emerge out
of great social transformation. Shakespeare is the artist of
the destruction of feudalism—and the emergence of capitalism. The mad Macbeths, bestial Richard III's, and other
feudal worthies are actually shown, like the whole class, as
degenerate—and degenerating. This is also why Shake-

speare deals with race (*Othello*), anti-Semitism (*The Merchant of Venice*), and feminism (*The Taming of the Shrew*); because these *will be* the continuing dilemmas of the bourgeois epoch! If we—opponents of racism, sexism, and the degeneracies of capitalism today—were to write Richard the Nix and Ronnie the Rex, we would not be called the Bard's heirs, although it is the bourgeoisie who came to shower celebration on Shakespeare—now they provide sterile, dead productions to hide the real texts.

Hansberry's play, too, was political agitation. It dealt with the very same issues of democratic rights and equality that were being aired in the streets. It dealt with them with an unabating dramatic force, vision, political concreteness and clarity that, in retrospect, are awesome. But it dealt with them not as abstractions, fit only for infantile-left pamphlets, but as they are *lived*. In reality.

All of *Raisin*'s characters speak *to* the text and are critical to its dramatic tensions and understanding. They are necessarily larger than life—in impact—but crafted meticulously from living social material.

When the play opened on Broadway, Lena Younger, the emotional adhesive of the family, was given a broad, aggressive reading by Claudia McNeil. Indeed, her reading has been taken as the model and somewhat institutionalized in various productions I've seen.

The role itself—of family head, folksy counsel, upholder of tradition—has caused many people to see her as the stereotyped "black matriarch" of establishment and commercial sociological fame. Carrying with them (or rebelling against) the preconceived baggage of that stereotype, and recalling the play through the haze of memory (or from the compromised movie version), they have not bothered to look more closely at the actual woman Hansberry created—and at *what* tradition she in fact upholds.

When my wife and I and three of our children went to

the recent New York revival by the Roundabout Theatre, Olivia Cole was playing the role. Her reading was revelation and renewal.

Ms. Cole came at the role from the inside out. Her Lena is a woman, black, poor, struggle-worn but proud and loving. She was in the world *before* the rest of the family, before many of us viewing the play. She has seen and felt what we have not, or what we cannot yet identify. She is no quaint, folksy artifact; she is truth, history, love—and struggle—as they can be manifest only in real life.

At this writing, Esther Rolle has taken over the role for the Kennedy Center production in Washington, and I have not seen her. But with Harold Scott's inspired direction, I would expect (and all accounts confirm) an equally fulfilling performance. For Scott has dug beneath the easy mis-seeing of the work as "soap opera," "stereotype," "well-made melodrama," and given us the emotional depths of these real people. He has done it by allowing the text to be heard, the boiling and lyrical words to strike home and be connected by the social actuality of real life impeccably rendered (and analyzed and criticized).

Similarly, the new interpreters of Walter Lee (James Pickens in New York, Delroy Lindo at Yale and in Washington) are something "fresh," like our kids say. They bring a contemporary flavoring to the work that consists of knowing—with more certainty than, say, Sidney Poitier could have in the original—the frustration and rage animating the healthy black male, *post*-civil rights era. They play Walter Lee more aggressively, more self-consciously, so that when he does fall we can actually hate him—hate the frivolous, selfish male-chauvinist part of ourselves. And when he stands up at the finale and will not be beaten, we can cry with joy.

Part of the renewed impact of the play comes with the fresh interpretation of both director and actors. But we cannot stop there! The social materials that Hansberry so brilliantly shaped into drama are not lightweight. For me this is the test of the writer: no matter the skill of the execution—*what* has been executed? What is it he or she is talking about? Form can never be dismissed, to say the least, particularly by an artist. But in the contradiction between form and content, content must be the bottom line—though unless the form be an extension of (and correctly serve) that content, obviously even understanding of the content will be flawed.

Formalist artists must resort to all kinds of superficial aberrations of form because usually they have nothing to say. Brecht said how much safer the red is in a "non-objective" painting than the red of blood rushing out of the slain worker's chest. This is why one expects to see more Pollocks in the banks than Orozcos or Riveras or John Biggers or Jake Lawrences. And it is one reason why some critics will always have a problem with the realism of a Hansberry—and ignore the multilayered richness of her form.

*A Raisin in the Sun* is about *dreams,* ironically enough. And how those psychological projections of human life can come into conflict like any other product of that life. For Lena, a new house, the stability and happiness of her children, are her principal dream. And as such this is the completion of a dream she and her late husband—who has literally, like the slaves, been *worked* to death—conceived together.

Ruth's dream, as mother and wife, is somewhat similar. A room for her son, an inside toilet. She dreams as one of those triply oppressed by society—as worker, as African American, and as woman. But her dream, and her mother-in-law's, conflicts with Walter Lee's. He is the chauffeur to a rich white man and dreams of owning all and doing all the things he sees "Mr. Arnold" do and own. On one level Walter Lee is merely aspiring to full and acknowledged humanity; on another level he yearns to strut his "manhood," a predictable mix of *machismo* and fantasy.

But Hansberry takes it even further to show us that on still another level Walter Lee, worker though he be, has the "realizable" dream of the black petty bourgeoisie. "There he is! *Monsieur le petit bourgeois noir*—himself!," cries Beneatha, the other of Lena Younger's children. "There he is—Symbol of a Rising Class! Entrepreneur! Titan of the system!" The deepness of this is that Hansberry can see that the conflict of dreams is not just that of individuals but, more importantly, of classes. Not since Theodore Ward's *Big White Fog* (1938) has there been a play so thoroughly and expertly reflective of class struggle within a black family.

Beneatha dreams of medical school. She is already socially mobile, finding a place, as her family cannot, among other petty bourgeois aspirants on the rungs of "education," where their hard work has put her. Her aspiration is less caustic, more attainable than Walter's. But she yearns for something more. Her name Beneatha (as who ain't?) should instruct us. She is, on the one hand, secure in the collegiate world of "ideas" and elitism, above the mass; on the other, undeceived by the myths and symbols of class and status. Part militant, part dilletante, "liberated" woman, little girl, she questions everything and dreams of service to humanity, an identity beyond self and family in the liberation struggles of her people. Ah, but will she have the strength to stay the course?

Hansberry has Beneatha grappling with key controversies of the period, but also some that had yet to clearly surface. And she grapples with some that will remain with us until society itself is changed: The relationship of the intellectual to the masses. The relationship of African Americans to Africans. The liberation movement itself and the gnawing necessity of black self-respect in its many guises (e.g., "straightened" hair vs. "the natural"). Written in 1956 and first seen by audiences in the new revivals, the part of the text in which Beneatha unveils her hair—the "perm" cut off and she glowing with her original woolly crown—precedes the "Afro" by a decade. Dialogue between Beneatha and her mother, brother, Asagai and George Murchison digs into all these still-burning concerns.

Similarly, Walter Lee and Ruth's dialogues lay out his male chauvinism and even self- and group-hate born of the frustration of too many dreams too long deferred: the powerlessness of black people to control their own fate or that of their families in capitalist America where race is place, white is right, and money makes and defines the man. Walter dreams of using his father's insurance money to buy a liquor store. This dream is in conflict not only with the dreams of the Younger women, but with reality. But Walter appreciates only his differences with—and blames—the women. Throughout the work, Hansberry addresses herself to issues that the very young might feel only *The Color Purple* has raised. Walter's relationship to his wife and sister, and Beneatha's with George and Asagai, gives us a variety of male chauvinism—working class, petty bourgeois, African.

Asagai, the Nigerian student who courts Beneatha, dreams of the liberation of Africa and even of taking Beneatha there: "We will pretend that . . . you have only been away for a day." But that's not reality either, though his discussion of the dynamics and dialectics of revolution —and of the continuity of human struggle, the only means of progress—still rings with truth!

Hansberry's warnings about neo-colonialism and the growth (and corruption) of a post-colonial African bourgeoisie—"the servants of empire," as Asagai calls them— are dazzling because of their subsequent replication by reality. As is, above all, her sense of the pressures mounting inexorably in this one typical household, and in Walter Lee especially, and of where they must surely lead. It was the "explosion" Langston Hughes talked about in his great poem "Harlem"—centerpiece of his incomparable

*Montage of a Dream Deferred,* from which the play's title was taken—and it informs the play as its twinned projection: dream or coming reality.

These are the categories Langston proposes for the dream:

> *Does it dry up*
> *Like a raisin in the sun?*

Dried up is what Walter Lee and Ruth's marriage had become, because their respective dreams have been deferred. When Mama Lena and Beneatha are felled by news of Walter Lee's weakness and dishonesty, their life's will—the desired greening of their humanity—is defoliated.

> *Or fester like a sore—*
> *And then run?*

Walter Lee's dream has festered, and in his dealings with the slack-jawed con man Willie (merchant of the stuff of dreams), his dream is "running."

We speak of the American Dream. Malcolm X said that for the Afro-American it was the American Nightmare. The little ferret man (played again tellingly by John Fiedler, one of the original cast on Broadway and in the film) is the dream's messenger, and the only white person in the play. His name is Lindner (as in "neither a borrower nor a Lindner be"), and the thirty or so "pieces of silver" he proffers are meant to help the niggers understand the dichotomous dream.

"But you've got to admit that a man, right or wrong, has the right to want to have the neighborhood he lives in a certain kind of way," says Lindner. Except black folks. Yes, these "not rich and fancy" representatives of white lower-middle America have a dream, too. A class dream, though it does not even serve them. But they are kept ignorant enough not to understand that the real dimensions

of that dream—white supremacy, black "inferiority," and
with them ultimately, though they know it not, fascism and
war—are revealed every day throughout the world as
deadly to human life and development—even their own.

In the post-civil rights era, in "polite" society, theirs is
a dream too gross even to speak of *directly* anymore. And
this is another legacy of the play: It was one of the shots
fired (and still being fired) at the aberrant white-supremacy
dream that is American reality. And the play is also a
summation of those shots, that battle, its heightened statement. Yet the man, Lindner, explains him/them self, and
there is even a hint of compassion for Lindner the man as
he bumbles on in outrageous innocence of all he is actually
saying—that "innocence" for which Americans are famous, which begs you to love and understand me for hating
you, the innocence that kills. Through him we see this
other dream:

> *Does it stink like rotten meat?*
> *Or crust and sugar over—*
> *Like a syrupy sweet?*

Almost everyone else in the play would sound like
Martin Luther King at the march on Washington were we
to read their speeches closely and project them broadly.
An exception is George Murchison (merchant's son), the
"assimilated" good bourgeois whose boldest dream, if one
can call it that, is to "get the grades . . . to pass the course
. . . to get a degree" en route to making it the American
way. George wants only to "pop" Beneatha after she, looking good, can be seen with him in the "proper" places.
He is opposed to a woman's "thinking" at all, and black
heritage to him "is nothing but a bunch of raggedy-ass
spirituals and some grass huts." The truth of this portrait
is one reason the black bourgeoisie has not created the
black national theaters, publishing houses, journals, gal-
leries, film corporations, and newspapers the African

American people desperately need. So lacking in self-respect are members of this class of George's, they even let the Kentucky Colonel sell us fried chicken and giblets.

The clash between Walter Lee and George, one of the high points of class struggle in the play and a dramatic tour de force, gives us the dialogue between the *sons* of the house and of the field slaves. And Joseph Phillips' portrayal of George's dumb behind in the production I saw is so striking because he understands that George thinks he is "cool." He does not understand he is corny!

When *Raisin* appeared the movement itself was in transition, which is why Hansberry could sum up its throbbing profile with such clarity. The baton was ready to pass from "George's father" as leader of the "Freedom Movement" (when its real muscle was always the Lena Youngers and their husbands) to the Walter Lees and Beneathas and Asagais and even the Georges.

In February 1960, black students at North Carolina A & T began to "sit in" at Woolworth's in a more forceful attack on segregated public facilities. By the end of 1960, some 96,000 students across the country had gotten involved in these sit-ins. In 1961, Patrice Lumumba was assassinated, and black intellectuals and activists in New York stormed the United Nations gallery. While Ralph Bunche (George's spiritual father) shrank back "embarrassed"—probably more so than by slavery and colonialism! But the Pan African thrust had definitely returned.

And by this time, too, Malcolm X, "the fire prophet," had emerged as the truest reflector of black mass feelings. It was of someone like Malcolm that Walter Lee spoke as in a trance in prophecy while he mounts the table to deliver his liquor-fired call to arms. (Nation of Islam headquarters was Chicago where the play is set!) Walter Lee embodies the explosion to be—what happens when the dream is deferred past even the patience of the Lena Youngers.

Young militants like myself were taken with Malcolm's

coming, with the immanence of explosion (e.g., Birmingham, when black Walters and Ruths struck back with icepicks and clubs in response to the bombing of a black church and the killing of four little girls in Sunday school.

We thought Hansberry's play was part of the "passive resistance" phase of the movement, which was over the minute Malcolm's penetrating eyes and words began to charge through the media with deadly force. We thought her play "middle class" in that its focus seemed to be on "moving into white folks' neighborhoods," when most blacks were just trying to pay their rent in ghetto shacks.

We missed the essence of the work—that Hansberry had created a family on the cutting edge of the same class and ideological struggles as existed in the movement itself and among the people. What is most telling about our ignorance is that Hansberry's play still remains overwhelmingly popular and evocative of black and white reality, and the masses of black people dug it true.

The next two explosions in black drama, Baldwin's *Blues for Mr. Charlie* and my own *Dutchman* (both 1964) raise up the militance and self-defense clamor of the movement as it came fully into the Malcolm era: Jimmy by constructing a debate between King (Meridian) and Richard (Malcolm), and I by having Clay openly advocate armed resistance. But neither of these plays is as much a statement from the African American majority as is *Raisin*. For one thing, they are both (regardless of their "power") too concerned with white people.

It is Lorraine Hansberry's play which, though it seems "conservative" in form and content to the radical petty bourgeoisie (as opposed to revolutionaries), is the accurate telling and stunning vision of the real struggle. Both Clay and Richard are rebellious scions of the middle class. The Younger family is part of the black majority, and the concerns I once dismissed as "middle class"—buying a house and moving into "white folks' neighborhoods"—are actually reflective of the essence of black people's striving and the will to defeat segregation, discrimination, and national oppression. There is no such thing as a "white folks' neighborhood" except to racists *and to those submitting to racism*.

The Younger family is the incarnation—*before* they burst from the bloody Southern backroads and the burning streets of Watts and Newark onto TV screens and the *world* stage—of our common ghetto-variey Fanny Lou Hamers, Malcolm X's, and Angela Davises. And their burden surely will be lifted, or one day it certainly will "explode."

November, 1986

A RAISIN IN THE SUN *was first presented by Philip Rose and David J. Cogan at the Ethel Barrymore Theatre, New York City, March 11, 1959, with the following cast:*

(In order of appearance)

| | |
|---|---|
| RUTH YOUNGER | Ruby Dee |
| TRAVIS YOUNGER | Glynn Turman |
| WALTER LEE YOUNGER (BROTHER) | Sidney Poitier |
| BENEATHA YOUNGER | Diana Sands |
| LENA YOUNGER (MAMA) | Claudia McNeil |
| JOSEPH ASAGAI | Ivan Dixon |
| GEORGE MURCHISON | Louis Gossett |
| KARL LINDNER | John Fiedler |
| BOBO | Lonne Elder III |
| MOVING MEN | Ed Hall, Douglas Turner Ward |

*Directed by* Lloyd Richards

*Designed and Lighted by* Ralph Alswang

*Costumes by* Virginia Volland

The action of the play is set in Chicago's Southside, sometime between World War II and the present.

## Act I

Scene One:    Friday morning.
Scene Two:    The following morning.

## Act II

Scene One:    Later, the same day.
Scene Two:    Friday night, a few weeks later.
Scene Three:  Moving day, one week later.

## Act III

An hour later.

# ACT I

## SCENE ONE

*The* YOUNGER *living room would be a comfortable and well-ordered room if it were not for a number of indestructible contradictions to this state of being. Its furnishings are typical and undistinguished and their primary feature now is that they have clearly had to accommodate the living of too many people for too many years—and they are tired. Still, we can see that at some time, a time probably no longer remembered by the family (except perhaps for* MAMA*), the furnishings of this room were actually selected with care and love and even hope—and brought to this apartment and arranged with taste and pride.*

*That was a long time ago. Now the once loved pattern of the couch upholstery has to fight to show itself from under acres of crocheted doilies and couch covers which have themselves finally come to be more important than the upholstery. And here a table or a chair has been moved to disguise the worn places in the carpet; but the carpet has fought back by showing its weariness, with depressing uniformity, elsewhere on its surface.*

*Weariness has, in fact, won in this room. Everything has been polished, washed, sat on, used, scrubbed too*

23

*often. All pretenses but living itself have long since vanished from the very atmosphere of this room.*

*Moreover, a section of this room, for it is not really a room unto itself, though the landlord's lease would make it seem so, slopes backward to provide a small kitchen area, where the family prepares the meals that are eaten in the living room proper, which must also serve as dining room. The single window that has been provided for these "two" rooms is located in this kitchen area. The sole natural light the family may enjoy in the course of a day is only that which fights its way through this little window.*

*At left, a door leads to a bedroom which is shared by* MAMA *and her daughter,* BENEATHA. *At right, opposite, is a second room (which in the beginning of the life of this apartment was probably a breakfast room) which serves as a bedroom for* WALTER *and his wife,* RUTH.

*Time: Sometime between World War II and the present.*
*Place: Chicago's Southside.*

*At Rise: It is morning dark in the living room.* TRAVIS *is asleep on the make-down bed at center. An alarm clock sounds from within the bedroom at right, and presently* RUTH *enters from that room and closes the door behind her. She crosses sleepily toward the window. As she passes her sleeping son she reaches down and shakes him a little. At the window she raises the shade and a dusky Southside morning light comes in feebly. She fills a pot with water and puts it on to boil. She calls to the boy, between yawns, in a slightly muffled voice.*

RUTH *is about thirty. We can see that she was a pretty girl, even exceptionally so, but now it is apparent that life has been little that she expected, and disappointment has already begun to hang in her face. In a few years, before thirty-five even, she will be known among her people as a "settled woman."*

*She crosses to her son and gives him a good, final, rousing shake.*

RUTH   Come on now, boy, it's seven thirty! (*Her son sits up at last, in a stupor of sleepiness*) I say hurry up, Travis! You ain't the only person in the world got to use a bathroom! (*The child, a sturdy, handsome little boy of ten or eleven, drags himself out of the bed and almost blindly takes his towels and "today's clothes" from drawers and a closet and goes out to the bathroom, which is in an outside hall and which is shared by another family or families on the same floor.* RUTH *crosses to the bedroom door at right and opens it and calls in to her husband*) Walter Lee! . . . It's after seven thirty! Lemme see you do some waking up in there now! (*She waits*) You better get up from there, man! It's after seven thirty I tell you. (*She waits again*) All right, you just go ahead and lay there and next thing you know Travis be finished and Mr. Johnson'll be in there and you'll be fussing and cussing round here like a madman! And be late too! (*She waits, at the end of patience*) Walter Lee—it's time for you to GET UP!

(*She waits another second and then starts to go into the bedroom, but is apparently satisfied that her husband has begun to get up. She stops, pulls the door to, and returns to the kitchen area. She wipes her face with a moist cloth and runs her fingers through her sleep-disheveled hair in a vain effort and ties an apron around her housecoat. The bedroom door at right opens and her husband stands in the doorway in his pajamas, which are rumpled and mismated. He is a lean, intense young man in his middle thirties, inclined to quick nervous movements and erratic speech habits—and always in his voice there is a quality of indictment*)

WALTER   Is he out yet?

RUTH   What you mean *out*? He ain't hardly got in there good yet.

WALTER (*Wandering in, still more oriented to sleep than to a new day*) Well, what was you doing all that yelling for if I can't even get in there yet? (*Stopping and thinking*) Check coming today?

RUTH They *said* Saturday and this is just Friday and I hopes to God you ain't going to get up here first thing this morning and start talking to me 'bout no money— 'cause I 'bout don't want to hear it.

WALTER Something the matter with you this morning?

RUTH No—I'm just sleepy as the devil. What kind of eggs you want?

WALTER Not scrambled. (RUTH *starts to scramble eggs*) Paper come? (RUTH *points impatiently to the rolled up* Tribune *on the table, and he gets it and spreads it out and vaguely reads the front page*) Set off another bomb yesterday.

RUTH (*Maximum indifference*) Did they?

WALTER (*Looking up*) What's the matter with you?

RUTH Ain't nothing the matter with me. And don't keep asking me that this morning.

WALTER Ain't nobody bothering you. (*Reading the news of the day absently again*) Say Colonel McCormick is sick.

RUTH (*Affecting tea-party interest*) Is he now? Poor thing.

WALTER (*Sighing and looking at his watch*) Oh, me. (*He waits*) Now what is that boy doing in that bathroom all this time? He just going to have to start getting up earlier. I can't be being late to work on account of him fooling around in there.

RUTH (*Turning on him*) Oh, no he ain't going to be getting up no earlier no such thing! It ain't his fault that he can't get to bed no earlier nights 'cause he got a bunch of crazy good-for-nothing clowns sitting up running their mouths in what is supposed to be his bedroom after ten o'clock at night . . .

WALTER  That's what you mad about, ain't it? The things I want to talk about with my friends just couldn't be important in your mind, could they?

*(He rises and finds a cigarette in her handbag on the table and crosses to the little window and looks out, smoking and deeply enjoying this first one)*

RUTH *(Almost matter of factly, a complaint too automatic to deserve emphasis)*  Why you always got to smoke before you eat in the morning?

WALTER *(At the window)*  Just look at 'em down there . . . Running and racing to work . . . *(He turns and faces his wife and watches her a moment at the stove, and then, suddenly)* You look young this morning, baby.

RUTH *(Indifferently)*  Yeah?

WALTER  Just for a second—stirring them eggs. Just for a second it was—you looked real young again. *(He reaches for her; she crosses away. Then, drily)* It's gone now—you look like yourself again!

RUTH  Man, if you don't shut up and leave me alone.

WALTER *(Looking out to the street again)*  First thing a man ought to learn in life is not to make love to no colored woman first thing in the morning. You all some eeeevil people at eight o'clock in the morning.

*(TRAVIS appears in the hall doorway, almost fully dressed and quite wide awake now, his towels and pajamas across his shoulders. He opens the door and signals for his father to make the bathroom in a hurry)*

TRAVIS  (*Watching the bathroom*)  Daddy, come on! (WALTER *gets his bathroom utensils and flies out to the bathroom*)

RUTH  Sit down and have your breakfast, Travis.

TRAVIS  Mama, this is Friday. (*Gleefully*) Check coming tomorrow, huh?

RUTH  You get your mind off money and eat your breakfast.

TRAVIS  (*Eating*)  This is the morning we supposed to bring the fifty cents to school.

RUTH  Well, I ain't got no fifty cents this morning.

TRAVIS  Teacher say we have to.

RUTH  I don't care what teacher say. I ain't got it. Eat your breakfast, Travis.

TRAVIS  I *am* eating.

RUTH  Hush up now and just eat!
(*The boy gives her an exasperated look for her lack of understanding, and eats grudgingly*)

TRAVIS  You think Grandmama would have it?

RUTH  No! And I want you to stop asking your grandmother for money, you hear me?

TRAVIS  (*Outraged*)  Gaaaleee! I don't ask her, she just gimme it sometimes!

RUTH  Travis Willard Younger—I got too much on me this morning to be—

TRAVIS  Maybe Daddy—

RUTH  *Travis!*
(*The boy hushes abruptly. They are both quiet and tense for several seconds*)

TRAVIS (*Presently*)   Could I maybe go carry some groceries in front of the supermarket for a little while after school then?

RUTH   Just hush, I said. (*Travis jabs his spoon into his cereal bowl viciously, and rests his head in anger upon his fists*) If you through eating, you can get over there and make up your bed.
(*The boy obeys stiffly and crosses the room, almost mechanically, to the bed and more or less folds the bedding into a heap, then angrily gets his books and cap*)

TRAVIS (*Sulking and standing apart from her unnaturally*) I'm gone.

RUTH (*Looking up from the stove to inspect him automatically*)   Come here. (*He crosses to her and she studies his head*) If you don't take this comb and fix this here head, you better! (TRAVIS *puts down his books with a great sigh of oppression, and crosses to the mirror. His mother mutters under her breath about his "slubbornness"*) 'Bout to march out of here with that head looking just like chickens slept in it! I just don't know where you get your slubborn ways . . . And get your jacket, too. Looks chilly out this morning.

TRAVIS (*With conspicuously brushed hair and jacket*)   I'm gone.

RUTH   Get carfare and milk money—(*Waving one finger*) —and not a single penny for no caps, you hear me?

TRAVIS (*With sullen politeness*)   Yes'm.
(*He turns in outrage to leave. His mother watches after him as in his frustration he approaches the door almost comically. When she speaks to him, her voice has become a very gentle tease*)

RUTH (*Mocking; as she thinks he would say it*)   Oh, Mama makes me so mad sometimes, I don't know what to do! (*She waits and continues to his back as he stands stock-still in front of the door*) I wouldn't kiss that woman good-bye for nothing in this world this morning! (*The boy finally turns around and rolls his eyes at her, knowing the mood has changed and he is vindicated; he does not, however, move toward her yet*) Not for nothing in this world! (*She finally laughs aloud at him and holds out her arms to him and we see that it is a way between them, very old and practiced. He crosses to her and allows her to embrace him warmly but keeps his face fixed with masculine rigidity. She holds him back from her presently and looks at him and runs her fingers over the features of his face. With utter gentleness—*) Now—whose little old angry man are you?

TRAVIS (*The masculinity and gruffness start to fade at last*)  Aw gaalee—Mama . . .

RUTH (*Mimicking*)  Aw—gaaaaalleeeee, Mama! (*She pushes him, with rough playfulness and finality, toward the door*) Get on out of here or you going to be late.

TRAVIS (*In the face of love, new aggressiveness*)  Mama, could I *please* go carry groceries?

RUTH  Honey, it's starting to get so cold evenings.

WALTER (*Coming in from the bathroom and drawing a make-believe gun from a make-believe holster and shooting at his son*)  What is it he wants to do?

RUTH  Go carry groceries after school at the supermarket.

WALTER  Well, let him go . . .

TRAVIS (*Quickly, to the ally*)  I *have* to—she won't gimme the fifty cents . . .

WALTER (*To his wife only*)  Why not?

RUTH (*Simply, and with flavor*)  'Cause we don't have it.

WALTER (*To* RUTH *only*)  What you tell the boy things like that for? (*Reaching down into his pants with a rather important gesture*) Here, son—
>    (*He hands the boy the coin, but his eyes are directed to his wife's.* TRAVIS *takes the money happily*)

TRAVIS  Thanks, Daddy.
>    (*He starts out.* RUTH *watches both of them with murder in her eyes.* WALTER *stands and stares back at her with defiance, and suddenly reaches into his pocket again on an afterthought*)

WALTER (*Without even looking at his son, still staring hard at his wife*)  In fact, here's another fifty cents . . . Buy yourself some fruit today—or take a taxicab to school or something!

TRAVIS  Whoopee—
>    (*He leaps up and clasps his father around the middle with his legs, and they face each other in mutual appreciation; slowly* WALTER LEE *peeks around the boy to catch the violent rays from his wife's eyes and draws his head back as if shot*)

WALTER  You better get down now—and get to school, man.

TRAVIS  (*At the door*)  O.K. Good-bye.
>    (*He exits*)

WALTER (*After him, pointing with pride*)  That's *my* boy. (*She looks at him in disgust and turns back to her work*) You know what I was thinking 'bout in the bathroom this morning?

RUTH  No.

WALTER  How come you always try to be so pleasant!

RUTH  What is there to be pleasant 'bout!

WALTER   You want to know what I was thinking 'bout in the bathroom or not!

RUTH   I know what you thinking 'bout.

WALTER (*Ignoring her*)   'Bout what me and Willy Harris was talking about last night.

RUTH (*Immediately—a refrain*)   Willy Harris is a good-for-nothing loudmouth.

WALTER   Anybody who talks to me has got to be a good-for-nothing loudmouth, ain't he? And what you know about who is just a good-for-nothing loudmouth? Charlie Atkins was just a "good-for-nothing loud-mouth" too, wasn't he! When he wanted me to go in the dry-cleaning business with him. And now—he's grossing a hundred thousand a year. A hundred thousand dollars a year! You still call *him* a loudmouth!

RUTH (*Bitterly*)   Oh, Walter Lee . . .
    (*She folds her head on her arms over the table*)

WALTER (*Rising and coming to her and standing over her*) You tired, ain't you? Tired of everything. Me, the boy, the way we live—this beat-up hole—everything. Ain't you? (*She doesn't look up, doesn't answer*) So tired—moaning and groaning all the time, but you wouldn't do nothing to help, would you? You couldn't be on my side that long for nothing, could you?

RUTH   Walter, please leave me alone.

WALTER   A man needs for a woman to back him up . . .

RUTH   Walter—

WALTER   Mama would listen to you. You know she listen to you more than she do me and Bennie. She think more of you. All you have to do is just sit down with her when you drinking your coffee one morning and talking 'bout things like you do and—(*He sits down be-*

*side her and demonstrates graphically what he thinks her
methods and tone should be*)—you just sip your coffee,
see, and say easy like that you been thinking 'bout that
deal Walter Lee is so interested in, 'bout the store and
all, and sip some more coffee, like what you saying ain't
really that important to you— And the next thing you
know, she be listening good and asking you questions
and when I come home—I can tell her the details. This
ain't no fly-by-night proposition, baby. I mean we
figured it out, me and Willy and Bobo.

RUTH (*With a frown*)   Bobo?

WALTER   Yeah. You see, this little liquor store we got in
mind cost seventy-five thousand and we figured the
initial investment on the place be 'bout thirty thousand,
see. That be ten thousand each. Course, there's a couple
of hundred you got to pay so's you don't spend your
life just waiting for them clowns to let your license get
approved—

RUTH   You mean graft?

WALTER (*Frowning impatiently*)   Don't call it that. See
there, that just goes to show you what women understand about the world. Baby, don't *nothing* happen
for you in this world 'less you pay *somebody* off!

RUTH   Walter, leave me alone! (*She raises her head and
stares at him vigorously—then says, more quietly*) *Eat*
your eggs, they gonna be cold.

WALTER (*Straightening up from her and looking off*)
That's it. There you are. Man say to his woman: I got
me a dream. His woman say: Eat your eggs. (*Sadly,
but gaining in power*) Man say: I got to take hold of
this here world, baby! And a woman will say: Eat your
eggs and go to work. (*Passionately now*) Man say: I
got to change my life, I'm choking to death, baby! And

his woman say—(*In utter anguish as he brings his fists down on his thighs*)—Your eggs is getting cold!

RUTH (*Softly*)  Walter, that ain't none of our money.

WALTER (*Not listening at all or even looking at her*)  This morning, I was lookin' in the mirror and thinking about it . . . I'm thirty-five years old; I been married eleven years and I got a boy who sleeps in the living room— (*Very, very quietly*)—and all I got to give him is stories about how rich white people live . . .

RUTH  Eat your eggs, Walter.

WALTER (*Slams the table and jumps up*)—DAMN MY EGGS—DAMN ALL THE EGGS THAT EVER WAS!

RUTH  Then go to work.

WALTER (*Looking up at her*)  See—I'm trying to talk to you 'bout myself—(*Shaking his head with the repetition*) —and all you can say is eat them eggs and go to work.

RUTH (*Wearily*)  Honey, you never say nothing new. I listen to you every day, every night and every morning, and you never say nothing new. (*Shrugging*) So you would rather *be* Mr. Arnold than be his chauffeur. So— I would *rather* be living in Buckingham Palace.

WALTER  That is just what is wrong with the colored woman in this world . . . Don't understand about building their men up and making 'em feel like they somebody. Like they can do something.

RUTH (*Drily, but to hurt*)  There *are* colored men who do things.

WALTER  No thanks to the colored woman.

RUTH  Well, being a colored woman, I guess I can't help myself none.

    (*She rises and gets the ironing board and sets it*

*up and attacks a huge pile of rough-dried clothes,*
*sprinkling them in preparation for the ironing and*
*then rolling them into tight fat balls*)

WALTER (*Mumbling*)   We one group of men tied to a race
of women with small minds!

    (*His sister* BENEATHA *enters. She is about twenty,*
*as slim and intense as her brother. She is not as*
*pretty as her sister-in-law, but her lean, almost*
*intellectual face has a handsomeness of its own.*
*She wears a bright-red flannel nightie, and her*
*thick hair stands wildly about her head. Her speech*
*is a mixture of many things; it is different from the*
*rest of the family's insofar as education has per-*
*meated her sense of English—and perhaps the*
*Midwest rather than the South has finally—at last*
*—won out in her inflection; but not altogether, be-*
*cause over all of it is a soft slurring and trans-*
*formed use of vowels which is the decided influ-*
*ence of the Southside. She passes through the*
*room without looking at either* RUTH *or* WALTER
*and goes to the outside door and looks, a little*
*blindly, out to the bathroom. She sees that it has*
*been lost to the Johnsons. She closes the door with*
*a sleepy vengeance and crosses to the table and sits*
*down a little defeated*)

BENEATHA   I am going to start timing those people.

WALTER   You should get up earlier.

BENEATHA (*Her face in her hands. She is still fighting the*
*urge to go back to bed*)   Really—would you suggest
dawn? Where's the paper?

WALTER (*Pushing the paper across the table to her as he*
*studies her almost clinically, as though he has never*
*seen her before*)   You a horrible-looking chick at this
hour.

BENEATHA (*Drily*)   Good morning, everybody.

WALTER (*Senselessly*)   How is school coming?

BENEATHA (*In the same spirit*)   Lovely. Lovely. And you know, biology is the greatest. (*Looking up at him*) I dissected something that looked just like you yesterday.

WALTER   I just wondered if you've made up your mind and everything.

BENEATHA (*Gaining in sharpness and impatience*)   And what did I answer yesterday morning—and the day before that?

RUTH (*From the ironing board, like someone disinterested and old*)   Don't be so nasty, Bennie.

BENEATHA (*Still to her brother*)   And the day before that and the day before that!

WALTER (*Defensively*)   I'm interested in you. Something wrong with that? Ain't many girls who decide—

WALTER *and* BENEATHA (*In unison*)   —"to be a doctor." (*Silence*)

WALTER   Have we figured out yet just exactly how much medical school is going to cost?

RUTH   Walter Lee, why don't you leave that girl alone and get out of here to work?

BENEATHA (*Exits to the bathroom and bangs on the door*) Come on out of there, please! (*She comes back into the room*)

WALTER (*Looking at his sister intently*)   You know the check is coming tomorrow.

BENEATHA (*Turning on him with a sharpness all her own*) That money belongs to Mama, Walter, and it's for her to decide how she wants to use it. I don't care if she wants to buy a house or a rocket ship or just nail it up somewhere and look at it. It's hers. Not ours—*hers*.

WALTER (*Bitterly*)   Now ain't that fine! You just got your mother's interest at heart, ain't you, girl? You such a nice girl—but if Mama got that money she can always take a few thousand and help you through school too —can't she?

BENEATHA   I have never asked anyone around here to do anything for me!

WALTER   No! And the line between asking and just accepting when the time comes is big and wide—ain't it!

BENEATHA (*With fury*)   What do you want from me, Brother—that I quit school or just drop dead, which!

WALTER   I don't want nothing but for you to stop acting holy 'round here. Me and Ruth done made some sacrifices for you—why can't you do something for the family?

RUTH   Walter, don't be dragging me in it.

WALTER   You are in it— Don't you get up and go work in somebody's kitchen for the last three years to help put clothes on her back?

RUTH   Oh, Walter—that's not fair . . .

WALTER   It ain't that nobody expects you to get on your knees and say thank you, Brother; thank you, Ruth; thank you, Mama—and thank you, Travis, for wearing the same pair of shoes for two semesters—

BENEATHA (*Dropping to her knees*)   Well—I *do*—all right?—thank everybody! And forgive me for ever wanting to be anything at all! (*Pursuing him on her knees across the floor*) FORGIVE ME, FORGIVE ME, FORGIVE ME!

RUTH  Please stop it! Your mama'll hear you.

WALTER  Who the hell told you you had to be a doctor? If you so crazy 'bout messing 'round with sick people —then go be a nurse like other women—or just get married and be quiet . . .

BENEATHA  Well—you finally got it said . . . It took you three years but you finally got it said. Walter, give up; leave me alone—it's Mama's money.

WALTER  *He was my father, too!*

BENEATHA  So what? He was mine, too—and Travis' grandfather—but the insurance money belongs to Mama. Picking on me is not going to make her give it to you to invest in any liquor stores—(*Underbreath, dropping into a chair*)—and I for one say, God bless Mama for that!

WALTER (*To* RUTH)  See—did you hear? Did you hear!

RUTH  Honey, please go to work.

WALTER  Nobody in this house is ever going to understand me.

BENEATHA  Because you're a nut.

WALTER  Who's a nut?

BENEATHA  You—you are a nut. Thee is mad, boy.

WALTER (*Looking at his wife and his sister from the door, very sadly*)  The world's most backward race of people, and that's a fact.

BENEATHA (*Turning slowly in her chair*)  And then there are all those prophets who would lead us out of the wilderness—(WALTER *slams out of the house*)—into the swamps!

RUTH  Bennie, why you always gotta be pickin' on your brother? Can't you be a little sweeter sometimes? (*Door *opens.* WALTER *walks in. He fumbles with his cap, starts to speak, clears throat, looks everywhere but at* RUTH. *Finally:*)

WALTER (*To* RUTH)    I need some money for carfare.

RUTH (*Looks at him, then warms; teasing, but tenderly*) Fifty cents? (*She goes to her bag and gets money*) Here—take a taxi!

(WALTER *exits.* MAMA *enters. She is a woman in her early sixties, full-bodied and strong. She is one of those women of a certain grace and beauty who wear it so unobtrusively that it takes a while to notice. Her dark-brown face is surrounded by the total whiteness of her hair, and, being a woman who has adjusted to many things in life and overcome many more, her face is full of strength. She has, we can see, wit and faith of a kind that keep her eyes lit and full of interest and expectancy. She is, in a word, a beautiful woman. Her bearing is perhaps most like the noble bearing of the women of the Hereros of Southwest Africa— rather as if she imagines that as she walks she still bears a basket or a vessel upon her head. Her speech, on the other hand, is as careless as her carriage is precise—she is inclined to slur everything —but her voice is perhaps not so much quiet as simply soft*)

MAMA    Who that 'round here slamming doors at this hour?
(*See crosses through the room, goes to the window, opens it, and brings in a feeble little plant growing doggedly in a small pot on the window sill. She feels the dirt and puts it back out*)

RUTH    That was Walter Lee. He and Bennie was at it again.

MAMA   My children and they tempers. Lord, if this little old plant don't get more sun than it's been getting it ain't never going to see spring again. (*She turns from the window*) What's the matter with you this morning, Ruth? You looks right peaked. You aiming to iron all them things? Leave some for me. I'll get to 'em this afternoon. Bennie honey, it's too drafty for you to be sitting 'round half dressed. Where's your robe?

BENEATHA   In the cleaners.

MAMA   Well, go get mine and put it on.

BENEATHA   I'm not cold, Mama, honest.

MAMA   I know—but you so thin . . .

BENEATHA (*Irritably*)   Mama, I'm not cold.

MAMA (*Seeing the make-down bed as* TRAVIS *has left it*) Lord have mercy, look at that poor bed. Bless his heart—he tries, don't he?
      (*She moves to the bed* TRAVIS *has sloppily made up*)

RUTH   No—he don't half try at all 'cause he knows you going to come along behind him and fix everything. That's just how come he don't know how to do nothing right now—you done spoiled that boy so.

MAMA (*Folding bedding*)   Well—he's a little boy. Ain't supposed to know 'bout housekeeping. My baby, that's what he is. What you fix for his breakfast this morning?

RUTH (*Angrily*)   I feed my son, Lena!

MAMA   I ain't meddling—(*Underbreath; busy-bodyish*) I just noticed all last week he had cold cereal, and when it starts getting this chilly in the fall a child ought to have some hot grits or something when he goes out in the cold—

RUTH (*Furious*)   I gave him hot oats—is that all right!

MAMA   I ain't meddling. (*Pause*) Put a lot of nice butter on it? (RUTH *shoots her an angry look and does not reply*) He likes lots of butter.

RUTH (*Exasperated*)   Lena—

MAMA (*To* BENEATHA. MAMA *is inclined to wander conversationally sometimes*)   What was you and your brother fussing 'bout this morning?

BENEATHA   It's not important, Mama.
    (*She gets up and goes to look out at the bathroom, which is apparently free, and she picks up her towels and rushes out*)

MAMA   What was they fighting about?

RUTH   Now you know as well as I do.

MAMA (*Shaking her head*)   Brother still worrying hisself sick about that money?

RUTH   You know he is.

MAMA   You had breakfast?

RUTH   Some coffee.

MAMA   Girl, you better start eating and looking after yourself better. You almost thin as Travis.

RUTH   Lena—

MAMA   Un-hunh?

RUTH   What are you going to do with it?

MAMA   Now don't you start, child. It's too early in the morning to be talking about money. It ain't Christian.

RUTH   It's just that he got his heart set on that store—

MAMA  You mean that liquor store that Willy Harris want him to invest in?

RUTH  Yes—

MAMA  We ain't no business people, Ruth. We just plain working folks.

RUTH  Ain't nobody business people till they go into business. Walter Lee say colored people ain't never going to start getting ahead till they start gambling on some different kinds of things in the world—investments and things.

MAMA  What done got into you, girl? Walter Lee done finally sold you on investing.

RUTH  No. Mama, something is happening between Walter and me. I don't know what it is—but he needs something—something I can't give him any more. He needs this chance, Lena.

MAMA  (*Frowning deeply*)  But liquor, honey—

RUTH  Well—like Walter say—I spec people going to always be drinking themselves some liquor.

MAMA  Well—whether they drinks it or not ain't none of my business. But whether I go into business selling it to 'em *is,* and I don't want that on my ledger this late in life. (*Stopping suddenly and studying her daughter-in-law*) Ruth Younger, what's the matter with you today? You look like you could fall over right there.

RUTH  I'm tired.

MAMA  Then you better stay home from work today.

RUTH  I can't stay home. She'd be calling up the agency and screaming at them, "My girl didn't come in today— send me somebody! My girl didn't come in!" Oh, she just have a fit . . .

MAMA    Well, let her have it. I'll just call her up and say you got the flu—

RUTH (*Laughing*)    Why the flu?

MAMA    'Cause it sounds respectable to 'em. Something white people get, too. They know 'bout the flu. Otherwise they think you been cut up or something when you tell 'em you sick.

RUTH    I got to go in. We need the money.

MAMA    Somebody would of thought my children done all but starved to death the way they talk about money here late. Child, we got a great big old check coming tomorrow.

RUTH (*Sincerely, but also self-righteously*)    Now that's your money. It ain't got nothing to do with me. We all feel like that—Walter and Bennie and me—even Travis.

MAMA (*Thoughtfully, and suddenly very far away*)    Ten thousand dollars—

RUTH    Sure is wonderful.

MAMA    Ten thousand dollars.

RUTH    You know what you should do, Miss Lena? You should take yourself a trip somewhere. To Europe or South America or someplace—

MAMA (*Throwing up her hands at the thought*)    Oh, child!

RUTH    I'm serious. Just pack up and leave! Go on away and enjoy yourself some. Forget about the family and have yourself a ball for once in your life—

MAMA (*Drily*)    You sound like I'm just about ready to die. Who'd go with me? What I look like wandering 'round Europe by myself?

RUTH   Shoot—these here rich white women do it all the time. They don't think nothing of packing up they suitcases and piling on one of them big steamships and—swoosh!—they gone, child.

MAMA   Something always told me I wasn't no rich white woman.

RUTH   Well—what are you going to do with it then?

MAMA   I ain't rightly decided. (*Thinking. She speaks now with emphasis*) Some of it got to be put away for Beneatha and her schoolin'—and ain't nothing going to touch that part of it. Nothing. (*She waits several seconds, trying to make up her mind about something, and looks at* RUTH *a little tentatively before going on*) Been thinking that we maybe could meet the notes on a little old two-story somewhere, with a yard where Travis could play in the summertime, if we use part of the insurance for a down payment and everybody kind of pitch in. I could maybe take on a little day work again, few days a week—

RUTH   (*Studying her mother-in-law furtively and concentrating on her ironing, anxious to encourage without seeming to*)   Well, Lord knows, we've put enough rent into this here rat trap to pay for four houses by now . . .

MAMA   (*Looking up at the words "rat trap" and then looking around and leaning back and sighing—in a suddenly reflective mood—*)   "Rat trap"—yes, that's all it is. (*Smiling*) I remember just as well the day me and Big Walter moved in here. Hadn't been married but two weeks and wasn't planning on living here no more than a year. (*She shakes her head at the dissolved dream*) We was going to set away, little by little, don't you know, and buy a little place out in Morgan Park. We had even picked out the house. (*Chuckling a little*)

Looks right dumpy today. But Lord, child, you should know all the dreams I had 'bout buying that house and fixing it up and making me a little garden in the back— (*She waits and stops smiling*) And didn't none of it happen.

(*Dropping her hands in a futile gesture*)

RUTH (*Keeps her head down, ironing*)   Yes, life can be a barrel of disappointments, sometimes.

MAMA   Honey, Big Walter would come in here some nights back then and slump down on that couch there and just look at the rug, and look at me and look at the rug and then back at me—and I'd know he was down then . . . really down. (*After a second very long and thoughtful pause; she is seeing back to times that only she can see*) And then, Lord, when I lost that baby—little Claude—I almost thought I was going to lose Big Walter too. Oh, that man grieved hisself! He was one man to love his children.

RUTH   Ain't nothin' can tear at you like losin' your baby.

MAMA   I guess that's how come that man finally worked hisself to death like he done. Like he was fighting his own war with this here world that took his baby from him.

RUTH   He sure was a fine man, all right. I always liked Mr. Younger.

MAMA   Crazy 'bout his children! God knows there was plenty wrong with Walter Younger—hard-headed, mean, kind of wild with women—plenty wrong with him. But he sure loved his children. Always wanted them to have something—be something. That's where Brother gets all these notions, I reckon. Big Walter used to say, he'd get right wet in the eyes sometimes, lean his head back with the water standing in his eyes and say, "Seem like God didn't see fit to give the black man nothing but dreams—but He did give us children to make them dreams seem worth while." (*She smiles*) He could talk like that, don't you know.

RUTH    Yes, he sure could. He was a good man, Mr. Younger.

MAMA    Yes, a fine man—just couldn't never catch up with his dreams, that's all.

(BENEATHA *comes in, brushing her hair and looking up to the ceiling, where the sound of a vacuum cleaner has started up*)

BENEATHA    What could be so dirty on that woman's rugs that she has to vacuum them every single day?

RUTH    I wish certain young women 'round here who I could name would take inspiration about certain rugs in a certain apartment I could also mention.

BENEATHA (*Shrugging*)    How much cleaning can a house need, for Christ's sakes.

MAMA (*Not liking the Lord's name used thus*)    Bennie!

RUTH    Just listen to her—just listen!

BENEATHA    Oh, God!

MAMA    If you use the Lord's name just one more time—

BENEATHA (*A bit of a whine*)    Oh, Mama—

RUTH    Fresh—just fresh as salt, this girl!

BENEATHA (*Drily*)    Well—if the salt loses its savor—

MAMA    Now that will do. I just ain't going to have you 'round here reciting the scriptures in vain—you hear me?

BENEATHA    How did I manage to get on everybody's wrong side by just walking into a room?

RUTH   If you weren't so fresh—

BENEATHA   Ruth, I'm twenty years old.

MAMA   What time you be home from school today?

BENEATHA   Kind of late. (*With enthusiasm*) Madeline is going to start my guitar lessons today.
(MAMA *and* RUTH *look up with the same expression*)

MAMA   Your *what* kind of lessons?

BENEATHA   Guitar.

RUTH   Oh, Father!

MAMA   How come you done taken it in your mind to learn to play the guitar?

BENEATHA   I just want to, that's all.

MAMA (*Smiling*)   Lord, child, don't you know what to do with yourself? How long it going to be before you get tired of this now—like you got tired of that little play-acting group you joined last year? (*Looking at* RUTH) And what was it the year before that?

RUTH   The horseback-riding club for which she bought that fifty-five-dollar riding habit that's been hanging in the closet ever since!

MAMA (*To* BENEATHA)   Why you got to flit so from one thing to another, baby?

BENEATHA (*Sharply*)   I just want to learn to play the guitar. Is there anything wrong with that?

MAMA   Ain't nobody trying to stop you. I just wonders sometimes why you has to flit so from one thing to another all the time. You ain't never done nothing with all that camera equipment you brought home—

BENEATHA I don't flit! I—I experiment with different forms of expression—

RUTH Like riding a horse?

BENEATHA —People have to express themselves one way or another.

MAMA What is it you want to express?

BENEATHA (*Angrily*) Me! (MAMA *and* RUTH *look at each other and burst into raucous laughter*) Don't worry— I don't expect you to understand.

MAMA (*To change the subject*) Who you going out with tomorrow night?

BENEATHA (*With displeasure*) George Murchison again.

MAMA (*Pleased*) Oh—you getting a little sweet on him?

RUTH You ask me, this child ain't sweet on nobody but herself—(*Underbreath*) Express herself!
(*They laugh*)

BENEATHA Oh—I like George all right, Mama. I mean I like him enough to go out with him and stuff, but—

RUTH (*For devilment*) What does *and stuff* mean?

BENEATHA Mind your own business.

MAMA Stop picking at her now, Ruth. (*She chuckles— then a suspicious sudden look at her daughter as she turns in her chair for emphasis*) What DOES it mean?

BENEATHA (*Wearily*) Oh, I just mean I couldn't ever really be serious about George. He's—he's so shallow.

RUTH Shallow—what do you mean he's shallow? He's *Rich!*

MAMA Hush, Ruth.

BENEATHA I know he's rich. He knows he's rich, too.

RUTH   Well—what other qualities a man got to have to satisfy you, little girl?

BENEATHA   You wouldn't even begin to understand. Anybody who married Walter could not possibly understand.

MAMA (*Outraged*)   What kind of way is that to talk about your brother?

BENEATHA   Brother is a flip—let's face it.

MAMA (*To* RUTH, *helplessly*)   What's a flip?

RUTH (*Glad to add kindling*)   She's saying he's crazy.

BENEATHA   Not crazy. Brother isn't really crazy yet—he—he's an elaborate neurotic.

MAMA   Hush your mouth!

BENEATHA   As for George. Well. George looks good—he's got a beautiful car and he takes me to nice places and, as my sister-in-law says, he is probably the richest boy I will ever get to know and I even like him sometimes—but if the Youngers are sitting around waiting to see if their little Bennie is going to tie up the family with the Murchisons, they are wasting their time.

RUTH   You mean you wouldn't marry George Murchison if he asked you someday? That pretty, rich thing? Honey, I knew you was odd—

BENEATHA   No I would not marry him if all I felt for him was what I feel now. Besides, George's family wouldn't really like it.

MAMA   Why not?

BENEATHA   Oh, Mama—The Murchisons are honest-to-God-real-*live*-rich colored people, and the only people in the world who are more snobbish than rich white people are rich colored people. I thought everybody knew that. I've met Mrs. Murchison. She's a scene!

MAMA  You must not dislike people 'cause they well off, honey.

BENEATHA  Why not? It makes just as much sense as disliking people 'cause they are poor, and lots of people do that.

RUTH (*A wisdom-of-the-ages manner. To* MAMA)  Well, she'll get over some of this—

BENEATHA  Get over it? What are you talking about, Ruth? Listen, I'm going to be a doctor. I'm not worried about who I'm going to marry yet—if I ever get married.

MAMA *and* RUTH    *If!*

MAMA  Now, Bennie—

BENEATHA  Oh, I probably will . . . but first I'm going to be a doctor, and George, for one, still thinks that's pretty funny. I couldn't be bothered with that. I am going to be a doctor and everybody around here better understand that!

MAMA (*Kindly*)  'Course you going to be a doctor, honey, God willing.

BENEATHA (*Drily*)  God hasn't got a thing to do with it.

MAMA  Beneatha—that just wasn't necessary.

BENEATHA  Well—neither is God. I get sick of hearing about God.

MAMA  Beneatha!

BENEATHA  I mean it! I'm just tired of hearing about God all the time. What has He got to do with anything? Does he pay tuition?

MAMA   You 'bout to get your fresh little jaw slapped!

RUTH   That's just what she needs, all right!

BENEATHA   Why? Why can't I say what I want to around here, like everybody else?

MAMA   It don't sound nice for a young girl to say things like that—you wasn't brought up that way. Me and your father went to trouble to get you and Brother to church every Sunday.

BENEATHA   Mama, you don't understand. It's all a matter of ideas, and God is just one idea I don't accept. It's not important. I am not going out and be immoral or commit crimes because I don't believe in God. I don't even think about it. It's just that I get tired of Him getting credit for all the things the human race achieves through its own stubborn effort. There simply is no blasted God—there is only man and it is *he* who makes miracles!

(MAMA *absorbs this speech, studies her daughter and rises slowly and crosses to* BENEATHA *and slaps her powerfully across the face. After, there is only silence and the daughter drops her eyes from her mother's face, and* MAMA *is very tall before her*)

MAMA   Now—you say after me, in my mother's house there is still God. (*There is a long pause and* BENEATHA *stares at the floor wordlessly.* MAMA *repeats the phrase with precision and cool emotion*) In my mother's house there is still God.

BENEATHA   In my mother's house there is still God.
(*A long pause*)

MAMA (*Walking away from* BENEATHA, *too disturbed for triumphant posture. Stopping and turning back to her daughter*)   There are some ideas we ain't going to have in this house. Not long as I am at the head of this family.

BENEATHA   Yes, ma'am.
(MAMA *walks out of the room*)

RUTH (*Almost gently, with profound understanding*)
You think you a woman, Bennie—but you still a little
girl. What you did was childish—so you got treated
like a child.

BENEATHA.  I see. (*Quietly*) I also see that everybody
thinks it's all right for Mama to be a tyrant. But all the
tyranny in the world will never put a God in the
heavens!
(*She picks up her books and goes out. Pause*)

RUTH (*Goes to* MAMA's *door*)   She said she was sorry.

MAMA (*Coming out, going to her plant*)   They frightens
me, Ruth. My children.

RUTH   You got good children, Lena. They just a little off
sometimes—but they're good.

MAMA   No—there's something come down between me
and them that don't let us understand each other and
I don't know what it is. One done almost lost his mind
thinking 'bout money all the time and the other done
commence to talk about things I can't seem to understand in no form or fashion. What is it that's changing,
Ruth.

RUTH (*Soothingly, older than her years*)   Now . . . you
taking it all too seriously. You just got strong-willed
children and it takes a strong woman like you to keep
'em in hand.

MAMA (*Looking at her plant and sprinkling a little water
on it*)   They spirited all right, my children. Got to admit they got spirit—Bennie and Walter. Like this little
old plant that ain't never had enough sunshine or nothing—and look at it . . .

*(She has her back to* RUTH, *who has had to stop ironing and lean against something and put the back of her hand to her forehead)*

RUTH *(Trying to keep* MAMA *from noticing)*  You . . . sure . . . loves that little old thing, don't you? . . .

MAMA  Well, I always wanted me a garden like I used to see sometimes at the back of the houses down home. This plant is close as I ever got to having one. *(She looks out of the window as she replaces the plant)* Lord, ain't nothing as dreary as the view from this window on a dreary day, is there? Why ain't you singing this morning, Ruth? Sing that "No Ways Tired." That song always lifts me up so—*(She turns at last to see that* RUTH *has slipped quietly to the floor, in a state of semiconsciousness)* Ruth! Ruth honey—what's the matter with you . . . Ruth!

*Curtain*

## SCENE TWO

*It is the following morning; a Saturday morning, and
house cleaning is in progress at the* YOUNGERS. *Furniture
has been shoved hither and yon and* MAMA *is giving the
kitchen-area walls a washing down.* BENEATHA, *in dungarees, with a handkerchief tied around her face, is
spraying insecticide into the cracks in the walls. As they
work, the radio is on and a Southside disk-jockey pro-
gram is inappropriately filling the house with a rather
exotic saxophone blues.* TRAVIS, *the sole idle one, is leaning on his arms, looking out of the window.*

TRAVIS  Grandmama, that stuff Bennie is using smells
awful. Can I go downstairs, please?

MAMA  Did you get all them chores done already? I ain't
seen you doing much.

TRAVIS  Yes'm—finished early. Where did Mama go this
morning?

MAMA (*Looking at* BENEATHA)  She had to go on a little
errand.
       (*The phone rings.* BENEATHA *runs to answer it and
       reaches it before* WALTER, *who has entered from
       bedroom*)

TRAVIS  Where?

MAMA  To tend to her business.

BENEATHA  Haylo . . . (*Disappointed*) Yes, he is. (*She
tosses the phone to* WALTER, *who barely catches it*) It's
Willie Harris again.

WALTER (*As privately as possible under* MAMA's *gaze*)
Hello, Willie. Did you get the papers from the lawyer?

54

. . . No, not yet. I told you the mailman doesn't get here till ten-thirty . . . No, I'll come there . . . Yeah! Right away. (*He hangs up and goes for his coat*)

BENEATHA   Brother, where did Ruth go?

WALTER (*As he exits*)   How should I know!

TRAVIS   Aw come on, Grandma. Can I go outside?

MAMA   Oh, I guess so. You stay right in front of the house, though, and keep a good lookout for the postman.

TRAVIS   Yes'm. (*He darts into bedroom for stickball and bat, reenters, and sees* BENEATHA *on her knees spraying under sofa with behind upraised. He edges closer to the target, takes aim, and lets her have it. She screams*) Leave them poor little cockroaches alone, they ain't bothering you none! (*He runs as she swings the spray-gun at him viciously and playfully*) Grandma! Grandma!

MAMA   Look out there, girl, before you be spilling some of that stuff on that child!

TRAVIS (*Safely behind the bastion of* MAMA)   That's right—look out, now! (*He exits*)

BENEATHA (*Drily*)   I can't imagine that it would hurt him —it has never hurt the roaches.

MAMA   Well, little boys' hides ain't as tough as Southside roaches. You better get over there behind the bureau. I seen one marching out of there like Napoleon yesterday.

BENEATHA   There's really only one way to get rid of them, Mama—

MAMA   How?

BENEATHA   Set fire to this building! Mama, where did Ruth go?

MAMA (*Looking at her with meaning*)   To the doctor, I think.

BENEATHA   The doctor? What's the matter? (*They exchange glances*) You don't think—

MAMA (*With her sense of drama*)   Now I ain't saying what I think. But I ain't never been wrong 'bout a woman neither.
(*The phone rings*)

BENEATHA (*At the phone*)   Hay-lo . . . (*Pause, and a moment of recognition*) Well—when did you get back! . . . And how was it? . . . Of course I've missed you— in my way . . . This morning? No . . . house cleaning and all that and Mama hates it if I let people come over when the house is like this . . . You *have?* Well, that's different . . . What is it— Oh, what the hell, come on over . . . Right, see you then. *Arrividerci.*
(*She hangs up*)

MAMA (*Who has listened vigorously, as is her habit*) Who is that you inviting over here with this house looking like this? You ain't got the pride you was born with!

BENEATHA   Asagai doesn't care how houses look, Mama —he's an intellectual.

MAMA   *Who?*

BENEATHA   Asagai—Joseph Asagai. He's an African boy I met on campus. He's been studying in Canada all summer.

MAMA   What's his name?

BENEATHA   Asagai, Joseph. Ah-sah-guy . . . He's from Nigeria.

MAMA   Oh, that's the little country that was founded by slaves way back . . .

BENEATHA No, Mama—that's Liberia.

MAMA I don't think I never met no African before.

BENEATHA Well, do me a favor and don't ask him a whole lot of ignorant questions about Africans. I mean, do they wear clothes and all that—

MAMA Well, now, I guess if you think we so ignorant 'round here maybe you shouldn't bring your friends here—

BENEATHA It's just that people ask such crazy things. All anyone seems to know about when it comes to Africa is Tarzan—

MAMA (*Indignantly*) Why should I know anything about Africa?

BENEATHA Why do you give money at church for the missionary work?

MAMA Well, that's to help save people.

BENEATHA You mean save them from *heathenism*—

MAMA (*Innocently*) Yes.

BENEATHA I'm afraid they need more salvation from the British and the French.
    (RUTH *comes in forlornly and pulls off her coat with dejection. They both turn to look at her*)

RUTH (*Dispiritedly*) Well, I guess from all the happy faces—everybody knows.

BENEATHA You pregnant?

MAMA Lord have mercy, I sure hope it's a little old girl. Travis ought to have a sister.
    (BENEATHA *and* RUTH *give her a hopeless look for this grandmotherly enthusiasm*)

BENEATHA   How far along are you?

RUTH   Two months.

BENEATHA   Did you mean to? I mean did you plan it or was it an accident?

MAMA   What do you know about planning or not planning?

BENEATHA   Oh, Mama.

RUTH (*Wearily*)   She's twenty years old, Lena.

BENEATHA   Did you plan it, Ruth?

RUTH   Mind your own business.

BENEATHA   It is my business—where is he going to live, on the *roof? (There is silence following the remark as the three women react to the sense of it)* Gee—I didn't mean that, Ruth, honest. Gee, I don't feel like that at all. I—I think it is wonderful.

RUTH (*Dully*)   Wonderful.

BENEATHA   Yes—really.

MAMA (*Looking at* RUTH, *worried*)   Doctor say everything going to be all right?

RUTH (*Far away*)   Yes—she says everything is going to be fine . . .

MAMA (*Immediately suspicious*)   "She"— What doctor you went to?
     (RUTH *folds over, near hysteria*)

MAMA (*Worriedly hovering over* RUTH)   Ruth honey—what's the matter with you—you sick?
     (RUTH *has her fists clenched on her thighs and is fighting hard to suppress a scream that seems to be rising in her*)

BENEATHA   What's the matter with her, Mama?

MAMA (*Working her fingers in* RUTH'S *shoulders to relax her*)   She be all right. Women gets right depressed sometimes when they get her way. (*Speaking softly, expertly, rapidly*) Now you just relax. That's right . . . just lean back, don't think 'bout nothing at all . . . nothing at all—

RUTH   I'm all right . . .
(*The glassy-eyed look melts and then she collapses into a fit of heavy sobbing. The bell rings*)

BENEATHA   Oh, my God—that must be Asagai.

MAMA (*To* RUTH)   Come on now, honey. You need to lie down and rest awhile . . . then have some nice hot food.
(*They exit,* RUTH'S *weight on her mother-in-law.* BENEATHA, *herself profoundly disturbed, opens the door to admit a rather dramatic-looking young man with a large package*)

ASAGAI   Hello, Alaiyo—

BENEATHA (*Holding the door open and regarding him with pleasure*)   Hello . . . (*Long pause*) Well—come in. And please excuse everything. My mother was very upset about my letting anyone come here with the place like this.

ASAGAI (*Coming into the room*)   You look disturbed too . . . Is something wrong?

BENEATHA (*Still at the door, absently*)   Yes . . . we've all got acute ghetto-itus. (*She smiles and comes toward him, finding a cigarette and sitting*) So—sit down! No! Wait! (*She whips the spraygun off sofa where she had left it and puts the cushions back. At last perches on arm of sofa. He sits*) So, how was Canada?

ASAGAI (*A sophisticate*)   Canadian.

BENEATHA (*Looking at him*)   Asagai, I'm very glad you are back.

ASAGAI (*Looking back at her in turn*)   Are you really?

BENEATHA   Yes—very.

ASAGAI   Why?—you were quite glad when I went away. What happened?

BENEATHA   You went away.

ASAGAI   Ahhhhhhhh.

BENEATHA   Before—you wanted to be so serious before there was time.

ASAGAI   How much time must there be before one knows what one feels?

BENEATHA (*Stalling this particular conversation. Her hands pressed together, in a deliberately childish gesture*) What did you bring me?

ASAGAI (*Handing her the package*)   Open it and see.

BENEATHA (*Eagerly opening the package and drawing out some records and the colorful robes of a Nigerian woman*)   Oh, Asagai! . . . You got them for me! . . . How beautiful . . . and the records too! (*She lifts out the robes and runs to the mirror with them and holds the drapery up in front of herself*)

ASAGAI (*Coming to her at the mirror*)   I shall have to teach you how to drape it properly. (*He flings the material about her for the moment and stands back to look at her*) Ah—Oh-pay-gay-day, oh-gbah-mu-shay. (*A Yoruba exclamation for admiration*) You wear it well . . . very well . . . mutilated hair and all.

BENEATHA (*Turning suddenly*)   My hair—what's wrong with my hair?

ASAGAI (*Shrugging*)   Were you born with it like that?

BENEATHA (*Reaching up to touch it*)   No . . . of course not.
      (*She looks back to the mirror, disturbed*)

ASAGAI (*Smiling*)   How then?

BENEATHA   You know perfectly well how . . . as crinkly as yours . . . that's how.

ASAGAI   And it is ugly to you that way?

BENEATHA (*Quickly*)   Oh, no—not ugly . . . (*More slowly, apologetically*) But it's so hard to manage when it's, well—raw.

ASAGAI   And so to accommodate that—you mutilate it every week?

BENEATHA   It's not mutilation!

ASAGAI (*Laughing aloud at her seriousness*)   Oh . . . please! I am only teasing you because you are so very serious about these things. (*He stands back from her and folds his arms across his chest as he watches her pulling at her hair and frowning in the mirror*) Do you remember the first time you met me at school? . . . (*He laughs*) You came up to me and you said—and I thought you were the most serious little thing I had ever seen—you said: (*He imitates her*) "Mr. Asagai—I want very much to talk with you. About Africa. You see, Mr. Asagai, I am looking for my *identity!*"
      (*He laughs*)

BENEATHA (*Turning to him, not laughing*)   Yes—
      (*Her face is quizzical, profoundly disturbed*)

ASAGAI (*Still teasing and reaching out and taking her face in his hands and turning her profile to him*)    Well . . . it is true that this is not so much a profile of a Hollywood queen as perhaps a queen of the Nile—(*A mock dismissal of the importance of the question*) But what does it matter? Assimilationism is so popular in your country.

BENEATHA (*Wheeling, passionately, sharply*)    I am not an assimilationist!

ASAGAI (*The protest hangs in the room for a moment and* ASAGAI *studies her, his laughter fading*)    Such a serious one. (*There is a pause*) So—you like the robes? You must take excellent care of them—they are from my sister's personal wardrobe.

BENEATHA (*With incredulity*)    You—you sent all the way home—for me?

ASAGAI (*With charm*)    For you—I would do much more . . . Well, that is what I came for. I must go.

BENEATHA    Will you call me Monday?

ASAGAI    Yes . . . We have a great deal to talk about. I mean about identity and time and all that.

BENEATHA    Time?

ASAGAI    Yes. About how much time one needs to know what one feels.

BENEATHA    You see! You never understood that there is more than one kind of feeling which can exist between a man and a woman—or, at least, there should be.

ASAGAI (*Shaking his head negatively but gently*)    No. Between a man and a woman there need be only one kind of feeling. I have that for you . . . Now even . . . right this moment . . .

BENEATHA   I know—and by itself—it won't do. I can find that anywhere.

ASAGAI   For a woman it should be enough.

BENEATHA   I know—because that's what it says in all the novels that men write. But it isn't. Go ahead and laugh—but I'm not interested in being someone's little episode in America or—(*With feminine vengeance*)—one of them! (ASAGAI *has burst into laughter again*) That's funny as hell, huh!

ASAGAI   It's just that every American girl I have known has said that to me. White—black—in this you are all the same. And the same speech, too!

BENEATHA (*Angrily*)   Yuk, yuk, yuk!

ASAGAI   It's how you can be sure that the world's most liberated women are not liberated at all. You all talk about it too much!
   (MAMA *enters and is immediately all social charm because of the presence of a guest*)

BENEATHA   Oh—Mama—this is Mr. Asagai.

MAMA   How do you do?

ASAGAI (*Total politeness to an elder*)   How do you do, Mrs. Younger. Please forgive me for coming at such an outrageous hour on a Saturday.

MAMA   Well, you are quite welcome. I just hope you understand that our house don't always look like this. (*Chatterish*) You must come again. I would love to here all about—(*Not sure of the name*)—your country. I think it's so sad the way our American Negroes don't know nothing about Africa 'cept Tarzan and all that. And all that money they pour into these churches when they ought to be helping you people over there drive out them French and Englishmen done taken away your land.

>(*The mother flashes a slightly superior look at her daughter upon completion of the recitation*)

ASAGAI (*Taken aback by this sudden and acutely unrelated expression of sympathy*)  Yes . . . yes . . .

MAMA (*Smiling at him suddenly and relaxing and looking him over*)  How many miles is it from here to where you come from?

ASAGAI  Many thousands.

MAMA (*Looking at him as she would* WALTER)  I bet you don't half look after yourself, being away from your mama either. I spec you better come 'round here from time to time to get yourself some decent home-cooked meals . . .

ASAGAI (*Moved*)  Thank you. Thank you very much. (*They are all quiet, then*—) Well . . . I must go. I will call you Monday, Alaiyo.

MAMA  What's that he call you?

ASAGAI  Oh—"Alaiyo." I hope you don't mind. It is what you would call a nickname, I think. It is a Yoruba word. I am a Yoruba.

MAMA (*Looking at* BENEATHA)  I—I thought he was from— (*Uncertain*)

ASAGAI (*Understanding*)  Nigeria is my country. Yoruba is my tribal origin—

BENEATHA  You didn't tell us what Alaiyo means . . . for all I know, you might be calling me Little Idiot or something . . .

ASAGAI  Well . . . let me see . . . I do not know how just to explain it . . . The sense of a thing can be so different when it changes languages.

BENEATHA  You're evading.

ASAGAI  No—really it is difficult . . . (*Thinking*) It means . . . it means One for Whom Bread—Food—Is Not Enough. (*He looks at her*) Is that all right?

BENEATHA (*Understanding, softly*)  Thank you.

MAMA (*Looking from one to the other and not understanding any of it*)  Well . . . that's nice . . . You must come see us again—Mr. ——

ASAGAI  Ah-sah-guy . . .

MAMA  Yes . . . Do come again.

ASAGAI  Good-bye.
  (*He exits*)

MAMA (*After him*)  Lord, that's a pretty thing just went out here! (*Insinuatingly, to her daughter*) Yes, I guess I see why we done commence to get so interested in Africa 'round here. Missionaries my aunt Jenny!
  (*She exits*)

BENEATHA  Oh, Mama! . . .
  (*She picks up the Nigerian dress and holds it up to her in front of the mirror again. She sets the headdress on haphazardly and then notices her hair again and clutches at it and then replaces the headdress and frowns at herself. Then she starts to wriggle in front of the mirror as she thinks a Nigerian woman might. TRAVIS enters and stands regarding her*)

TRAVIS  What's the matter, girl, you cracking up?

BENEATHA   Shut up.
>   (*She pulls the headdress off and looks at herself in the mirror and clutches at her hair again and squinches her eyes as if trying to imagine something. Then, suddenly, she gets her raincoat and kerchief and hurriedly prepares for going out*)

MAMA (*Coming back into the room*)   She's resting now. Travis, baby, run next door and ask Miss Johnson to please let me have a little kitchen cleanser. This here can is empty as Jacob's kettle.

TRAVIS   I just came in.

MAMA   Do as you told. (*He exits and she looks at her daughter*) Where you going?

BENEATHA (*Halting at the door*)   To become a queen of the Nile!
>   (*She exits in a breathless blaze of glory.* RUTH *appears in the bedroom doorway*)

MAMA   Who told you to get up?

RUTH   Ain't nothing wrong with me to be lying in no bed for. Where did Bennie go?

MAMA (*Drumming her fingers*)   Far as I could make out—to Egypt. (RUTH *just looks at her*) What time is it getting to?

RUTH   Ten twenty. And the mailman going to ring that bell this morning just like he done every morning for the last umpteen years.
>   (TRAVIS *comes in with the cleanser can*)

TRAVIS   She say to tell you that she don't have much.

MAMA (*Angrily*)   Lord, some people I could name sure is tight-fisted! (*Directing her grandson*) Mark two cans of cleanser down on the list there. If she that hard up for kitchen cleanser, I sure don't want to forget to get her none!

RUTH   Lena—maybe the woman is just short on cleanser—

MAMA (*Not listening*)   —Much baking powder as she done borrowed from me all these years, she could of done gone into the baking business!
       (*The bell sounds suddenly and sharply and all three are stunned—serious and silent—mid-speech. In spite of all the other conversations and distractions of the morning, this is what they have been waiting for, even* TRAVIS, *who looks helplessly from his mother to his grandmother.* RUTH *is the first to come to life again*)

RUTH (*To* TRAVIS)   Get down them steps, boy!
       (TRAVIS *snaps to life and flies out to get the mail*)

MAMA (*Her eyes wide, her hand to her breast*)   You mean it done really come?

RUTH (*Excited*)   Oh, Miss Lena!

MAMA (*Collecting herself*)   Well . . . I don't know what we all so excited about 'round here for. We known it was coming for months.

RUTH   That's a whole lot different from having it come and being able to hold it in your hands . . . a piece of paper worth ten thousand dollars . . . (TRAVIS *bursts back into the room. He holds the envelope high above his head, like a little dancer, his face is radiant and he is breathless. He moves to his grandmother with sudden slow ceremony and puts the envelope into her hands. She accepts it, and then merely holds it and looks at it*) Come on! Open it . . . Lord have mercy, I wish Walter Lee was here!

TRAVIS   Open it, Grandmama!

MAMA (*Staring at it*)  Now you all be quiet. It's just a check.

RUTH  Open it . . .

MAMA (*Still staring at it*)  Now don't act silly . . . We ain't never been no people to act silly 'bout no money—

RUTH (*Swiftly*)  We ain't never had none before—OPEN IT!
> (MAMA *finally makes a good strong tear and pulls out the thin blue slice of paper and inspects it closely. The boy and his mother study it raptly over* MAMA'S *shoulders*)

MAMA  Travis! (*She is counting off with doubt*) Is that the right number of zeros.

TRAVIS  Yes'm . . . ten thousand dollars. Gaalee, Grandmama, you rich.

MAMA (*She holds the check away from her, still looking at it. Slowly her face sobers into a mask of unhappiness*)  Ten thousand dollars. (*She hands it to* RUTH) Put it away somewhere, Ruth. (*She does not look at* RUTH; *her eyes seem to be seeing something somewhere very far off*) Ten thousand dollars they give you. Ten thousand dollars.

TRAVIS (*To his mother, sincerely*)  What's the matter with Grandmama—don't she want to be rich?

RUTH (*Distractedly*)  You go on out and play now, baby. (TRAVIS *exits.* MAMA *starts wiping dishes absently, humming intently to herself.* RUTH *turns to her, with kind exasperation*) You've gone and got yourself upset.

MAMA (*Not looking at her*)  I spec if it wasn't for you all . . . I would just put that money away or give it to the church or something.

RUTH   Now what kind of talk is that. Mr. Younger would just be plain mad if he could hear you talking foolish like that.

MAMA  (*Stopping and staring off*)   Yes . . . he sure would. (*Sighing*) We got enough to do with that money, all right. (*She halts then, and turns and looks at her daughter-in-law hard;* RUTH *avoids her eyes and* MAMA *wipes her hands with finality and starts to speak firmly to* RUTH) Where did you go today, girl?

RUTH   To the doctor.

MAMA  (*Impatiently*)   Now, Ruth . . . you know better than that. Old Doctor Jones is strange enough in his way but there ain't nothing 'bout him make somebody slip and call him "she"—like you done this morning.

RUTH   Well, that's what happened—my tongue slipped.

MAMA   You went to see that woman, didn't you?

RUTH  (*Defensively, giving herself away*)   What woman you talking about?

MAMA  (*Angrily*)   That woman who—
     (WALTER *enters in great excitement*)

WALTER   Did it come?

MAMA  (*Quietly*)   Can't you give people a Christian greeting before you start asking about money?

WALTER  (*To* RUTH)   Did it come? (RUTH *unfolds the check and lays it quietly before him, watching him intently with thoughts of her own.* WALTER *sits down and grasps it close and counts off the zeros*) Ten thousand dollars—(*He turns suddenly, frantically to his mother and draws some papers out of his breast pocket*) Mama—look. Old Willy Harris put everything on paper—

MAMA    Son—I think you ought to talk to your wife . . . I'll go on out and leave you alone if you want—

WALTER    I can talk to her later— Mama, look—

MAMA    Son—

WALTER    WILL SOMEBODY PLEASE LISTEN TO ME TODAY!

MAMA (*Quietly*)    I don't 'low no yellin' in this house, Walter Lee, and you know it—(WALTER *stares at them in frustration and starts to speak several times*) And there ain't going to be no investing in no liquor stores.

WALTER    But, Mama, you ain't even looked at it.

MAMA    I don't aim to have to speak on that again.
          (*A long pause*)

WALTER    You ain't looked at it and you don't aim to have to speak on that again? You ain't even looked at it and *you* have decided— (*Crumpling his papers*) Well, *you* tell that to my boy tonight when you put him to sleep on the living-room couch . . . (*Turning to* MAMA *and speaking directly to her*) Yeah—and tell it to my wife, Mama, tomorrow when she has to go out of here to look after somebody else's kids. And tell it to *me,* Mama, every time we need a new pair of curtains and I have to watch *you* go out and work in somebody's kitchen. Yeah, you tell me then!
          (WALTER *starts out*)

RUTH    Where you going?

WALTER    I'm going out!

RUTH    Where?

WALTER    Just out of this house somewhere—

RUTH (*Getting her coat*)    I'll come too.

WALTER  I don't want you to come!

RUTH  I got something to talk to you about, Walter.

WALTER  That's too bad.

MAMA  (*Still quietly*)  Walter Lee—(*She waits and he finally turns and looks at her*) Sit down.

WALTER  I'm a grown man, Mama.

MAMA  Ain't nobody said you wasn't grown. But you still in my house and my presence. And as long as you are—you'll talk to your wife civil. Now sit down.

RUTH  (*Suddenly*)  Oh, let him go on out and drink himself to death! He makes me sick to my stomach! (*She flings her coat against him and exits to bedroom*)

WALTER  (*Violently flinging the coat after her*)  And you turn mine too, baby! (*The door slams behind her*) That was my biggest mistake—

MAMA  (*Still quietly*)  Walter, what is the matter with you?

WALTER  Matter with me? Ain't nothing the matter with *me!*

MAMA  Yes there is. Something eating you up like a crazy man. Something more than me not giving you this money. The past few years I been watching it happen to you. You get all nervous acting and kind of wild in the eyes—(WALTER *jumps up impatiently at her words*) I said sit there now, I'm talking to you!

WALTER  Mama—I don't need no nagging at me today.

MAMA  Seem like you getting to a place where you always tied up in some kind of knot about something. But if anybody ask you 'bout it you just yell at 'em and bust out the house and go out and drink somewheres. Walter Lee, people can't live with that. Ruth's a good, patient girl in her way—but you getting to be too much. Boy, don't make the mistake of driving that girl away from you.

WALTER   Why—what she do for me?

MAMA   She loves you.

WALTER   Mama—I'm going out. I want to go off somewhere and be by myself for a while.

MAMA   I'm sorry 'bout your liquor store, son. It just wasn't the thing for us to do. That's what I want to tell you about—

WALTER   I got to go out, Mama—
        (*He rises*)

MAMA   It's dangerous, son.

WALTER   What's dangerous?

MAMA   When a man goes outside his home to look for peace.

WALTER (*Beseechingly*)   Then why can't there never be no peace in this house then?

MAMA   You done found it in some other house?

WALTER   No—there ain't no woman! Why do women always think there's a woman somewhere when a man gets restless. (*Picks up the check*) Do you know what this money means to me? Do you know what this money can do for us? (*Puts it back*) Mama—Mama—I want so many things . . .

MAMA   Yes, son—

WALTER   I want so many things that they are driving me kind of crazy . . . Mama—look at me.

MAMA   I'm looking at you. You a good-looking boy. You got a job, a nice wife, a fine boy and—

WALTER   A job. (*Looks at her*) Mama, a job? I open
and close car doors all day long. I drive a man around
in his limousine and I say, "Yes, sir; no, sir; very
good, sir; shall I take the Drive, sir?" Mama, that ain't
no kind of job . . . that ain't nothing at all. (*Very
quietly*) Mama, I don't know if I can make you understand.

MAMA   Understand what, baby?

WALTER (*Quietly*)   Sometimes it's like I can see the future stretched out in front of me—just plain as day.
The future, Mama. Hanging over there at the edge of
my days. Just waiting for me—a big, looming blank
space—full of *nothing*. Just waiting for *me*. But it don't
have to be. (*Pause. Kneeling beside her chair*) Mama—
sometimes when I'm downtown and I pass them cool,
quiet-looking restaurants where them white boys are
sitting back and talking 'bout things . . . sitting there
turning deals worth millions of dollars . . . sometimes I
see guys don't look much older than me—

MAMA   Son—how come you talk so much 'bout money?

WALTER (*With immense passion*)   Because it is life,
Mama!

MAMA (*Quietly*)   Oh—(*Very quietly*) So now it's life.
Money is life. Once upon a time freedom used to be
life—now it's money. I guess the world really do
change . . .

WALTER   No—it was always money, Mama. We just
didn't know about it.

MAMA   No . . . something has changed. (*She looks at
him*) You something new, boy. In my time we was
worried about not being lynched and getting to the
North if we could and how to stay alive and still have
a pinch of dignity too . . . Now here come you and

Beneatha—talking 'bout things we ain't never even thought about hardly, me and your daddy. You ain't satisfied or proud of nothing we done. I mean that you had a home; that we kept you out of trouble till you was grown; that you don't have to ride to work on the back of nobody's streetcar— You my children—but how different we done become.

WALTER (*A long beat. He pats her hand and gets up*) You just don't understand, Mama, you just don't understand.

MAMA    Son—do you know your wife is expecting another baby? (WALTER *stands, stunned, and absorbs what his mother has said*) That's what she wanted to talk to you about. (WALTER *sinks down into a chair*) This ain't for me to be telling—but you ought to know. (*She waits*) I think Ruth is thinking 'bout getting rid of that child.

WALTER (*Slowly understanding*)—No — no — Ruth wouldn't do that.

MAMA    When the world gets ugly enough—a woman will do anything for her family. *The part that's already living.*

WALTER    You don't know Ruth, Mama, if you think she would do that.
          (RUTH *opens the bedroom door and stands there a little limp*)

RUTH (*Beaten*)    Yes I would too, Walter. (*Pause*) I gave her a five-dollar down payment.
          (*There is total silence as the man stares at his wife and the mother stares at her son*)

MAMA (*Presently*)    Well — (*Tightly*) Well — son, I'm waiting to hear you say something . . . (*She waits*) I'm waiting to hear how you be your father's son. Be the man he was . . . (*Pause. The silence shouts*) Your wife say she going to destroy your child. And I'm waiting to hear you talk like him and say we a people who give children life, not who destroys them—(*She rises*) I'm waiting to see you stand up and look like your daddy and say we done give up one baby to poverty and that we ain't going to give up nary another one . . . I'm waiting.

WALTER   Ruth— (*He can say nothing*)

MAMA   If you a son of mine, tell her! (WALTER *picks up his keys and his coat and walks out. She continues, bitterly*) You . . . you are a disgrace to your father's memory. Somebody get me my hat!

*Curtain*

# ACT II

## Scene One

*Time: Later the same day.*
*At rise:* RUTH *is ironing again. She has the radio going. Presently* BENEATHA'S *bedroom door opens and* RUTH'S *mouth falls and she puts down the iron in fascination.*

RUTH   What have we got on tonight!

BENEATHA (*Emerging grandly from the doorway so that we can see her thoroughly robed in the costume Asagai brought*)   You are looking at what a well-dressed Nigerian woman wears—(*She parades for* RUTH, *her hair completely hidden by the headdress; she is coquettishly fanning herself with an ornate oriental fan, mistakenly more like Butterfly than any Nigerian that ever was*) Isn't it beautiful? (*She promenades to the radio and, with an arrogant flourish, turns off the good loud blues that is playing*) Enough of this assimilationist junk! (*RUTH follows her with her eyes as she goes to the phonograph and puts on a record and turns and waits ceremoniously for the music to come up. Then, with a shout*—) OCOMOGOSIAY!

(*RUTH jumps. The music comes up, a lovely Nigerian melody.* BENEATHA *listens, enraptured, her*

76

*eyes far away—"back to the past." She begins to dance.* RUTH *is dumfounded*)

RUTH   What kind of dance is that?

BENEATHA   A folk dance.

RUTH (*Pearl Bailey*)   What kind of folks do that, honey?

BENEATHA   It's from Nigeria. It's a dance of welcome.

RUTH   Who you welcoming?

BENEATHA   The men back to the village.

RUTH   Where they been?

BENEATHA   How should I know—out hunting or something. Anyway, they are coming back now . . .

RUTH   Well, that's good.

BENEATHA (*With the record*)
*Alundi, alundi*
*Alundi alunya*
*Jop pu a jeepua*
*Ang gu sooooooooooo*

*Ai yai yae . . .*
*Ayehaye—alundi . . .*
(WALTER *comes in during this performance; he has obviously been drinking. He leans against the door heavily and watches his sister, at first with distaste. Then his eyes look off—"back to the past"—as he lifts both his fists to the roof, screaming*)

WALTER   YEAH . . . AND ETHIOPIA STRETCH FORTH HER HANDS AGAIN! . . .

RUTH (*Drily, looking at him*)   Yes—and Africa sure is claiming her own tonight. (*She gives them both up and starts ironing again*)

WALTER (*All in a drunken, dramatic shout*)  Shut up!
. . . I'm digging them drums . . . them drums move me!
. . . (*He makes his weaving way to his wife's face and
leans in close to her*) In my *heart of hearts*—(*He
thumps his chest*)—I am much warrior!

RUTH (*Without even looking up*)  In your heart of hearts
you are much drunkard.

WALTER (*Coming away from her and starting to wander
around the room, shouting*)  Me and Jomo . . . (*Intently, in his sister's face. She has stopped dancing to
watch him in this unknown mood*) That's my man,
Kenyatta. (*Shouting and thumping his chest*) FLAM-
ING SPEAR! HOT DAMN! (*He is suddenly in pos-
session of an imaginary spear and actively spearing
enemies all over the room*) OCOMOGOSIAY . . .

BENEATHA (*To encourage* WALTER, *thoroughly caught up
with this side of him*)  OCOMOGOSIAY, FLAMING
SPEAR!

WALTER   THE LION IS WAKING . . . OWIMOWEH!
(*He pulls his shirt open and leaps up on the table and
gestures with his spear*)

BENEATHA   OWIMOWEH!

WALTER (*On the table, very far gone, his eyes pure glass
sheets. He sees what we cannot, that he is a leader of
his people, a great chief, a descendant of Chaka, and
that the hour to march has come*)  Listen, my black
brothers—

BENEATHA   OCOMOGOSIAY!

WALTER   —Do you hear the waters rushing against the
shores of the coastlands—

BENEATHA   OCOMOGOSIAY!

WALTER    —Do you hear the screeching of the cocks in yonder hills beyond where the chiefs meet in council for the coming of the mighty war—

BENEATHA   OCOMOGOSIAY!
> (*And now the lighting shifts subtly to suggest the world of* WALTER'S *imagination, and the mood shifts from pure comedy. It is the inner* WALTER *speaking: the Southside chauffeur has assumed an unexpected majesty*)

WALTER    —Do you hear the beating of the wings of the birds flying low over the mountains and the low places of our land—

BENEATHA   OCOMOGOSIAY!

WALTER    —Do you hear the singing of the women, singing the war songs of our fathers to the babies in the great houses? Singing the sweet war songs! (*The doorbell rings*) OH, DO YOU HEAR, MY *BLACK* BROTHERS!

BENEATHA (*Completely gone*)   We hear you, Flaming Spear—
> (RUTH *shuts off the phonograph and opens the door.* GEORGE MURCHISON *enters*)

WALTER    Telling us to prepare for the GREATNESS OF THE TIME! (*Lights back to normal. He turns and sees* GEORGE) Black Brother!
> (*He extends his hand for the fraternal clasp*)

GEORGE    Black Brother, hell!

RUTH (*Having had enough, and embarrassed for the family*) Beneatha, you got company—what's the matter with you? Walter Lee Younger, get down off that table and stop acting like a fool . . .

(WALTER *comes down off the table suddenly and makes a quick exit to the bathroom*)

RUTH    He's had a little to drink . . . I don't know what her excuse is.

GEORGE (*To* BENEATHA)    Look honey, we're going *to* the theatre—we're not going to be *in* it . . . so go change, huh?
(BENEATHA *looks at him and slowly, ceremoniously, lifts her hands and pulls off the headdress. Her hair is close-cropped and unstraightened.* GEORGE *freezes mid-sentence and* RUTH'S *eyes all but fall out of her head*)

GEORGE    What in the name of—

RUTH (*Touching* BENEATHA'S *hair*)    Girl, you done lost your natural mind!? Look at your head!

GEORGE    What have you done to your head—I mean your hair!

BENEATHA    Nothing—except cut it off.

RUTH    Now that's the truth—it's what ain't been done to it! You expect this boy to go out with you with your head all nappy like that?

BENEATHA (*Looking at* GEORGE)    That's up to George. If he's ashamed of his heritage—

GEORGE    Oh, don't be so proud of yourself, Bennie—just because you look eccentric.

BENEATHA    How can something that's natural be eccentric?

GEORGE    That's what being eccentric means—being natural. Get dressed.

BENEATHA    I don't like that, George.

RUTH   Why must you and your brother make an argument out of everything people say?

BENEATHA   Because I hate assimilationist Negroes!

RUTH   Will somebody please tell me what assimila-whoever means!

GEORGE   Oh, it's just a college girl's way of calling people Uncle Toms—but that isn't what it means at all.

RUTH   Well, what does it mean?

BENEATHA   (*Cutting* GEORGE *off and staring at him as she replies to* RUTH)   It means someone who is willing to give up his own culture and submerge himself completely in the dominant, and in this case *oppressive* culture!

GEORGE   Oh, dear, dear, dear! Here we go! A lecture on the African past! On our Great West African Heritage! In one second we will hear all about the great Ashanti empires; the great Songhay civilizations; and the great sculpture of Bénin—and then some poetry in the Bantu—and the whole monologue will end with the word *heritage!* (*Nastily*) Let's face it, baby, your heritage is nothing but a bunch of raggedy-assed spirituals and some grass huts!

BENEATHA   GRASS HUTS! (RUTH *crosses to her and forcibly pushes her toward the bedroom*) See there . . . you are standing there in your splendid ignorance talking about people who were the first to smelt iron on the face of the earth! (RUTH *is pushing her through the door*) The Ashanti were performing surgical operations when the English—(RUTH *pulls the door to, with* BENEATHA *on the other side, and smiles graciously at* GEORGE. BENEATHA *opens the door and shouts the end of the sentence defiantly at* GEORGE)—were still tatooing themselves with blue dragons! (*She goes back inside*)

RUTH  Have a seat, George (*They both sit.* RUTH *folds her hands rather primly on her lap, determined to demonstrate the civilization of the family*) Warm, ain't it? I mean for September. (*Pause*) Just like they always say about Chicago weather: If it's too hot or cold for you, just wait a minute and it'll change. (*She smiles happily at this cliché of clichés*) Everybody say it's got to do with them bombs and things they keep setting off. (*Pause*) Would you like a nice cold beer?

GEORGE  No, thank you. I don't care for beer. (*He looks at his watch*) I hope she hurries up.

RUTH  What time is the show?

GEORGE  It's an eight-thirty curtain. That's just Chicago, though. In New York standard curtain time is eight forty.
    (*He is rather proud of this knowledge*)

RUTH (*Properly appreciating it*)  You get to New York a lot?

GEORGE (*Offhand*)  Few times a year.

RUTH  Oh—that's nice. I've never been to New York.
    (WALTER *enters. We feel he has relieved himself, but the edge of unreality is still with him*)

WALTER  New York ain't got nothing Chicago ain't. Just a bunch of hustling people all squeezed up together— being "Eastern."
    (*He turns his face into a screw of displeasure*)

GEORGE  Oh—you've been?

WALTER  *Plenty* of times.

RUTH (*Shocked at the lie*)  Walter Lee Younger!

WALTER (*Staring her down*)  Plenty! (*Pause*) What we got to drink in this house? Why don't you offer this man some refreshment. (*To* GEORGE) They don't know how to entertain people in this house, man.

GEORGE     Thank you—I don't really care for anything.

WALTER (*Feeling his head; sobriety coming*)     Where's Mama?

RUTH     She ain't come back yet.

WALTER (*Looking* MURCHISON *over from head to toe, scrutinizing his carefully casual tweed sports jacket over cashmere V-neck sweater over soft eyelet shirt and tie, and soft slacks, finished off with white buckskin shoes*) Why all you college boys wear them faggoty-looking white shoes?

RUTH     Walter Lee!
     (GEORGE MURCHISON *ignores the remark*)

WALTER (*To* RUTH)     Well, they look crazy as hell— white shoes, cold as it is.

RUTH (*Crushed*)     You have to excuse him—

WALTER     No he don't! Excuse me for what? What you always excusing me for! I'll excuse myself when I needs to be excused! (*A pause*) They look as funny as them black knee socks Beneatha wears out of here all the time.

RUTH     It's the college *style*, Walter.

WALTER     Style, hell. She looks like she got burnt legs or something!

RUTH     Oh, Walter—

WALTER (*An irritable mimic*)     Oh, Walter! Oh, Walter! (*To* MURCHISON) How's your old man making out? I understand you all going to buy that big hotel on the Drive? (*He finds a beer in the refrigerator, wanders over to* MURCHISON, *sipping and wiping his lips with the back of his hand, and straddling a chair backwards to talk to the other man*) Shrewd move. Your old man is all right, man. (*Tapping his head and half winking for emphasis*) I mean he knows how to operate. I mean he thinks *big,* you know what I mean, I mean for a *home,* you know? But I think he's kind of running out of ideas now. I'd like to talk to him. Listen, man, I got some plans that could turn this city upside down. I mean think like he does. *Big.* Invest big, gamble big, hell, lose *big* if you have to, you know what I mean. It's hard to find a man on this whole Southside who understands my kind of thinking—you dig? (*He scrutinizes* MURCHISON *again, drinks his beer, squints his eyes and leans in close, confidential, man to man*) Me and you ought to sit down and talk sometimes, man. Man, I got me some ideas . . .

MURCHISON (*With boredom*) Yeah — sometimes we'll have to do that, Walter.

WALTER (*Understanding the indifference, and offended*) Yeah—well, when you get the time, man. I know you a busy little boy.

RUTH  Walter, please—

WALTER (*Bitterly, hurt*) I know ain't nothing in this world as busy as you colored college boys with your fraternity pins and white shoes . . .

RUTH (*Covering her face with humiliation*) Oh, Walter Lee—

WALTER  I see you all all the time—with the books tucked under your arms—going to your (*British A—a mimic*) "clahsses." And for what! What the hell you learning over there? Filling up your heads—(*Counting off on his fingers*)—with the sociology and the psychology—but they teaching you how to be a man?

How to take over and run the world? They teaching
you how to run a rubber plantation or a steel mill?
Naw—just to talk proper and read books and wear
them faggoty-looking white shoes . . .

GEORGE (*Looking at him with distaste, a little above it
all*)  You're all wacked up with bitterness, man.

WALTER (*Intently, almost quietly, between the teeth,
glaring at the boy*)  And you—ain't you bitter, man?
Ain't you just about had it yet? Don't you see no stars
gleaming that you can't reach out and grab? You
happy?—You contented son-of-a-bitch—you happy?
You got it made? Bitter? Man, I'm a volcano. Bitter?
Here I am a giant—surrounded by ants! Ants who
can't even understand what it is the giant is talking
about.

RUTH (*Passionately and suddenly*)  Oh, Walter—ain't
you with nobody!

WALTER (*Violently*)  No! 'Cause ain't nobody with me!
Not even my own mother!

RUTH  Walter, that's a terrible thing to say!
(BENEATHA *enters, dressed for the evening in a
cocktail dress and earrings, hair natural*)

GEORGE  Well—hey—(*Crosses to* BENEATHA; *thoughtful,
with emphasis, since this is a reversal*) You look great!

WALTER (*Seeing his sister's hair for the first time*)  What's
the matter with your head?

BENEATHA (*Tired of the jokes now*)  I cut it off, Brother.

WALTER (*Coming close to inspect it and walking around
her*)  Well, I'll be damned. So that's what they mean
by the African bush . . .

BENEATHA  Ha ha. Let's go, George.

GEORGE (*Looking at her*)    You know something? I like it. It's sharp. I mean it really is. (*Helps her into her wrap*)

RUTH    Yes—I think so, too. (*She goes to the mirror and starts to clutch at her hair*)

WALTER    Oh no! You leave yours alone, baby. You might turn out to have a pin-shaped head or something!

BENEATHA    See you all later.

RUTH    Have a nice time.

GEORGE    Thanks. Good night. (*Half out the door, he re-opens it. To* WALTER) Good night, Prometheus!
    (BENEATHA *and* GEORGE *exit*)

WALTER (*To* RUTH)    Who is Prometheus?

RUTH    I don't know. Don't worry about it.

WALTER (*In fury, pointing after* GEORGE)    See there—they get to a point where they can't insult you man to man—they got to go talk about something ain't nobody never heard of!

RUTH    How do you know it was an insult? (*To humor him*) Maybe Prometheus is a nice fellow.

WALTER    Prometheus! I bet there ain't even no such thing! I bet that simple-minded clown—

RUTH    Walter—
    (*She stops what she is doing and looks at him*)

WALTER (*Yelling*)    Don't start!

RUTH    Start what?

WALTER    Your nagging! Where was I? Who was I with? How much money did I spend?

RUTH (*Plaintively*)    Walter Lee—why don't we just try to talk about it . . .

WALTER (*Not listening*)  I been out talking with people who understand me. People who care about the things I got on my mind.

RUTH (*Wearily*)  I guess that means people like Willy Harris.

WALTER  Yes, people like Willy Harris.

RUTH (*With a sudden flash of impatience*)  Why don't you all just hurry up and go into the banking business and stop talking about it!

WALTER  Why? You want to know why? 'Cause we all tied up in a race of people that don't know how to do nothing but moan, pray and have babies!
(*The line is too bitter even for him and he looks at her and sits down*)

RUTH  Oh, Walter . . . (*Softly*) Honey, why can't you stop fighting me?

WALTER (*Without thinking*)  Who's fighting you? Who even cares about you?
(*This line begins the retardation of his mood*)

RUTH  Well—(*She waits a long time, and then with resignation starts to put away her things*) I guess I might as well go on to bed . . . (*More or less to herself*) I don't know where we lost it . . . but we have . . . (*Then, to him*) I—I'm sorry about this new baby, Walter. I guess maybe I better go on and do what I started . . . I guess I just didn't realize how bad things was with us . . . I guess I just didn't really realize—(*She starts out to the bedroom and stops*) You want some hot milk?

WALTER  Hot milk?

RUTH  Yes—hot milk.

WALTER  Why hot milk?

RUTH  'Cause after all that liquor you come home with you ought to have something hot in your stomach.

WALTER   I don't want no milk.

RUTH   You want some coffee then?

WALTER   No, I don't want no coffee. I don't want nothing hot to drink. (*Almost plaintively*) Why you always trying to give me something to eat?

RUTH (*Standing and looking at him helplessly*)   What *else* can I give you, Walter Lee Younger?
(*She stands and looks at him and presently turns to go out again. He lifts his head and watches her going away from him in a new mood which began to emerge when he asked her "Who cares about you?"*)

WALTER   It's been rough, ain't it, baby? (*She hears and stops but does not turn around and he continues to her back*) I guess between two people there ain't never as much understood as folks generally thinks there is. I mean like between me and you—(*She turns to face him*) How we gets to the place where we scared to talk softness to each other. (*He waits, thinking hard himself*) Why you think it got to be like that? (*He is thoughtful, almost as a child would be*) Ruth, what is it gets into people ought to be close?

RUTH   I don't know, honey. I think about it a lot.

WALTER   On account of you and me, you mean? The way things are with us. The way something done come down between us.

RUTH   There ain't so much between us, Walter . . . Not when you come to me and try to talk to me. Try to be with me . . . a little even.

WALTER (*Total honesty*) Sometimes . . . sometimes . . .
I don't even know how to try.

RUTH  Walter—

WALTER  Yes?

RUTH (*Coming to him, gently and with misgiving, but
coming to him*) Honey . . . life don't have to be like
this. I mean sometimes people can do things so that
things are better . . . You remember how we used to
talk when Travis was born . . . about the way we were
going to live . . . the kind of house . . . (*She is strok-
ing his head*) Well, it's all starting to slip away from
us . . .

> (*He turns her to him and they look at each other
> and kiss, tenderly and hungrily. The door opens
> and* MAMA *enters—*WALTER *breaks away and
> jumps up. A beat*)

WALTER  Mama, where have you been?

MAMA  My—them steps is longer than they used to be.
Whew! (*She sits down and ignores him*) How you feeling this evening, Ruth?

> (RUTH *shrugs, disturbed at having been interrupted
> and watching her husband knowingly*)

WALTER  Mama, where have you been all day?

MAMA (*Still ignoring him and leaning on the table and
changing to more comfortable shoes*) Where's Travis?

RUTH  I let him go out earlier and he ain't come back
yet. Boy, is he going to get it!

WALTER  Mama!

MAMA (*As if she has heard him for the first time*) Yes,
son?

WALTER    Where did you go this afternoon?

MAMA    I went downtown to tend to some business that I had to tend to.

WALTER    What kind of business?

MAMA    You know better than to question me like a child, Brother.

WALTER (*Rising and bending over the table*)    Where were you, Mama? (*Bringing his fists down and shouting*) Mama, you didn't go do something with that insurance money, something crazy?
     (*The front door opens slowly, interrupting him, and* TRAVIS *peeks his head in, less than hopefully*)

TRAVIS (*To his mother*)    Mama, I—

RUTH    "Mama I" nothing! You're going to get it, boy! Get on in that bedroom and get yourself ready!

TRAVIS    But I—

MAMA    Why don't you all never let the child explain hisself.

RUTH    Keep out of it now, Lena.
     (MAMA *clamps her lips together, and* RUTH *advances toward her son menacingly*)

RUTH    A thousand times I have told you not to go off like that—

MAMA (*Holding out her arms to her grandson*)    Well— at least let me tell him something. I want him to be the first one to hear . . . Come here, Travis. (*The boy obeys, gladly*) Travis—(*She takes him by the shoulder and looks into his face*)—you know that money we got in the mail this morning?

TRAVIS    Yes'm—

MAMA  Well—what you think your grandmama gone and done with that money?

TRAVIS  I don't know, Grandmama.

MAMA (*Putting her finger on his nose for emphasis*)  She went out and she bought you a house! (*The explosion comes from* WALTER *at the end of the revelation and he jumps up and turns away from all of them in a fury.* MAMA *continues, to* TRAVIS)  You glad about the house? It's going to be yours when you get to be a man.

TRAVIS  Yeah—I always wanted to live in a house.

MAMA  All right, gimme some sugar then—(TRAVIS *puts his arms around her neck as she watches her son over the boy's shoulder. Then, to* TRAVIS, *after the embrace*) Now when you say your prayers tonight, you thank God and your grandfather—'cause it was him who give you the house—in his way.

RUTH (*Taking the boy from* MAMA *and pushing him toward the bedroom*)  Now you get out of here and get ready for your beating.

TRAVIS  Aw, Mama—

RUTH  Get on in there—(*Closing the door behind him and turning radiantly to her mother-in-law*) So you went and did it!

MAMA (*Quietly, looking at her son with pain*)  Yes, I did.

RUTH (*Raising both arms classically*)  PRAISE GOD! (*Looks at* WALTER *a moment, who says nothing. She crosses rapidly to her husband*) Please, honey—let me be glad . . . you be glad too. (*She has laid her hands on his shoulders, but he shakes himself free of her roughly, without turning to face her*) Oh, Walter . . .

a home . . . *a home*. (*She comes back to* MAMA) Well
—where is it? How big is it? How much it going to
cost?

MAMA   Well—

RUTH   When we moving?

MAMA (*Smiling at her*)   First of the month.

RUTH (*Throwing back her head with jubilance*)   *Praise
God!*

MAMA (*Tentatively, still looking at her son's back turned
against her and* RUTH)   It's—it's a nice house too . . .
(*She cannot help speaking directly to him. An im-
ploring quality in her voice, her manner, makes her
almost like a girl now*)   Three bedrooms—nice big one
for you and Ruth. . . . Me and Beneatha still have to
share our room, but Travis have one of his own—and
(*With difficulty*) I figure if the—new baby—is a boy,
we could get one of them double-decker outfits . . .
And there's a yard with a little patch of dirt where I
could maybe get to grow me a few flowers . . . And a
nice big basement . . .

RUTH   Walter honey, be glad—

MAMA (*Still to his back, fingering things on the table*)
'Course I don't want to make it sound fancier than it
is . . . It's just a plain little old house—but it's made
good and solid—and it will be *ours*. Walter Lee—it
makes a difference in a man when he can walk on
floors that belong to *him* . . .

RUTH   Where is it?

MAMA (*Frightened at this telling*)   Well—well—it's out
there in Clybourne Park—
         (RUTH'S *radiance fades abruptly, and* WALTER
         *finally turns slowly to face his mother with incre-
         dulity and hostility*)

RUTH  Where?

MAMA (*Matter-of-factly*)  Four o six Clybourne Street, Clybourne Park.

RUTH  Clybourne Park? Mama, there ain't no colored people living in Clybourne Park.

MAMA (*Almost idiotically*)  Well, I guess there's going to be some now.

WALTER (*Bitterly*)  So that's the peace and comfort you went out and bought for us today!

MAMA (*Raising her eyes to meet his finally*)  Son—I just tried to find the nicest place for the least amount of money for my family.

RUTH (*Trying to recover from the shock*)  Well—well— 'course I ain't one never been 'fraid of no crackers, mind you—but—well, wasn't there no other houses nowhere?

MAMA  Them houses they put up for colored in them areas way out all seem to cost twice as much as other houses. I did the best I could.

RUTH (*Struck senseless with the news, in its various degrees of goodness and trouble, she sits a moment, her fists propping her chin in thought, and then she starts to rise, bringing her fists down with vigor, the radiance spreading from cheek to cheek again*)  Well —well!—All I can say is—if this is my time in life— MY TIME—to say good-bye—(*And she builds with momentum as she starts to circle the room with an exuberant, almost tearfully happy release*)—to these Goddamned cracking walls!—(*She pounds the walls*) —and these marching roaches!—(*She wipes at an imaginary army of marching roaches*)—and this cramped little closet which ain't now or never was no kitchen! . . . then I say it loud and good, HALLELUJAH! AND

GOOD-BYE MISERY . . . I DON'T NEVER WANT
TO SEE YOUR UGLY FACE AGAIN! (*She laughs
joyously, having practically destroyed the apartment,
and flings her arms up and lets them come down happily,
slowly, reflectively, over her abdomen, aware for the
first time perhaps that the life therein pulses with happiness and not despair*) Lena?

MAMA (*Moved, watching her happiness*)   Yes, honey?

RUTH (*Looking off*)   Is there—is there a whole lot of
sunlight?

MAMA (*Understanding*)   Yes, child, there's a whole lot
of sunlight.
(*Long pause*)

RUTH (*Collecting herself and going to the door of the
room* TRAVIS *is in*)   Well—I guess I better see 'bout
Travis. (*To* MAMA) Lord, I sure don't feel like whip-
ping nobody today!
(*She exits*)

MAMA (*The mother and son are left alone now and the
mother waits a long time, considering deeply, before
she speaks*)   Son—you—you understand what I done,
don't you? (WALTER *is silent and sullen*) I—I just
seen my family falling apart today . . . just falling to
pieces in front of my eyes . . . We couldn't of gone on
like we was today. We was going backwards 'stead of
forwards—talking 'bout killing babies and wishing each
other was dead . . . When it gets like that in life—you
just got to do something different, push on out and do
something bigger . . . (*She waits*) I wish you say something, son . . . I wish you'd say how deep inside you
you think I done the right thing—

WALTER (*Crossing slowly to his bedroom door and finally
turning there and speaking measuredly*)   What you
need me to say you done right for? *You* the head of this

family. You run our lives like you want to. It was your money and you did what you wanted with it. So what you need for me to say it was all right for? (*Bitterly, to hurt her as deeply as he knows is possible*) So you butchered up a dream of mine—you—who always talking 'bout your children's dreams . . .

MAMA    Walter Lee—
(*He just closes the door behind him.* MAMA *sits alone, thinking heavily*)

*Curtain*

*Time: Friday night. A few weeks later.*
*At rise: Packing crates mark the intention of the family*
*to move.* BENEATHA *and* GEORGE *come in, presumably from*
*an evening out again.*

GEORGE  O.K. . . . O.K., whatever you say . . . (*They*
*both sit on the couch. He tries to kiss her. She moves*
*away*) Look, we've had a nice evening; let's not spoil
it, huh? . . .
>  (*He again turns her head and tries to nuzzle in and*
>  *she turns away from him, not with distaste but*
>  *with momentary lack of interest; in a mood to pur-*
>  *sue what they were talking about*)

BENEATHA  I'm *trying* to talk to you.

GEORGE  We always talk.

BENEATHA  Yes—and I love to talk.

GEORGE  (*Exasperated; rising*)  I know it and I don't
mind it sometimes . . . I want you to cut it out, see—
The moody stuff, I mean. I don't like it. You're a nice-
looking girl . . . all over. That's all you need, honey,
forget the atmosphere. Guys aren't going to go for the
atmosphere—they're going to go for what they see.
Be glad for that. Drop the Garbo routine. It doesn't
go with you. As for myself, I want a nice—(*Groping*)
—simple (*Thoughtfully*)—sophisticated girl . . . not a
poet—O.K.?
>  (*He starts to kiss her, she rebuffs him again and*
>  *he jumps up*)

BENEATHA  Why are you angry, George?

GEORGE  Because this is stupid! I don't go out with you
to discuss the nature of "quiet desperation" or to hear

all about your thoughts—because the world will go on thinking what it thinks regardless—

BENEATHA  Then why read books? Why go to school?

GEORGE (*With artificial patience, counting on his fingers*) It's simple. You read books—to learn facts—to get grades—to pass the course—to get a degree. That's all —it has nothing to do with thoughts.
(*A long pause*)

BENEATHA  I see. (*He starts to sit*) Good night, George. (GEORGE *looks at her a little oddly, and starts to exit. He meets* MAMA *coming in*)

GEORGE  Oh—hello, Mrs. Younger.

MAMA  Hello, George, how you feeling?

GEORGE  Fine—fine, how are you?

MAMA  Oh, a little tired. You know them steps can get you after a day's work. You all have a nice time to-night?

GEORGE  Yes—a fine time. A fine time.

MAMA  Well, good night.

GEORGE  Good night. (*He exits.* MAMA *closes the door behind her*) Hello, honey. What you sitting like that for?

BENEATHA  I'm just sitting.

MAMA  Didn't you have a nice time?

BENEATHA  No.

MAMA  No? What's the matter?

BENEATHA  Mama, George is a fool—honest. (*She rises*)

MAMA (*Hustling around unloading the packages she has entered with. She stops*)  Is he, baby?

BENEATHA  Yes.
(BENEATHA *makes up* TRAVIS' *bed as she talks*)

MAMA  You sure?

BENEATHA  Yes.

MAMA  Well—I guess you better not waste your time with no fools.
(BENEATHA *looks up at her mother, watching her put groceries in the refrigerator. Finally she gathers up her things and starts into the bedroom. At the door she stops and looks back at her mother*)

BENEATHA  Mama—

MAMA  Yes, baby—

BENEATHA  Thank you.

MAMA  For what?

BENEATHA  For understanding me this time.
(*She exits quickly and the mother stands, smiling a little, looking at the place where* BENEATHA *just stood.* RUTH *enters*)

RUTH  Now don't you fool with any of this stuff, Lena—

MAMA  Oh, I just thought I'd sort a few things out. Is Brother here?

RUTH  Yes.

MAMA (*With concern*)  Is he—

RUTH (*Reading her eyes*)  Yes.
(MAMA *is silent and someone knocks on the door.* MAMA *and* RUTH *exchange weary and knowing glances and* RUTH *opens it to admit the neighbor,* MRS. JOHNSON,* *who is a rather squeaky wide-*

---

* This character and the scene of her visit were cut from the original production and early editions of the play.

*eyed lady of no particular age, with a newspaper
under her arm*)

MAMA (*Changing her expression to acute delight and a
ringing cheerful greeting*)   Oh—hello there, Johnson.

JOHNSON (*This is a woman who decided long ago to be
enthusiastic about EVERYTHING in life and she is
inclined to wave her wrist vigorously at the height of her
exclamatory comments*)   Hello there, yourself! H'you
this evening, Ruth?

RUTH (*Not much of a deceptive type*)   Fine, Mis' Johnson, h'you?

JOHNSON   Fine. (*Reaching out quickly, playfully, and
patting* RUTH'S *stomach*)   Ain't you starting to poke out
none yet! (*She mugs with delight at the over-familiar
remark and her eyes dart around looking at the crates
and packing preparation;* MAMA'S *face is a cold sheet
of endurance*)   Oh, ain't we getting ready round here,
though! Yessir! Lookathere! I'm telling you the
Youngers is really getting ready to "move on up a little
higher!"—Bless God!

MAMA (*A little drily, doubting the total sincerity of the
Blesser*)   Bless God.

JOHNSON   He's good, ain't He?

MAMA   Oh yes, He's good.

JOHNSON   I mean sometimes He works in mysterious
ways ... but He works, don't He!

MAMA (*The same*)   Yes, he does.

JOHNSON   I'm just soooooo happy for y'all. And this
here child—(*About* RUTH) looks like she could just
pop open with happiness, don't she. Where's all the rest
of the family?

MAMA   Bennie's gone to bed—

JOHNSON   Ain't no . . . (*The implication is pregnancy*) sickness done hit you—I hope . . . ?

MAMA   No—she just tired. She was out this evening.

JOHNSON   (*All is a coo, an emphatic coo*)   Aw—ain't that lovely. She still going out with the little Murchison boy?

MAMA (*Drily*)   Ummmm huh.

JOHNSON   That's lovely. You sure got lovely children, Younger. Me and Isaiah talks all the time 'bout what fine children you was blessed with. We sure do.

MAMA   Ruth, give Mis' Johnson a piece of sweet potato pie and some milk.

JOHNSON   Oh honey, I can't stay hardly a minute—I just dropped in to see if there was anything I could do. (*Accepting the food easily*) I guess y'all seen the news what's all over the colored paper this week . . .

MAMA   No—didn't get mine yet this week.

JOHNSON   (*Lifting her head and blinking with the spirit of catastrophe*)   You mean you ain't read 'bout them colored people that was bombed out their place out there?

> (RUTH *straightens with concern and takes the paper and reads it.* JOHNSON *notices her and feeds commentary*)

JOHNSON   Ain't it something how bad these here white folks is getting here in Chicago! Lord, getting so you think you right down in Mississippi! (*With a tremendous and rather insincere sense of melodrama*) 'Course I thinks it's wonderful how our folks keeps on pushing out. You hear some of these Negroes round here talking 'bout how they don't go where they ain't wanted and all that—but not me, honey! (*This is a lie*) Wilhemenia

Othella Johnson goes anywhere, any time she feels like it! (*With head movement for emphasis*) Yes I do! Why if we left it up to these here crackers, the poor niggers wouldn't have nothing—(*She clasps her hand over her mouth*) Oh, I always forgets you don't 'low that word in your house.

MAMA (*Quietly, looking at her*)   No—I don't 'low it.

JOHNSON (*Vigorously again*)   Me neither! I was just telling Isaiah yesterday when he come using it in front of me—I said, "Isaiah, it's just like Mis' Younger says all the time—"

MAMA   Don't you want some more pie?

JOHNSON   No—no thank you; this was lovely. I got to get on over home and have my midnight coffee. I hear some people say it don't let them sleep but I finds I can't close my eyes right lessen I done had that laaaast cup of coffee . . . (*She waits. A beat. Undaunte*d) My Goodnight coffee, I calls it!

MAMA (*With much eye-rolling and communication between herself and* RUTH)   Ruth, why don't you give Mis' Johnson some coffee.

    (RUTH *gives* MAMA *an unpleasant look for her kindness*)

JOHNSON (*Accepting the coffee*)   Where's Brother tonight?

MAMA   He's lying down.

JOHNSON   MMmmmmm, he sure gets his beauty rest, don't he? Good-looking man. Sure is a good-looking man! (*Reaching out to pat* RUTH'S *stomach again*) I guess that's how come we keep on having babies around here. (*She winks at* MAMA) One thing 'bout Brother, he always know how to have a *good* time. And soooooo ambitious! I bet it was his idea y'all moving out to

Clybourne Park. Lord—I bet this time next month y'all's names will have been in the papers plenty— (*Holding up her hands to mark off each word of the headline she can see in front of her*) "NEGROES INVADE CLYBOURNE PARK—BOMBED!"

MAMA (*She and* RUTH *look at the woman in amazement*) We ain't exactly moving out there to get bombed.

JOHNSON Oh, honey—you know I'm praying to God every day that don't nothing like that happen! But you have to think of life like it is—and these here Chicago peckerwoods is some baaaad peckerwoods.

MAMA (*Wearily*) We done thought about all that Mis' Johnson.

> (BENEATHA *comes out of the bedroom in her robe and passes through to the bathroom.* MRS. JOHNSON *turns*)

JOHNSON Hello there, Bennie!

BENEATHA (*Crisply*) Hello, Mrs. Johnson.

JOHNSON How is school?

BENEATHA (*Crisply*) Fine, thank you. (*She goes out.*)

JOHNSON (*Insulted*) Getting so she don't have much to say to nobody.

MAMA The child was on her way to the bathroom.

JOHNSON I know—but sometimes she act like ain't got time to pass the time of day with nobody ain't been to college. Oh—I ain't criticizing her none. It's just—you know how some of our young people gets when they get a little education. (MAMA *and* RUTH *say nothing, just look at her*) Yes—well. Well, I guess I better get on home. (*Unmoving*) 'Course I can understand how she must be proud and everything—being the only one in the family to make something of herself. I know just being a chauffeur ain't never satisfied Brother none. He shouldn't feel like that, though. Ain't nothing wrong with being a chauffeur.

MAMA    There's plenty wrong with it.

JOHNSON    What?

MAMA    Plenty. My husband always said being any kind of a servant wasn't a fit thing for a man to have to be. He always said a man's hands was made to make things, or to turn the earth with—not to drive nobody's car for 'em—or—(*She looks at her own hands*) carry they slop jars. And my boy is just like him—he wasn't meant to wait on nobody.

JOHNSON (*Rising, somewhat offended*)    Mmmmmmmmm. The Youngers is too much for me! (*She looks around*) You sure one proud-acting bunch of colored folks. Well —I always thinks like Booker T. Washington said that time—"Education has spoiled many a good plow hand"—

MAMA    Is that what old Booker T. said?

JOHNSON    He sure did.

MAMA    Well, it sounds just like him. The fool.

JOHNSON (*Indignantly*)    Well—he was one of our great men.

MAMA    Who said so?

JOHNSON (*Nonplussed*)    You know, me and you ain't never agreed about some things, Lena Younger. I guess I better be going—

RUTH (*Quickly*)    Good night.

JOHNSON    Good night. Oh—(*Thrusting it at her*) You can keep the paper! (*With a trill*) 'Night.

MAMA　Good night, Mis' Johnson.
(MRS. JOHNSON *exits*)

RUTH　If ignorance was gold . . .

MAMA　Shush. Don't talk about folks behind their backs.

RUTH　You do.

MAMA　I'm old and corrupted. (BENEATHA *enters*) You was rude to Mis' Johnson, Beneatha, and I don't like it at all.

BENEATHA (*At her door*)　Mama, if there are two things we, as a people, have got to overcome, one is the Klu Klux Klan—and the other is Mrs. Johnson. (*She exits*)

MAMA　Smart aleck.
(*The phone rings*)

RUTH　I'll get it.

MAMA　Lord, ain't this a popular place tonight.

RUTH (*At the phone*)　Hello—Just a minute. (*Goes to door*) Walter, it's Mrs. Arnold. (*Waits. Goes back to the phone. Tense*) Hello. Yes, this is his wife speaking . . . He's lying down now. Yes . . . well, he'll be in tomorrow. He's been very sick. Yes—I know we should have called, but we were so sure he'd be able to come in today. Yes—yes, I'm very sorry. Yes . . . Thank you very much. (*She hangs up.* WALTER *is standing in the doorway of the bedroom behind her*) That was Mrs. Arnold.

WALTER (*Indifferently*)　Was it?

RUTH　She said if you don't come in tomorrow that they are getting a new man . . .

WALTER　Ain't that sad—ain't that crying sad.

RUTH    She said Mr. Arnold has had to take a cab for
three days . . . Walter, you ain't been to work for three
days! (*This is a revelation to her*) Where you been,
Walter Lee Younger? (WALTER *looks at her and starts
to laugh*) You're going to lose your job.

WALTER    That's right . . . (*He turns on the radio*)

RUTH    Oh, Walter, and with your mother working like
a dog every day—
     (*A steamy, deep blues pours into the room*)

WALTER    That's sad too— Everything is sad.

MAMA    What you been doing for these three days, son?

WALTER    Mama—you don't know all the things a man
what got leisure can find to do in this city . . . What's
this—Friday night? Well—Wednesday I borrowed Willy
Harris' car and I went for a drive . . . just me and myself and I drove and drove . . . Way out . . . way past
South Chicago, and I parked the car and I sat and
looked at the steel mills all day long. I just sat in the
car and looked at them big black chimneys for hours.
Then I drove back and I went to the Green Hat.
(*Pause*) And Thursday—Thursday I borrowed the car
again and I got in it and I pointed it the other way and
I drove the other way—for hours—way, way up to
Wisconsin, and I looked at the farms. I just drove and
looked at the farms. Then I drove back and I went to
the Green Hat. (*Pause*) And today—today I didn't
get the car. Today I just walked. All over the Southside. And I looked at the Negroes and they looked at
me and finally I just sat down on the curb at Thirty-
ninth and South Parkway and I just sat there and
watched the Negroes go by. And then I went to the
Green Hat. You all sad? You all depressed? And you
know where I am going right now—.
     (RUTH *goes out quietly*)

MAMA   Oh, Big Walter, is this the harvest of our days?

WALTER   You know what I like about the Green Hat?
I like this little cat they got there who blows a sax . . .
He blows. He talks to me. He ain't but 'bout five feet
tall and he's got a conked head and his eyes is always
closed and he's all music—

MAMA (*Rising and getting some papers out of her handbag*)   Walter—

WALTER   And there's this other guy who plays the piano
. . . and they got a sound. I mean they can work on
some music . . . They got the best little combo in the
world in the Green Hat . . . You can just sit there and
drink and listen to them three men play and you realize that don't nothing matter worth a damn, but just
being there—

MAMA   I've helped do it to you, haven't I, son? Walter
I been wrong.

WALTER   Naw—you ain't never been wrong about nothing, Mama.

MAMA   Listen to me, now. I say I been wrong, son. That
I been doing to you what the rest of the world been
doing to you. (*She turns off the radio*) Walter—(*She
stops and he looks up slowly at her and she meets his
eyes pleadingly*) What you ain't never understood is that
I ain't got nothing, don't own nothing, ain't never really
wanted nothing that wasn't for you. There ain't nothing
as precious to me . . . There ain't nothing worth holding
on to, money, dreams, nothing else—if it means—if it
means it's going to destroy my boy. (*She takes an envelope out of her handbag and puts it in front of him
and he watches her without speaking or moving*) I paid
the man thirty-five hundred dollars down on the house.
That leaves sixty-five hundred dollars. Monday morning

I want you to take this money and take three thousand dollars and put it in a savings account for Beneatha's medical schooling. The rest you put in a checking account—with your name on it. And from now on any penny that come out of it or that go in it is for you to look after. For you to decide. (*She drops her hands a little helplessly*) It ain't much, but it's all I got in the world and I'm putting it in your hands. I'm telling you to be the head of this family from now on like you supposed to be.

WALTER (*Stares at the money*)  You trust me like that, Mama?

MAMA  I ain't never stop trusting you. Like I ain't never stop loving you.
(*She goes out, and* WALTER *sits looking at the money on the table. Finally, in a decisive gesture, he gets up, and, in mingled joy and desperation, picks up the money. At the same moment,* TRAVIS *enters for bed*)

TRAVIS  What's the matter, Daddy? You drunk?

WALTER (*Sweetly, more sweetly than we have ever known him*)  No, Daddy ain't drunk. Daddy ain't going to never be drunk again. . . .

TRAVIS  Well, good night, Daddy.
(*The* FATHER *has come from behind the couch and leans over, embracing his son*)

WALTER  Son, I feel like talking to you tonight.

TRAVIS  About what?

WALTER  Oh, about a lot of things. About you and what kind of man you going to be when you grow up. . . . Son—son, what do you want to be when you grow up?

TRAVIS  A bus driver.

WALTER  (*Laughing a little*)  A what? Man, that ain't nothing to want to be!

TRAVIS  Why not?

WALTER  'Cause, man—it ain't big enough—you know what I mean.

TRAVIS  I don't know then. I can't make up my mind. Sometimes Mama asks me that too. And sometimes when I tell her I just want to be like you—she says she don't want me to be like that and sometimes she says she does. . . .

WALTER  (*Gathering him up in his arms*)  You know what, Travis? In seven years you going to be seventeen years old. And things is going to be very different with us in seven years, Travis. . . . One day when you are seventeen I'll come home—home from my office downtown somewhere—

TRAVIS  You don't work in no office, Daddy.

WALTER  No—but after tonight. After what your daddy gonna do tonight, there's going to be offices—a whole lot of offices. . . .

TRAVIS  What you gonna do tonight, Daddy?

WALTER  You wouldn't understand yet, son, but your daddy's gonna make a transaction . . . a business transaction that's going to change our lives. . . . That's how come one day when you 'bout seventeen years old I'll come home and I'll be pretty tired, you know what I mean, after a day of conferences and secretaries getting things wrong the way they do . . . 'cause an executive's life is hell, man—(*The more he talks the farther away he gets*) And I'll pull the car up on the driveway . . . just a plain black Chrysler, I think, with white walls—no—black tires. More elegant. Rich people don't have to be flashy . . . though I'll have to get something a little sportier for Ruth—maybe a Cadillac convertible to do her shopping in. . . . And I'll come up the steps to the house and the gardener will be clipping away at the hedges and he'll say, "Good evening, Mr. Younger." And I'll say, "Hello, Jefferson, how are you this evening?" And I'll go inside and Ruth will come downstairs and meet me at the door and we'll kiss each other and she'll take my arm and we'll go up to your room to see you sitting on the floor with the catalogues of all the great schools in America around you. . . . All the great schools in the world! And—and I'll say, all right son—it's your seventeenth birthday, what is it you've decided? . . . Just tell me where you want to go to school and you'll *go*. Just tell me, what it is you want to be—and you'll *be* it. . . . Whatever you want to be—Yessir! (*He holds his arms open for* TRAVIS) You just name it, son . . . (TRAVIS *leaps into them*) and I hand you the world!

> (WALTER's *voice has risen in pitch and hysterical promise and on the last line he lifts* TRAVIS *high*)

(*Blackout*)

## Scene Three

*Time: Saturday, moving day, one week later.*
*Before the curtain rises,* RUTH'S *voice, a strident, dramatic church alto, cuts through the silence.*
*It is, in the darkness, a triumphant surge, a penetrating statement of expectation: "Oh, Lord, I don't feel no ways tired! Children, oh, glory hallelujah!"*
*As the curtain rises we see that* RUTH *is alone in the living room, finishing up the family's packing. It is moving day. She is nailing crates and tying cartons.* BENEATHA *enters, carrying a guitar case, and watches her exuberant sister-in-law.*

RUTH   Hey!

BENEATHA (*Putting away the case*)   Hi.

RUTH (*Pointing at a package*)   Honey—look in that package there and see what I found on sale this morning at the South Center. (RUTH *gets up and moves to the package and draws out some curtains*) Lookahere— hand-turned hems!

BENEATHA   How do you know the window size out there?

RUTH (*Who hadn't thought of that*)   Oh— Well, they bound to fit something in the whole house. Anyhow, they was too good a bargain to pass up. (RUTH *slaps her head, suddenly remembering something*) Oh, Bennie—I meant to put a special note on that carton over there. That's your mama's good china and she wants 'em to be very careful with it.

BENEATHA   I'll do it.
        (BENEATHA *finds a piece of paper and starts to draw large letters on it*)

*110*

RUTH   You know what I'm going to do soon as I get in that new house?

BENEATHA   What?

RUTH   Honey—I'm going to run me a tub of water up to here . . . (*With her fingers practically up to her nostrils*) And I'm going to get in it—and I am going to sit . . . and sit . . . and sit in that hot water and the first person who knocks to tell *me* to hurry up and come out—

BENEATHA   Gets shot at sunrise.

RUTH (*Laughing happily*)   You said it, sister! (*Noticing how large* BENEATHA *is absent-mindedly making the note*) Honey, they ain't going to read that from no airplane.

BENEATHA (*Laughing herself*)   I guess I always think things have more emphasis if they are big, somehow.

RUTH (*Looking up at her and smiling*)   You and your brother seem to have that as a philosophy of life. Lord, that man—done changed so 'round here. You know—you know what we did last night? Me and Walter Lee?

BENEATHA   What?

RUTH (*Smiling to herself*)   We went to the movies. (*Looking at* BENEATHA *to see if she understands*) We went to the movies. You know the last time me and Walter went to the movies together?

BENEATHA   No.

RUTH   Me neither. That's how long it been. (*Smiling again*) But we went last night. The picture wasn't much good, but that didn't seem to matter. We went—and we held hands.

BENEATHA   Oh, Lord!

RUTH    We held hands—and you know what?

BENEATHA    What?

RUTH    When we come out of the show it was late and dark and all the stores and things was closed up . . . and it was kind of chilly and there wasn't many people on the streets . . . and we was still holding hands, me and Walter.

BENEATHA    You're killing me.
(WALTER *enters with a large package. His happiness is deep in him; he cannot keep still with his new-found exuberance. He is singing and wiggling and snapping his fingers. He puts his package in a corner and puts a phonograph record, which he has brought in with him, on the record player. As the music, soulful and sensuous, comes up he dances over to* RUTH *and tries to get her to dance with him. She gives in at last to his raunchiness and in a fit of giggling allows herself to be drawn into his mood. They dip and she melts into his arms in a classic, body-melding "slow drag"*)

BENEATHA (*Regarding them a long time as they dance, then drawing in her breath for a deeply exaggerated comment which she does not particularly mean*)    Talk about—olddddddddd-fashioneddddddd—Negroes!

WALTER (*Stopping momentarily*)    What kind of Negroes?
(*He says this in fun. He is not angry with her today, nor with anyone. He starts to dance with his wife again*)

BENEATHA    Old-fashioned.

WALTER (*As he dances with* RUTH)    You know, when these *New Negroes* have their convention—(*Pointing at his sister*)—that is going to be the chairman of the

Committee on Unending Agitation. (*He goes on dancing, then stops*) Race, race, race! . . . Girl, I do believe you are the first person in the history of the entire human race to successfully brainwash yourself. (BENEATHA *breaks up and he goes on dancing. He stops again, enjoying his tease*) Damn, even the N double A C P takes a holiday sometimes! (BENEATHA *and* RUTH *laugh. He dances with* RUTH *some more and starts to laugh and stops and pantomimes someone over an operating table*) I can just see that chick someday looking down at some poor cat on an operating table and before she starts to slice him, she says . . . (*Pulling his sleeves back maliciously*) "By the way, what are your views on civil rights down there? . . ."

> (*He laughs at her again and starts to dance happily. The bell sounds*)

BENEATHA   Sticks and stones may break my bones but . . . words will never hurt me!

> (BENEATHA *goes to the door and opens it as* WALTER *and* RUTH *go on with the clowning.* BENEATHA *is somewhat surprised to see a quiet-looking middle-aged white man in a business suit holding his hat and a briefcase in his hand and consulting a small piece of paper*)

MAN   Uh—how do you do, miss. I am looking for a Mrs.—(*He looks at the slip of paper*) Mrs. Lena Younger? (*He stops short, struck dumb at the sight of the oblivious* WALTER *and* RUTH)

BENEATHA   (*Smoothing her hair with slight embarrassment*)   Oh—yes, that's my mother. Excuse me (*She closes the door and turns to quiet the other two*) Ruth! Brother! (*Enunciating precisely but soundlessly: "There's a white man at the door!" They stop dancing,* RUTH *cuts off the phonograph,* BENEATHA *opens the door. The*

*man casts a curious quick glance at all of them)* Uh—
come in please.

MAN (*Coming in*)   Thank you.

BENEATHA   My mother isn't here just now. Is it business?

MAN   Yes . . . well, of a sort.

WALTER (*Freely, the Man of the House*)   Have a seat.
I'm Mrs. Younger's son. I look after most of her business matters.
        (RUTH *and* BENEATHA *exchange amused glances*)

MAN (*Regarding* WALTER, *and sitting*)   Well— My name
is Karl Lindner . . .

WALTER (*Stretching out his hand*)   Walter Younger. This
is my wife—(RUTH *nods politely*)—and my sister.

LINDNER   How do you do.

WALTER (*Amiably, as he sits himself easily on a chair,
leaning forward on his knees with interest and looking
expectantly into the newcomer's face*)   What can we
do for you, Mr. Lindner!

LINDNER (*Some minor shuffling of the hat and briefcase
on his knees*)   Well—I am a representative of the Clybourne Park Improvement Association—

WALTER (*Pointing*)   Why don't you sit your things on
the floor?

LINDNER   Oh—yes. Thank you. (*He slides the briefcase
and hat under the chair*)   And as I was saying—I am
from the Clybourne Park Improvement Association and
we have had it brought to our attention at the last meeting that you people—or at least your mother—has
bought a piece of residential property at—(*He digs for
the slip of paper again*)—four o six Clybourne Street . . .

WALTER    That's right. Care for something to drink? Ruth, get Mr. Lindner a beer.

LINDNER (*Upset for some reason*)   Oh—no, really. I mean thank you very much, but no thank you.

RUTH (*Innocently*)   Some coffee?

LINDNER   Thank you, nothing at all.
(BENEATHA *is watching the man carefully*)

LINDNER   Well, I don't know how much you folks know about our organization. (*He is a gentle man; thoughtful and somewhat labored in his manner*) It is one of these community organizations set up to look after—oh, you know, things like block upkeep and special projects and we also have what we call our New Neighbors Orientation Committee . . .

BENEATHA (*Drily*)   Yes—and what do they do?

LINDNER (*Turning a little to her and then returning the main force to* WALTER)   Well—it's what you might call a sort of welcoming committee, I guess. I mean they, we—I'm the chairman of the committee—go around and see the new people who move into the neighborhood and sort of give them the lowdown on the way we do things out in Clybourne Park.

BENEATHA (*With appreciation of the two meanings, which escape* RUTH *and* WALTER)   Un-huh.

LINDNER   And we also have the category of what the association calls—(*He looks elsewhere*)—uh—special community problems . . .

BENEATHA   Yes—and what are some of those?

WALTER   Girl, let the man talk.

LINDNER (*With understated relief*)  Thank you. I would
sort of like to explain this thing in my own way. I
mean I want to explain to you in a certain way.

WALTER  Go ahead.

LINDNER  Yes. Well. I'm going to try to get right to the
point. I'm sure we'll all appreciate that in the long run.

BENEATHA  Yes.

WALTER  Be still now!

LINDNER  Well—

RUTH (*Still innocently*)  Would you like another chair—
you don't look comfortable.

LINDNER (*More frustrated than annoyed*)  No, thank
you very much. Please. Well—to get right to the point
I—(*A great breath, and he is off at last*) I am sure
you people must be aware of some of the incidents
which have happened in various parts of the city when
colored people have moved into certain areas—(BE-
NEATHA *exhales heavily and starts tossing a piece of
fruit up and down in the air*) Well—because we have
what I think is going to be a unique type of organization in American community life—not only do we
deplore that kind of thing—but we are trying to do
something about it. (BENEATHA *stops tossing and turns
with a new and quizzical interest to the man*) We feel
—(*gaining confidence in his mission because of the interest in the faces of the people he is talking to*)—we
feel that most of the trouble in this world, when you
come right down to it—(*He hits his knee for emphasis*)
—most of the trouble exists because people just don't
sit down and talk to each other.

RUTH (*Nodding as she might in church, pleased with the
remark*)  You can say that again, mister.

LINDNER (*More encouraged by such affirmation*) That we don't try hard enough in this world to understand the other fellow's problem. The other guy's point of view.

RUTH   Now that's right.
(BENEATHA *and* WALTER *merely watch and listen with genuine interest*)

LINDNER   Yes—that's the way we feel out in Clybourne Park. And that's why I was elected to come here this afternoon and talk to you people. Friendly like, you know, the way people should talk to each other and see if we couldn't find some way to work this thing out. As I say, the whole business is a matter of *caring* about the other fellow. Anybody can see that you are a nice family of folks, hard working and honest I'm sure. (BENEATHA *frowns slightly, quizzically, her head tilted regarding him*) Today everybody knows what it means to be on the outside of *something*. And of course, there is always somebody who is out to take advantage of people who don't always understand.

WALTER   What do you mean?

LINDNER   Well—you see our community is made up of people who've worked hard as the dickens for years to build up that little community. They're not rich and fancy people; just hard-working, honest people who don't really have much but those little homes and a dream of the kind of community they want to raise their children in. Now, I don't say we are perfect and there is a lot wrong in some of the things they want. But you've got to admit that a man, right or wrong, has the right to want to have the neighborhood he lives in a certain kind of way. And at the moment the overwhelming majority of our people out there feel that people get along better, take more of a common interest in the life of the community, when they share a common background. I want you to believe me when I tell you that race prejudice simply doesn't enter into it. It is a matter of the people of Clybourne Park believing, rightly or wrongly, as I say, that for the happiness of all concerned that our Negro families are happier when they live in their *own* communities.

BENEATHA (*With a grand and bitter gesture*) This, friends, is the Welcoming Committee!

WALTER (*Dumfounded, looking at* LINDNER) Is this what you came marching all the way over here to tell us?

LINDNER Well, now we've been having a fine conversation. I hope you'll hear me all the way through.

WALTER (*Tightly*) Go ahead, man.

LINDNER You see—in the face of all the things I have said, we are prepared to make your family a very generous offer . . .

BENEATHA Thirty pieces and not a coin less!

WALTER Yeah?

LINDNER (*Putting on his glasses and drawing a form out of the briefcase*) Our association is prepared, through the collective effort of our people, to buy the house from you at a financial gain to your family.

RUTH Lord have mercy, ain't this the living gall!

WALTER All right, you through?

LINDNER Well, I want to give you the exact terms of the financial arrangement—

WALTER We don't want to hear no exact terms of no arrangements. I want to know if you got any more to tell us 'bout getting together?

LINDNER (*Taking off his glasses*)    Well—I don't suppose that you feel . . .

WALTER    Never mind how I feel—you got any more to say 'bout how people ought to sit down and talk to each other? . . . Get out of my house, man.
(*He turns his back and walks to the door*)

LINDNER (*Looking around at the hostile faces and reaching and assembling his hat and briefcase*)    Well—I don't understand why you people are reacting this way. What do you think you are going to gain by moving into a neighborhood where you just aren't wanted and where some elements—well—people can get awful worked up when they feel that their whole way of life and everything they've ever worked for is threatened.

WALTER    Get out.

LINDNER (*At the door, holding a small card*)    Well—I'm sorry it went like this.

WALTER    Get out.

LINDNER (*Almost sadly regarding* WALTER)    You just can't force people to change their hearts, son.
(*He turns and put his card on a table and exits.* WALTER *pushes the door to with stinging hatred, and stands looking at it.* RUTH *just sits and* BE-NEATHA *just stands. They say nothing.* MAMA *and* TRAVIS *enter*)

MAMA    Well—this all the packing got done since I left out of here this morning. I testify before God that my children got all the energy of the *dead*! What time the moving men due?

BENEATHA    Four o'clock. You had a caller, Mama.
(*She is smiling, teasingly*)

MAMA    Sure enough—who?

BENEATHA (*Her arms folded saucily*)  The Welcoming Committee.
> (WALTER *and* RUTH *giggle*)

MAMA (*Innocently*)  Who?

BENEATHA  The Welcoming Committee. They said they're sure going to be glad to see you when you get there.

WALTER (*Devilishly*)  Yeah, they said they can't hardly wait to see your face.
> (*Laughter*)

MAMA (*Sensing their facetiousness*)  What's the matter with you all?

WALTER  Ain't nothing the matter with us. We just telling you 'bout the gentleman who came to see you this afternoon. From the Clybourne Park Improvement Association.

MAMA  What he want?

RUTH (*In the same mood as* BENEATHA *and* WALTER)  To welcome you, honey.

WALTER  He said they can't hardly wait. He said the one thing they don't have, that they just *dying* to have out there is a fine family of fine colored people! (*To* RUTH *and* BENEATHA) Ain't that right!

RUTH (*Mockingly*)  Yeah! He left his card—

BENEATHA (*Handing card to* MAMA)  In case.
> (MAMA *reads and throws it on the floor—understanding and looking off as she draws her chair up to the table on which she has put her plant and some sticks and some cord*)

MAMA  Father, give us strength. (*Knowingly—and without fun*) Did he threaten us?

BENEATHA   Oh—Mama—they don't do it like that any
more. He talked Brotherhood. He said everybody ought
to learn how to sit down and hate each other with good
Christian fellowship.

(*She and* WALTER *shake hands to ridicule the
remark*)

MAMA (*Sadly*)   Lord, protect us . . .

RUTH   You should hear the money those folks raised
to buy the house from us. All we paid and then some.

BENEATHA   What they think we going to do—eat 'em?

RUTH   No, honey, marry 'em.

MAMA (*Shaking her head*)   Lord, Lord, Lord . . .

RUTH   Well—that's the way the crackers crumble. (*A
beat*) Joke.

BENEATHA (*Laughingly noticing what her mother is doing*)   Mama, what are you doing?

MAMA   Fixing my plant so it won't get hurt none on the
way . . .

BENEATHA   Mama, you going to take *that* to the new
house?

MAMA   Un-huh—

BENEATHA   That raggedy-looking old thing?

MAMA (*Stopping and looking at her*)   It expresses ME!

RUTH (*With delight, to* BENEATHA)   So there, Miss
Thing!

(WALTER *comes to* MAMA *suddenly and bends
down behind her and squeezes her in his arms with
all his strength. She is overwhelmed by the sudden-
ness of it and, though delighted, her manner is
like that of* RUTH *and* TRAVIS)

MAMA    Look out now, boy! You make me mess up my thing here!

WALTER (*His face lit, he slips down on his knees beside her, his arms still about her*)  Mama . . . you know what it means to climb up in the chariot?

MAMA (*Gruffly, very happy*)  Get on away from me now . . .

RUTH (*Near the gift-wrapped package, trying to catch* WALTER'S *eye*)  Psst—

WALTER   What the old song say, Mama . . .

RUTH   Walter—Now?
      (*She is pointing at the package*)

WALTER  (*Speaking the lines, sweetly, playfully, in his mother's face*)
      *I got wings . . . you got wings . . .*
      *All God's Children got wings . . .*

MAMA    Boy—get out of my face and do some work . . .

WALTER
      *When I get to heaven gonna put on my wings,*
      *Gonna fly all over God's heaven . . .*

BENEATHA (*Teasingly, from across the room*)  Everybody talking 'bout heaven ain't going there!

WALTER (*To* RUTH, *who is carrying the box across to them*)  I don't know, you think we ought to give her that . . . Seems to me she ain't been very appreciative around here.

MAMA (*Eying the box, which is obviously a gift*)  What is that?

WALTER (*Taking it from* RUTH *and putting it on the table in front of* MAMA)  Well—what you all think? Should we give it to her?

RUTH    Oh—she was pretty good today.

MAMA    I'll good you—
(*She turns her eyes to the box again*)

BENEATHA    Open it, Mama.
(*She stands up, looks at it, turns and looks at all of them, and then presses her hands together and does not open the package*)

WALTER (*Sweetly*)    Open it, Mama. It's for you. (MAMA *looks in his eyes. It is the first present in her life without its being Christmas. Slowly she opens her package and lifts out, one by one, a brand-new sparkling set of gardening tools.* WALTER *continues, prodding*) Ruth made up the note—read it . . .

MAMA (*Picking up the card and adjusting her glasses*) "To our own Mrs. Miniver—Love from Brother, Ruth and Beneatha." Ain't that lovely . . .

TRAVIS (*Tugging at his father's sleeve*)    Daddy, can I give her mine now?

WALTER    All right, son. (TRAVIS *flies to get his gift*)

MAMA    Now I don't have to use my <u>knives</u> and forks no more . . .

WALTER    Travis didn't want to go in with the rest of us, Mama. He got his own. (*Somewhat amused*) We don't know what it is . . .

TRAVIS (*Racing back in the room with a large hatbox and putting it in front of his grandmother*)    Here!

MAMA    Lord have mercy, baby. You done gone and bought your grandmother a hat?

TRAVIS (*Very proud*)    Open it!
(*She does and lifts out an elaborate, but very elaborate, wide gardening hat, and all the adults break up at the sight of it*)

RUTH   Travis, honey, what is that?

TRAVIS (*Who thinks it is beautiful and appropriate*)   It's a gardening hat! Like the ladies always have on in the magazines when they work in their gardens.

BENEATHA (*Giggling fiercely*)   Travis—we were trying to make Mama Mrs. Miniver—not Scarlett O'Hara!

MAMA (*Indignantly*)   What's the matter with you all! This here is a beautiful hat! (*Absurdly*) I always wanted me one just like it!
> (*She pops it on her head to prove it to her grand-son, and the hat is ludicrous and considerably oversized*)

RUTH   Hot dog! Go, Mama!

WALTER (*Doubled over with laughter*)   I'm sorry, Mama —but you look like you ready to go out and chop you some cotton sure enough!
> (*They all laugh except* MAMA, *out of deference to* TRAVIS' *feelings*)

MAMA (*Gathering the boy up to her*)   Bless your heart —this is the prettiest hat I ever owned— (WALTER, RUTH *and* BENEATHA *chime in—noisily, festively and insincerely congratulating* TRAVIS *on his gift*) What are we all standing around here for? We ain't finished packin' yet. Bennie, you ain't packed one book.
> (*The bell rings*)

BENEATHA   That couldn't be the movers . . . it's not hardly two good yet—
> (BENEATHA *goes into her room.* MAMA *starts for door*)

WALTER (*Turning, stiffening*)   Wait—wait—I'll get it.
> (*He stands and looks at the door*)

MAMA  You expecting company, son?

WALTER (*Just looking at the door*)  Yeah—yeah . . .
 (MAMA *looks at* RUTH, *and they exchange innocent and unfrightened glances*)

MAMA (*Not understanding*)  Well, let them in, son.

BENEATHA (*From her room*)  We need some more string.

MAMA  Travis—you run to the hardware and get me
some string cord.
 (MAMA *goes out and* WALTER *turns and looks at*
 RUTH. TRAVIS *goes to a dish for money*)

RUTH  Why don't you answer the door, man?

WALTER (*Suddenly bounding across the floor to embrace
her*)  'Cause sometimes it hard to let the future begin!
(*Stooping down in her face*)
  *I got wings! You got wings!*
  *All God's children got wings!*
(*He crosses to the door and throws it open. Standing
there is a very slight little man in a not too prosperous
business suit and with haunted frightened eyes and a hat
pulled down tightly, brim up, around his forehead.*
TRAVIS *passes between the men and exits.* WALTER
*leans deep in the man's face, still in his jubilance*)
  *When I get to heaven gonna put on my wings,*
  *Gonna fly all over God's heaven . . .*
(*The little man just stares at him*)
  *Heaven—*
(*Suddenly he stops and looks past the little man into
the empty hallway*)  Where's Willy, man?

BOBO  He ain't with me.

WALTER (*Not disturbed*)  Oh—come on in. You know
my wife.

BOBO (*Dumbly, taking off his hat*) Yes—h'you, Miss Ruth.

RUTH (*Quietly, a mood apart from her husband already, seeing* BOBO) Hello, Bobo.

WALTER You right on time today . . . Right on time. That's the way! (*He slaps* BOBO *on his back*) Sit down . . . lemme hear.

> (RUTH *stands stiffly and quietly in back of them, as though somehow she senses death, her eyes fixed on her husband*)

BOBO (*His frightened eyes on the floor, his hat in his hands*) Could I please get a drink of water, before I tell you about it, Walter Lee?

> (WALTER *does not take his eyes off the man.* RUTH *goes blindly to the tap and gets a glass of water and brings it to* BOBO)

WALTER There ain't nothing wrong, is there?

BOBO Lemme tell you—

WALTER Man—didn't nothing go wrong?

BOBO Lemme tell you—Walter Lee. (*Looking at* RUTH *and talking to her more than to* WALTER) You know how it was. I got to tell you how it was. I mean first I got to tell you how it was all the way . . . I mean about the money I put in, Walter Lee . . .

WALTER (*With taut agitation now*) What about the money you put in?

BOBO Well—it wasn't much as we told you—me and Willy—(*He stops*) I'm sorry, Walter. I got a bad feeling about it. I got a real bad feeling about it . . .

WALTER Man, what you telling me about all this for? . . . Tell me what happened in Springfield . . .

**BOBO**  Springfield.

**RUTH** (*Like a dead woman*)  What was supposed to happen in Springfield?

**BOBO** (*To her*)  This deal that me and Walter went into with Willy— Me and Willy was going to go down to Springfield and spread some money 'round so's we wouldn't have to wait so long for the liquor license . . . That's what we were going to do. Everybody said that was the way you had to do, you understand, Miss Ruth?

**WALTER**  Man—what happened down there?

**BOBO** (*A pitiful man, near tears*)  I'm trying to tell you, Walter.

**WALTER** (*Screaming at him suddenly*)  THEN TELL ME, GODDAMMIT . . . WHAT'S THE MATTER WITH YOU?

**BOBO**  Man . . . I didn't go to no Springfield, yesterday.

**WALTER** (*Halted, life hanging in the moment*)  Why not?

**BOBO** (*The long way, the hard way to tell*)  'Cause I didn't have no reasons to . . .

**WALTER**  Man, what are you talking about!

**BOBO**  I'm talking about the fact that when I got to the train station yesterday morning—eight o'clock like we planned . . . Man—*Willy didn't never show up.*

**WALTER**  Why . . . where was he . . . where is he?

**BOBO**  That's what I'm trying to tell you . . . I don't know . . . I waited six hours . . . I called his house . . . and I waited . . . six hours . . . I waited in that train station six hours . . . (*Breaking into tears*) That was all the extra money I had in the world . . .

(*Looking up at* WALTER *with the tears running down his face*) Man, *Willy is gone.*

WALTER    Gone, what you mean Willy is gone? Gone where? You mean he went by himself. You mean he went off to Springfield by himself—to take care of getting the license—(*Turns and looks anxiously at* RUTH) You mean maybe he didn't want too many people in on the business down there? (*Looks to* RUTH *again, as before*) You know Willy got his own ways. (*Looks back to* BOBO) Maybe you was late yesterday and he just went on down there without you. Maybe—maybe —he's been callin' you at home tryin' to tell you what happened or something. Maybe—maybe—he just got sick. He's somewhere—he's got to be somewhere. We just got to find him—me and you got to find him. (*Grabs* BOBO *senselessly by the collar and starts to shake him*) We got to!

BOBO (*In sudden angry, frightened agony*)    What's the matter with you, Walter! *When a cat take off with your money he don't leave you no road maps!*

WALTER (*Turning madly, as though he is looking for* WILLY *in the very room*) Willy! . . . Willy . . . don't do it . . . Please don't do it . . . Man, not with that money . . . Man, please, not with that money . . . Oh, God . . . Don't let it be true . . . (*He is wandering around, crying out for* WILLY *and looking for him or perhaps for help from God*) Man . . . I trusted you . . . Man, I put my life in your hands . . . (*He starts to crumple down on the floor as* RUTH *just covers her face in horror.* MAMA *opens the door and comes into the room, with* BENEATHA *behind her*) Man . . . (*He starts to pound the floor with his fists, sobbing wildly*) THAT MONEY IS MADE OUT OF MY FATHER'S FLESH——

BOBO (*Standing over him helplessly*)   I'm sorry, Walter
. . . (*Only* WALTER'S *sobs reply.* BOBO *puts on his hat*)
I had my life staked on this deal, too . . .
      (*He exits*)

MAMA (*To* WALTER)   Son—(*She goes to him, bends
down to him, talks to his bent head*) Son . . . Is it
gone? Son, I gave you sixty-five hundred dollars. Is it
gone? All of it? Beneatha's money too?

WALTER (*Lifting his head slowly*)   Mama . . . I never
. . . went to the bank at all . . .

MAMA (*Not wanting to believe him*)   You mean . . .
your sister's school money . . . you used that too . . .
Walter? . . .

WALTER   Yessss! All of it . . . It's all gone . . .
      (*There is total silence.* RUTH *stands with her face
      covered with her hands;* BENEATHA *leans forlornly
      against a wall, fingering a piece of red ribbon from
      the mother's gift.* MAMA *stops and looks at her son
      without recognition and then, quite without think-
      ing about it, starts to beat him senselessly in the
      face.* BENEATHA *goes to them and stops it*)

BENEATHA   Mama!
      (MAMA *stops and looks at both of her children
      and rises slowly and wanders vaguely, aimlessly
      away from them*)

MAMA   I seen . . . him . . . night after night . . . come
in . . . and look at that rug . . . and then look at me
. . . the red showing in his eyes . . . the veins moving in
his head . . . I seen him grow thin and old before he
was forty . . . working and working and working like
somebody's old horse . . . killing himself . . . and you
—you give it all away in a day—(*She raises her arms to
strike him again*)

BENEATHA   Mama—

MAMA   Oh, God . . . (*She looks up to Him*) Look down here—and show me the strength.

BENEATHA   Mama—

MAMA (*Folding over*)   Strength . . .

BENEATHA (*Plaintively*)   Mama . . .

MAMA   Strength!

*Curtain*

# ACT III

*An hour later.*

*At curtain, there is a sullen light of gloom in the living room, gray light not unlike that which began the first scene of Act One. At left we can see* WALTER *within his room, alone with himself. He is stretched out on the bed, his shirt out and open, his arms under his head. He does not smoke, he does not cry out, he merely lies there, looking up at the ceiling, much as if he were alone in the world.*

*In the living room* BENEATHA *sits at the table, still surrounded by the now almost ominous packing crates. She sits looking off. We feel that this is a mood struck perhaps an hour before, and it lingers now, full of the empty sound of profound disappointment. We see on a line from her brother's bedroom the sameness of their attitudes. Presently the bell rings and* BENEATHA *rises without ambition or interest in answering. It is* ASAGAI, *smiling broadly, striding into the room with energy and happy expectation and conversation.*

ASAGAI   I came over . . . I had some free time. I thought I might help with the packing. Ah, I like the look of packing crates! A household in preparation for a journey! It depresses some people . . . but for me . . . it is another feeling. Something full of the flow of life, do you understand? Movement, progress ... It makes me think of Africa.

BENEATHA  Africa!

ASAGAI  What kind of a mood is this? Have I told you how deeply you move me?

BENEATHA  He gave away the money, Asagai ...

ASAGAI  Who gave away what money?

BENEATHA  The insurance money. My brother gave it away.

ASAGAI  Gave it away?

BENEATHA  He made an investment! With a man even Travis wouldn't have trusted with his most worn-out marbles.

ASAGAI  And it's gone?

BENEATHA  Gone!

ASAGAI  I'm very sorry ... And you, now?

BENEATHA  Me? ... Me? ... Me, I'm nothing ... Me. When I was very small ... we used to take our sleds out in the wintertime and the only hills we had were the ice-covered stone steps of some houses down the street. And we used to fill them in with snow and make them smooth and slide down them all day ... and it was very dangerous, you know ... far too steep ... and sure enough one day a kid named Rufus came down too fast and hit the sidewalk and we saw his face just split open right there in front of us ... And I remember standing there looking at his bloody open face thinking that was the end of Rufus. But the ambulance came and they took him to the hospital and they fixed the broken bones and they sewed it all up ... and the next time I saw

Rufus he just had a little line down the middle of his
face . . . I never got over that . . .

ASAGAI  What?

BENEATHA  That that was what one person could do for
another, fix him up—sew up the problem, make him
all right again. That was the most marvelous thing in
the world . . . I wanted to do that. I always thought
it was the one concrete thing in the world that a human
being could do. Fix up the sick, you know—and make
them whole again. This was truly being God . . .

ASAGAI  You wanted to be God?

BENEATHA  No—I wanted to cure. It used to be so important to me. I wanted to cure. It used to matter. I
used to care. I mean about people and how their bodies
hurt . . .

ASAGAI  And you've stopped caring?

BENEATHA  Yes—I think so.

ASAGAI  Why?

BENEATHA  (*Bitterly*) Because it doesn't seem deep
enough, close enough to what ails mankind! It was a
child's way of seeing things—or an idealist's.

ASAGAI  Children see things very well sometimes—and
idealists even better.

BENEATHA  I know that's what you think. Because you
are still where I left off. You with all your talk and
dreams about Africa! You still think you can patch up
the world. Cure the Great Sore of Colonialism—(*Loftily, mocking it*) with the Penicillin of Independence—!

ASAGAI  Yes!

BENEATHA  Independence *and then what?* What about all
the crooks and thieves and just plain idiots who will

come into power and steal and plunder the same as before—only now they will be black and do it in the name of the new Independence—WHAT ABOUT THEM?!

ASAGAI  That will be the problem for another time. First we must get there.

BENEATHA  And where does it end?

ASAGAI  End? Who even spoke of an end? To life? To living?

BENEATHA  An end to misery! To stupidity! Don't you see there isn't any real progress, Asagai, there is only one large circle that we march in, around and around, each of us with our own little picture in front of us—our own little mirage that we think is the future.

ASAGAI  That is the mistake.

BENEATHA  What?

ASAGAI  What you just said—about the circle. It isn't a circle—it is simply a long line—as in geometry, you know, one that reaches into infinity. And because we cannot see the end—we also cannot see how it changes. And it is very odd but those who see the changes—who dream, who will not give up—are called idealists . . . and those who see only the circle—we call *them* the "realists"!

BENEATHA  Asagai, while I was sleeping in that bed in there, people went out and took the future right out of my hands! And nobody asked me, nobody consulted me—they just went out and changed my life!

ASAGAI  Was it your money?

BENEATHA  What?

ASAGAI  Was it your money he gave away?

BENEATHA   It belonged to all of us.

ASAGAI   But did you earn it? Would you have had it at all if your father had not died?

BENEATHA   No.

ASAGAI   Then isn't there something wrong in a house— in a world—where all dreams, good or bad, must depend on the death of a man? I never thought to see *you* like this, Alaiyo. You! Your brother made a mistake and you are grateful to him so that now you can give up the ailing human race on account of it! You talk about what good is struggle, what good is anything! Where are we all going and why are we bothering!

BENEATHA   AND YOU CANNOT ANSWER IT!

ASAGAI *(Shouting over her)   I LIVE THE ANSWER!* *(Pause)* In my village at home it is the exceptional man who can even read a newspaper . . . or who ever sees a book at all. I will go home and much of what I will have to say will seem strange to the people of my village. But I will teach and work and things will happen, slowly and swiftly. At times it will seem that nothing changes at all . . . and then again the sudden dramatic events which make history leap into the future. And then quiet again. Retrogression even. Guns, murder, revolution. And I even will have moments when I wonder if the quiet was not better than all that death and hatred. But I will look about my village at the illiteracy and disease and ignorance and I will not wonder long. And perhaps . . . perhaps I will be a great man . . . I mean perhaps I will hold on to the substance of truth and find my way always with the right course . . . and perhaps for it I will be butchered in my bed some night by the servants of empire . . .

BENEATHA   *The martyr!*

ASAGAI (*He smiles*) ... or perhaps I shall live to be a very old man, respected and esteemed in my new nation ... And perhaps I shall hold office and this is what I'm trying to tell you, Alaiyo: Perhaps the things I believe now for my country will be wrong and outmoded, and I will not understand and do terrible things to have things my way or merely to keep my power. Don't you see that there will be young men and women—not British soldiers then, but my own black countrymen—to step out of the shadows some evening and slit my then useless throat? Don't you see they have always been there ... that they always will be. And that such a thing as my own death will be an advance? They who might kill me even ... actually replenish all that I was.

BENEATHA Oh, Asagai, I know all that.

ASAGAI Good! Then stop moaning and groaning and tell me what you plan to do.

BENEATHA Do?

ASAGAI I have a bit of a suggestion.

BENEATHA What?

ASAGAI (*Rather quietly for him*) That when it is all over —that you come home with me—

BENEATHA (*Staring at him and crossing away with exasperation*) Oh—Asagai—at this moment you decide to be romantic!

ASAGAI (*Quickly understanding the misunderstanding*) My dear, young creature of the New World—I do not mean across the city—I mean across the ocean: home— to Africa.

BENEATHA (*Slowly understanding and turning to him with murmured amazement*) To Africa?

ASAGAI   Yes! . . . (*Smiling and lifting his arms playfully*)
Three hundred years later the African Prince rose up
out of the seas and swept the maiden back across the
middle passage over which her ancestors had come—

BENEATHA (*Unable to play*)   To—to Nigeria?

ASAGIA   Nigeria. Home. (*Coming to her with genuine romantic flippancy*) I will show you our mountains and
our stars; and give you cool drinks from gourds and
teach you the old songs and the ways of our people—
and, in time, we will pretend that—(*Very Softly*)—you
have only been away for a day. Say that you'll come—
(*He swings her around and takes her full in his arms
in a kiss which proceeds to passion*)

BENEATHA (*Pulling away suddenly*)   You're getting me
all mixed up—

ASAGAI   Why?

BENEATHA   Too many things—too many things have
happened today. I must sit down and think. I don't
know what I feel about anything right this minute.
      (*She promptly sits down and props her chin on her
      fist*)

ASAGAI (*Charmed*)   All right, I shall leave you. No—
don't get up. (*Touching her, gently, sweetly*) Just sit
awhile and think . . . Never be afraid to sit awhile and
think. (*He goes to door and looks at her*) How often
I have looked at you and said, "Ah—so this is what
the New World hath finally wrought . . ."
      (*He exits. BENEATHA sits on alone. Presently
      WALTER enters from his room and starts to rum-
      mage through things, feverishly looking for some-
      thing. She looks up and turns in her seat*)

BENEATHA (*Hissingly*)   Yes—just look at what the New
World hath wrought! . . . Just look! (*She gestures with*

*bitter disgust*) There he is! *Monsieur le petit bourgeois noir*—himself! There he is—Symbol of a Rising Class! Entrepreneur! Titan of the system! (WALTER *ignores her completely and continues frantically and destructively looking for something and hurling things to floor and tearing things out of their place in his search.* BENEATHA *ignores the eccentricity of his actions and goes on with the monologue of insult*) Did you dream of yachts on Lake Michigan, Brother? Did you see yourself on that Great Day sitting down at the Conference Table, surrounded by all the mighty bald-headed men in America? All halted, waiting, breathless, waiting for your pronouncements on industry? Waiting for you—Chairman of the Board! (WALTER *finds what he is looking for—a small piece of white paper—and pushes it in his pocket and puts on his coat and rushes out without ever having looked at her. She shouts after him*) I look at you and I see the final triumph of stupidity in the world!

> (*The door slams and she returns to just sitting again.* RUTH *comes quickly out of* MAMA'S *room*)

RUTH   Who was that?

BENEATHA   Your husband.

RUTH   Where did he go?

BENEATHA   Who knows—maybe he has an appointment at U.S. Steel.

RUTH (*Anxiously, with frightened eyes*)   You didn't say nothing bad to him, did you?

BENEATHA   Bad? Say anything bad to him? No—I told him he was a sweet boy and full of dreams and everything is strictly peachy keen, as the ofay kids say!

> (MAMA *enters from her bedroom. She is lost, vague, trying to catch hold, to make some sense of*

*her former command of the world, but it still
eludes her. A sense of waste overwhelms her gait;
a measure of apology rides on her shoulders. She
goes to her plant, which has remained on the
table, looks at it, picks it up and takes it to the
window sill and sits it outside, and she stands and
looks at it a long moment. Then she closes the
window, straightens her body with effort and turns
around to her children)*

MAMA  Well—ain't it a mess in here, though? (*A false
cheerfulness, a beginning of something*) I guess we all
better stop moping around and get some work done.
All this unpacking and everything we got to do. (RUTH
*raises her head slowly in response to the sense of the
line; and* BENEATHA *in similar manner turns very slowly
to look at her mother*) One of you all better call the
moving people and tell 'em not to come.

RUTH  Tell 'em not to come?

MAMA  Of course, baby. Ain't no need in 'em coming all
the way here and having to go back. They charges for
that too. (*She sits down, fingers to her brow, thinking*)
Lord, ever since I was a little girl, I always remembers
people saying, "Lena—Lena Eggleston, you aims too
high all the time. You needs to slow down and see life
a little more like it is. Just slow down some." That's
what they always used to say down home—"Lord, that
Lena Eggleston is a high-minded thing. She'll get her
due one day!"

RUTH  No, Lena . . .

MAMA  Me and Big Walter just didn't never learn right.

RUTH  Lena, no! We gotta go. Bennie—tell her . . .
(*She rises and crosses to* BENEATHA *with her arms outstretched.* BENEATHA *doesn't respond*) Tell her we

can still move . . . the notes ain't but a hundred and twenty-five a month. We got four grown people in this house—we can work . . .

MAMA (*To herself*)  Just aimed too high all the time—

RUTH (*Turning and going to* MAMA *fast—the words pouring out with urgency and desperation*)  Lena—I'll work . . . I'll work twenty hours a day in all the kitchens in Chicago . . . I'll strap my baby on my back if I have to and scrub all the floors in America and wash all the sheets in America if I have to—but we got to MOVE! We got to get OUT OF HERE!!

> (MAMA *reaches out absently and pats* RUTH'S *hand*)

MAMA  No—I sees things differently now. Been thinking 'bout some of the things we could do to fix this place up some. I seen a second-hand bureau over on Maxwell Street just the other day that could fit right there. (*She points to where the new furniture might go.* RUTH *wanders away from her*) Would need some new handles on it and then a little varnish and it look like something brand-new. And—we can put up them new curtains in the kitchen . . . Why this place be looking fine. Cheer us all up so that we forget trouble ever come . . . (*To* RUTH) And you could get some nice screens to put up in your room round the baby's bassinet . . . (*She looks at both of them, pleadingly*) Sometimes you just got to know when to give up some things . . . and hold on to what you got. . . .

> (WALTER *enters from the outside, looking spent and leaning against the door, his coat hanging from him*)

MAMA  Where you been, son?

WALTER (*Breathing hard*)  Made a call.

MAMA   To who, son?

WALTER   To The Man. (*He heads for his room*)

MAMA   What man, baby?

WALTER (*Stops in the door*)   The Man, Mama. Don't
you know who The Man is?

RUTH   Walter Lee?

WALTER   *The Man.* Like the guys in the streets say—
The Man. Captain Boss—Mistuh Charley . . . Old
Cap'n Please Mr. Bossman . . .

BENEATHA (*Suddenly*)   Lindner!

WALTER   That's right! That's good. I told him to come
right over.

BENEATHA (*Fiercely, understanding*)   For what? What
do you want to see him for!

WALTER (*Looking at his sister*)   We going to do business with him.

MAMA   What you talking 'bout, son?

WALTER   Talking 'bout life, Mama. You all always telling me to see life like it is. Well—I laid in there on
my back today . . . and I figured it out. Life just like it
is. Who gets and who don't get. (*He sits down with his
coat on and laughs*) Mama, you know it's all divided
up. Life is. Sure enough. Between the takers and the
"tooken." (*He laughs*) I've figured it out finally. (*He
looks around at them*) Yeah. Some of us always getting
"tooken." (*He laughs*) People like Willy Harris, they
don't never get "tooken." And you know why the rest
of us do? 'Cause we all mixed up. Mixed up bad. We
get to looking 'round for the right and the wrong; and
we worry about it and cry about it and stay up nights

trying to figure out 'bout the wrong and the right of
things all the time . . . And all the time, man, them
takers is out there operating, just taking and taking.
Willy Harris? Shoot—Willy Harris don't even count.
He don't even count in the big scheme of things. But
I'll say one thing for old Willy Harris . . . he's taught
me something. He's taught me to keep my eye on
what counts in this world. Yeah—(*Shouting out a little*)
Thanks, Willy!

RUTH  What did you call that man for, Walter Lee?

WALTER  Called him to tell him to come on over to the
show. Gonna put on a show for the man. Just what
he wants to see. You see, Mama, the man came here
today and he told us that them people out there where
you want us to move—well they so upset they willing
to pay us *not* to move! (*He laughs again*) And—and
oh, Mama—you would of been proud of the way me
and Ruth and Bennie acted. We told him to get out . . .
Lord have mercy! We told the man to get out! Oh, we
was some proud folks this afternoon, yeah. (*He lights a
cigarette*) We were still full of that old-time stuff . . .

RUTH  (*Coming toward him slowly*)  You talking 'bout
taking them people's money to keep us from moving in
that house?

WALTER  I ain't just talking 'bout it, baby—I'm telling
you that's what's going to happen!

BENEATHA  Oh, God! Where is the bottom! Where is the
real honest-to-God bottom so he can't go any farther!

WALTER  See—that's the old stuff. You and that boy that
was here today. You all want everybody to carry a
flag and a spear and sing some marching songs, huh?
You wanna spend your life looking into things and trying to find the right and the wrong part, huh? Yeah.
You know what's going to happen to that boy someday

—he'll find himself sitting in a dungeon, locked in forever—and the takers will have the key! Forget it, baby! There ain't no causes—there ain't nothing but taking in this world, and he who takes most is smartest —and it don't make a damn bit of difference *how*.

MAMA  You making something inside me cry, son. Some awful pain inside me.

WALTER  Don't cry, Mama. Understand. That white man is going to walk in that door able to write checks for more money than we ever had. It's important to him and I'm going to help him . . . I'm going to put on the show, Mama.

MAMA  Son—I come from five generations of people who was slaves and sharecroppers—but ain't nobody in my family never let nobody pay 'em no money that was a way of telling us we wasn't fit to walk the earth. We ain't never been that poor. (*Raising her eyes and looking at him*) We ain't never been that—dead inside.

BENEATHA  Well—we are dead now. All the talk about dreams and sunlight that goes on in this house. It's all dead now.

WALTER  What's the matter with you all! I didn't make this world! It was give to me this way! Hell, yes, I want me some yachts someday! Yes, I want to hang some real pearls 'round my wife's neck. Ain't she supposed to wear no pearls? Somebody tell me—tell me, who decides which women is suppose to wear pearls in this world. I tell you I am a *man*—and I think my wife should wear some pearls in this world!
 (*This last line hangs a good while and* WALTER *begins to move about the room. The word "Man" has penetrated his consciousness; he mumbles it to himself repeatedly between strange agitated pauses as he moves about*)

MAMA    Baby, how you going to feel on the inside?

WALTER    Fine! . . . Going to feel fine . . . a man . . .

MAMA    You won't have nothing left then, Walter Lee.

WALTER (*Coming to her*)    I'm going to feel fine, Mama.
I'm going to look that son-of-a-bitch in the eyes and
say—(*He falters*)—and say, "All right, Mr. Lindner—
(*He falters even more*)—that's *your* neighborhood out
there! You got the right to keep it like you want! You
got the right to have it like you want! Just write the
check and—the house is yours." And—and I am going
to say—(*His voice almost breaks*) "And you—you
people just put the money in my hand and you won't
have to live next to this bunch of stinking niggers! . . ."
(*He straightens up and moves away from his mother,
walking around the room*) And maybe—maybe I'll just
get down on my black knees . . . (*He does so;* RUTH *and*
BENNIE *and* MAMA *watch him in frozen horror*) "Captain, Mistuh, Bossman—(*Groveling and grinning and
wringing his hands in profoundly anguished imitation of
the slow-witted movie stereotype*) A-hee-hee-hee! Oh,
yassuh boss! Yasssssuh! Great white—(*Voice breaking,
he forces himself to go on*)—Father, just gi' ussen de
money, fo' God's sake, and we's—we's ain't gwine come
out deh and dirty up yo' white folks neighborhood . . ."
(*He breaks down completely*) And I'll feel fine! Fine!
FINE! (*He gets up and goes into the bedroom*)

BENEATHA    That is not a man. That is nothing but a tooth-
less rat.

MAMA    Yes—death done come in this here house. (*She
is nodding, slowly, reflectively*) Done come, walking in
my house on the lips of my children. You what supposed to be my beginning again. You—what supposed
to be my harvest. (*To* BENEATHA) You—you mourning your brother?

BENEATHA    He's no brother of mine.

MAMA    What you say?

BENEATHA    I said that that individual in that room is no brother of mine.

MAMA    That's what I thought you said. You feeling like you better than he is today? (BENEATHA *does not answer*) Yes? What you tell him a minute ago? That he wasn't a man? Yes? You give him up for me? You done wrote his epitaph too—like the rest of the world? Well, who give you the privilege?

BENEATHA    Be on my side for once! You saw what he just did, Mama! You saw him—down on his knees. Wasn't it you who taught me to despise any man who would do that? Do what he's going to do?

MAMA    Yes—I taught you that. Me and your daddy. But I thought I taught you something else too . . . I thought I taught you to love him.

BENEATHA    Love him? There is nothing left to love.

MAMA    There is *always* something left to love. And if you ain't learned that, you ain't learned nothing. (*Looking at her*) Have you cried for that boy today? I don't mean for yourself and for the family 'cause we lost the money. I mean for him: what he been through and what it done to him. Child, when do you think is the time to love somebody the most? When they done good and made things easy for everybody? Well then, you ain't through learning—because that ain't the time at all. It's when he's at his lowest and can't believe in hisself 'cause the world done whipped him so! When you starts measuring somebody, measure him right, child, measure him right. Make sure you done taken into account what hills and valleys he come through before he got to wherever he is.

(TRAVIS *bursts into the room at the end of the speech, leaving the door open*)

TRAVIS    Grandmama—the moving men are downstairs! The truck just pulled up.

MAMA (*Turning and looking at him*)    Are they, baby? They downstairs?
(*She sighs and sits.* LINDNER *appears in the doorway. He peers in and knocks lightly, to gain attention, and comes in. All turn to look at him*)

LINDNER (*Hat and briefcase in hand*)    Uh—hello . . .
(RUTH *crosses mechanically to the bedroom door and opens it and lets it swing open freely and slowly as the lights come up on* WALTER *within, still in his coat, sitting at the far corner of the room. He looks up and out through the room to* LINDNER)

RUTH    He's here.
(*A long minute passes and* WALTER *slowly gets up*)

LINDNER (*Coming to the table with efficiency, putting his briefcase on the table and starting to unfold papers and unscrew fountain pens*)    Well, I certainly was glad to hear from you people. (WALTER *has begun the trek out of the room, slowly and awkwardly, rather like a small boy, passing the back of his sleeve across his mouth from time to time*) Life can really be so much simpler than people let it be most of the time. Well—with whom do I negotiate? You, Mrs. Younger, or your son here? (MAMA *sits with her hands folded on her lap and her eyes closed as* WALTER *advances.* TRAVIS *goes closer to* LINDNER *and looks at the papers curiously*) Just some official papers, sonny.

RUTH    Travis, you go downstairs—

MAMA (*Opening her eyes and looking into* WALTER'S) No. Travis, you stay right here. And you make him understand what you doing, Walter Lee. You teach him good. Like Willy Harris taught you. You show where our five generations done come to. (WALTER *looks from her to the boy, who grins at him innocently*) Go ahead, son—(*She folds her hands and closes her eyes*) Go ahead.

WALTER (*At last crosses to* LINDNER, *who is reviewing the contract*) Well, Mr. Lindner. (BENEATHA *turns away*) We called you—(*There is a profound, simple groping quality in his speech*)—because, well, me and my family (*He looks around and shifts from one foot to the other*) Well—we are very plain people . . .

LINDNER Yes—

WALTER I mean—I have worked as a chauffeur most of my life—and my wife here, she does domestic work in people's kitchens. So does my mother. I mean—we are plain people . . .

LINDNER Yes, Mr. Younger—

WALTER (*Really like a small boy, looking down at his shoes and then up at the man*) And—uh—well, my father, well, he was a laborer most of his life. . . .

LINDNER (*Absolutely confused*) Uh, yes—yes, I understand. (*He turns back to the contract*)

WALTER (*A beat; staring at him*) And my father— (*With sudden intensity*) My father almost *beat a man to death* once because this man called him a bad name or something, you know what I mean?

LINDNER (*Looking up, frozen*) No, no, I'm afraid I don't—

WALTER (*A beat. The tension hangs; then* WALTER *steps back from it*)  Yeah. Well—what I mean is that we come from people who had a lot of *pride*. I mean—we are very proud people. And that's my sister over there and she's going to be a doctor—and we are very proud—

LINDNER  Well—I am sure that is very nice, but—

WALTER  What I am telling you is that we called you over here to tell you that we are very proud and that this— (*Signaling to* TRAVIS) Travis, come here. (TRAVIS *crosses and* WALTER *draws him before him facing the man*) This is my son, and he makes the sixth generation our family in this country. And we have all thought about your offer—

LINDNER  Well, good ... good—

WALTER  And we have decided to move into our house because my father—my father—he earned it for us brick by brick. (MAMA *has her eyes closed and is rocking back and forth as though she were in church, with her head nodding the Amen yes*) We don't want to make no trouble for nobody or fight no causes, and we will try to be good neighbors. And that's *all* we got to say about that. (*He looks the man absolutely in the eyes*) We don't want your money. (*He turns and walks away*)

LINDNER (*Looking around at all of them*)  I take it then —that you have decided to occupy ...

BENEATHA  That's what the man said.

LINDNER (*To* MAMA *in her reverie*)  Then I would like to appeal to you, Mrs. Younger. You are older and wiser and understand things better I am sure ...

MAMA  I am afraid you don't understand. My son said we was going to move and there ain't nothing left for

me to say. (*Briskly*) You know how these young folks
is nowadays, mister. Can't do a thing with 'em! (*As he
opens his mouth, she rises*) Good-bye.

LINDNER (*Folding up his materials*)    Well—if you are
that final about it . . . there is nothing left for me to
say. (*He finishes, almost ignored by the family, who are
concentrating on* WALTER LEE. *At the door* LINDNER
*halts and looks around*) I sure hope you people know
what you're getting into.
    (*He shakes his head and exits*)

RUTH (*Looking around and coming to life*)    Well, for
God's sake—if the moving men are here—LET'S GET
THE HELL OUT OF HERE!

MAMA (*Into action*)    Ain't it the truth! Look at all this
here mess. Ruth, put Travis' good jacket on him . . .
Walter Lee, fix your tie and tuck your shirt in, you
look like somebody's hoodlum! Lord have mercy, where
is my plant? (*She flies to get it amid the general bustling
of the family, who are deliberately trying to ignore the
nobility of the past moment*)    You all start on down
. . . Travis child, don't go empty-handed . . . Ruth, where
did I put that box with my skillets in it? I want to be in
charge of it myself . . . I'm going to make us the biggest
dinner we ever ate tonight . . . Beneatha, what's the
matter with them stockings? Pull them things up, girl . . .
    (*The family starts to file out as two moving men
    appear and begin to carry out the heavier pieces
    of furniture, bumping into the family as they move
    about*)

BENEATHA    Mama, Asagai asked me to marry him today
and go to Africa—

MAMA (*In the middle of her getting-ready activity*)    He
did? You ain't old enough to marry nobody—(*Seeing
the moving men lifting one of her chairs precariously*)

Darling, that ain't no bale of cotton, please handle it so we can sit in it again! I had that chair twenty-five years . . .

(*The movers sigh with exasperation and go on with their work*)

BENEATHA (*Girlishly and unreasonably trying to pursue the conversation*)   To go to Africa, Mama—be a doctor in Africa . . .

MAMA (*Distracted*)   Yes, baby—

WALTER   *Africa!* What he want you to go to Africa for?

BENEATHA   To practice there . . .

WALTER   Girl, if you don't get all them silly ideas out your head! You better marry yourself a man with some loot . . .

BENEATHA (*Angrily, precisely as in the first scene of the play*)   What have you got to do with who I marry!

WALTER   Plenty. Now I think George Murchison—

BENEATHA   *George Murchison!* I wouldn't marry him if he was Adam and I was Eve!

(WALTER *and* BENEATHA *go out yelling at each other vigorously and the anger is loud and real till their voices diminish.* RUTH *stands at the door and turns to* MAMA *and smiles knowingly*)

MAMA (*Fixing her hat at last*)   Yeah—they something all right, my children . . .

RUTH   Yeah—they're something. Let's go, Lena.

MAMA (*Stalling, starting to look around at the house*)   Yes—I'm coming. Ruth—

RUTH   Yes?

MAMA (*Quietly, woman to woman*)  He finally come into his manhood today, didn't he? Kind of like a rainbow after the rain . . .

RUTH (*Biting her lip lest her own pride explode in front of* MAMA)  Yes, Lena.
>   (WALTER'S *voice calls for them raucously*)

WALTER (*Off stage*)  Y'all come on! These people charges by the hour, you know!

MAMA (*Waving* RUTH *out vaguely*)  All right, honey— go on down. I be down directly.
>   (RUTH *hesitates, then exits.* MAMA *stands, at last alone in the living room, her plant on the table before her as the lights start to come down. She looks around at all the walls and ceilings and suddenly, despite herself, while the children call below, a great heaving thing rises in her and she puts her fist to her mouth to stifle it, takes a final desperate look, pulls her coat about her, pats her hat and goes out. The lights dim down. The door opens and she comes back in, grabs her plant, and goes out for the last time*)

*Curtain*

# THE SIGN IN SIDNEY BRUSTEIN'S WINDOW

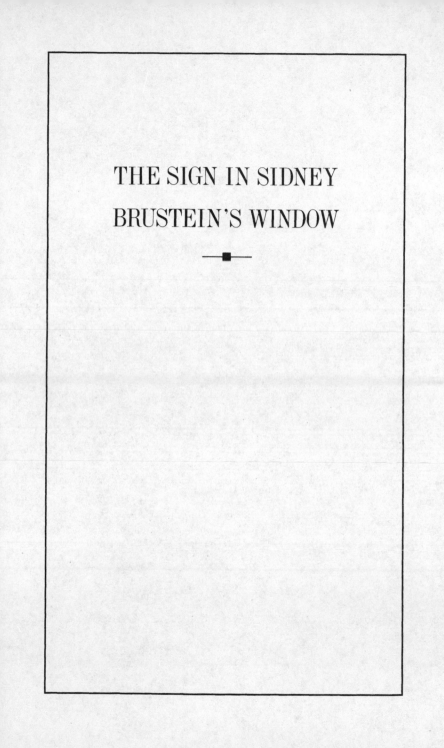

For

Robert Nemiroff

AND

Burt D'Lugoff

AND

*the committed everywhere*

*A Portrait:*

# The 101 "Final" Performances
# of SIDNEY BRUSTEIN

by Robert Nemiroff

> I care. I care about it all. It takes too much energy *not* to
> care . . . The *why* of why we are here is an intrigue for
> adolescents; the *how* is what must command the living.
> Which is why I have lately become an insurgent again.
> —Lorraine Hansberry

At 8:50 on the morning of Tuesday, January 12, 1965,
Lorraine Hansberry, aged thirty-four, died of cancer. That
same night, in respect to her memory, Henry Miller's Theatre stayed dark. It did not reopen thereafter and *"The Sign
in Sidney Brustein's Window* went into the record books"
—as the *Herald Tribune* reported it—"after an extraordinary run on Broadway of 101 performances."

At some midpoint in those 101 improbable performances the press began to call *Sidney Brustein* "one of the
most talked about plays in years," and it certainly was that;
but this is the least of a story that has already become
something of theatrical legend. It is the quality of all leg-
ends (even in realms not nearly so fanciful as the theater)
that they tend to grow out of all proportion to the facts.
But in the case of *Sidney Brustein* the facts themselves are
impressive enough. I was present throughout the two years
in which the author—the remarkable, beautiful woman
who meant more to me than any other person in life—bat-
tled so valiantly and, to the end, indomitably, against the
foe that finally took her. These were the same two years in
which *Sidney Brustein* came to life. And in the last months
it was my job, as one of the producers, at each of these 101
performances to share with the audience the day-to-day

*159*

facts of the struggle to keep it alive. I cannot pretend to objectivity about either the play or its author; I must leave that to time and to others. But the facts are another matter; they should be allowed to speak for themselves. It is thus appropriate to set them down, for they are not unrelated to the quality of the play—and of the life it embodied.

In the weeks just prior to the opening of *The Sign in Sidney Brustein's Window,* Lorraine resided, with a nurse in attendance, at the Hotel Victoria, where she might be close to rehearsals. She did not know the nature of her illness, only that she was terribly sick and that it might be some time before she could work again at full capacity. Nights were the worst—when she would often waken in agony. And she had developed, too, a corollary ailment to her lowered resistance: shingles—a blistering of the skin that girdled her torso with fire. Medication brought some degree of relief and at times she was, in fact, relatively free of pain. In a piece written for *Playbill* years earlier she had described how a friend, a much older woman "who had lived a purposeful and courageous life and who was then dying of cancer, . . . saluted it [this enemy] without despondency, but with a lively, beautiful and quite ribald anger. . . . There was one thing, she felt, which would prove equal to its relentless ravages, and that was the genius of man. Not his mysticism, but man with tubes and slides and the stubborn human notion that the stars are very much within our reach."

It was that way with Lorraine Hansberry. The "beautiful, ribald anger" with which she greeted fate and the humor without which she could never approach any one of her characters, even those she most admired, were not reserved for the stage. Even in the last months, she would often sit up with her dear friend Dorothy Secules, or myself, in some mugging pose or another, with a hot-water bottle perched debonairly atop her head, her lips turned up, and her eyes wide. And then she would collapse with laughter.

Autumn being ever her favorite season—"melancholy autumn," as she always called it—she was able to take in its vistas and watch the leaves turning on "jaunts" about Central Park in a wheel chair. She managed to attend a certain number of rehearsals and previews—most often she would force herself to take a taxi the three blocks to the Longacre Theatre and then walk, for the wheel chair embarrassed her—and she did an amount of writing.

In a Sunday *Times* article written in this period, for the opening, she summed up what she considered to be "the core" of her play:

Few things are more natural than that the tortures of the *engagé* should attract me thematically. Being 34 years old at this writing means that I am of the generation which grew up in the swirl and dash of the Sartre-Camus debate of the postwar years. The silhouette of the Western intellectual poised in hesitation before the flames of involvement was an accurate symbolism of some of my closest friends, some of whom crossed each other leaping in and out, for instance, of the Communist Party. Others searched, as agonizingly, for some ultimate justification of their lives in the abstractions flowing out of London or Paris. Still others were contorted into seeking a meaningful repudiation of *all* justifications of anything and had, accordingly, turned to Zen, action painting or even just Jack Kerouac.

Mine is, after all, the generation that had come to maturity drinking in the forebodings of the Silones, Koestlers and Richard Wrights. It had left us ill-prepared for decisions that had to be made in our own time about Algeria, Birmingham or the Bay of Pigs. By the 1960's few enough American Intellectuals had it within them to be ashamed that their discovery of the "betrayal" of the Cuban Revolution by Castro just happened to coincide with the change of heart of official American government policy. They left it to TV humorists to defend the Agrarian Reform in the end. It is the climate and mood of such intellectuals, if not these particular events, which constitute the core of a play called *The Sign in Sidney Brustein's Window*.

The play opened Thursday, October 15, 1964, to mixed notices, not surprisingly, as I look back on it now. For apart from its human essences and the distinctively irrepressible humor without which Lorraine Hansberry could never approach any character, even those she most admired, *Sidney Brustein* was among other things a "play of ideas"—and thus, from the start, a somewhat alien visitation to Broadway. At best such plays, which have never been entirely at home here, tend to make us nervous, save on the special occasions when they bear the prior stamp of British approval. To make matters worse, it was a play of ideas that are not popular: ideas that ran deliberately counter to the entire vogue of sophisticated *ennui*, the self-absorption, negation, disenchantment and despair that pass for "depth" in the theatre today—again, in those rare instances when "ideas" are admitted at all.

At a critical moment Sidney Brustein, who like so many of us has transformed the tensions of our age into a personal internal ulcer, is offered the only remedy that seems within his ken: a tranquilizing pill. He reaches out for the pill and, lifting it aloft—as the stage directions say, "like Poor Yorick's skull"—he exclaims: "Yes, by all means hand me the chloroform of my passions; the sweetening of my conscience; the balm of my glands. Oh blessed age! That has provided that I need never live again in the full temper of my rage. . . ." And then, setting it down again on the table, he continues: In another day, Sidney laments, his ancestors might have confronted evil with a sword: "But how does one confront these thousand nameless faceless vapors that are the evil of our time? Could a sword pierce it? . . . Wrath has become a poisoned gastric juice in the intestine. One does not *smite* evil anymore: one holds one's gut, thus—and takes a pill."

In the face of such a world, in which passion has all but lost the name of meaningful action, a world faced at any conceivable moment with extinction beyond the control of any man, it is understandable that the fashion should be despair: that all appears absurdity and that nothing could seem more irrelevant than the quest for alternatives. The very day the play opened Khrushchev fell from power in Russia, the Labor Party rose in England, and the Chinese set off their atom bomb; where such events can occupy twenty-four hours, what power can a single man feel over the shaping of his destiny? Belief, confidence, hope—commitment of any kind, any act or movement designed to achieve anything at all—the very words become gauche and embarrassing.

And yet it was in the face of just this world, and moreover, with full and unblinking recognition of the *actuality* of the evil within it; and with awareness too, awareness only too personal, of the ultimate absurdity of individual fate, the inevitability of the pain and suffering inherent in the "human condition"—that she set out to *realistically* affirm the species. It was Lorraine Hansberry's stubborn notion that mankind might yet muddle through. Or that, in any event, we deserved the *chance* and that only this was worth the candle.

Distance, however, seems to lend perspective. The goal she set herself, in all her work, was a task possible—or at any rate, easier of achievement—in the crucible of a John Procter, the court of a Hamlet or the Thirty Years' War of a Mother Courage: those moments of man's past when he stood on the brink of a great decision, and heroic action could have clear meaning. It was a task possible even in the slums of Walter Lee Younger's Chicago where black and white are, still, more pronounced than our intermediate gray. If the playwright's commitment were less universal, bounded by race or restricted by color, she might have turned for her affirmation, for example, to Mississippi. Instead, she chose to look for it in the most unlikely place of all: the lives most of us lead today. Precisely, in short, where *we* cannot find it. It was the mark of her respect for us all.

The play she wrote was not neat, simple or "well-made" for easy assimilation at one sitting. Rather than essaying a single domestic situation or even several themes, which would ignore the complexity we live with, she deliberately chose to confront the "thousand nameless faceless vapors" of evil that preoccupy and compel us. It was a sprawling canvas on which are juxtaposed, with varying degrees of success, the dominant themes and conflicts which, *only* in their totality and terribly complicated interrelationship, motivate and define our generation. And she did not even allow herself the cover of obscurity. Lorraine Hansberry insisted on clarity *in* complexity. She tackled sacred cows quite as if she did not acknowledge their sanctity, and she had the temerity to discuss ideas *per se* quite as if she did not know she was *not* George Bernard Shaw.

Nor was the play easily classifiable; it could not be comfortably pigeonholed by the first-night critic with a deadline to meet. It was not the exercise in "naturalism" we blithely tend to assume for the social playwright. Neither did it have the familiar tone or attitude that makes more experimental forms acceptable. It was too *popular*—too hopeful, too readily accessible to—and respectful of—the intelligence of the mass audience to be taken for "serious" drama; there was too damn much fun in it. And not one symbol you could not understand. *"There are no squares, Sidney: everybody is his own hipster, believe me when I tell you."* In the simplistic universe of a theatre that has discovered "guilt" and the great new revelation, "original sin," there is something obviously disconcerting—and therefore "sentimental"—about a 34-year-old author who can, after properly nailing the "bourgeois Philistine" that is Mavis Parodus, proceed to turn right around and pay her tribute—and, moreover, actually raise fists to the gods in her behalf, as Sidney does. There is something almost indecent about this; it is an unforgivable lapse, the final fall from sophistication. For it smacks of the suggestion that there is perhaps a potential in her (and if in Mavis, why not in us all?) greater than environment has permitted. And didn't this go "out" with the thirties, at least among "serious" men?

Finally—the cardinal sin—*Sidney Brustein* mixed *styles!* For all the oft-remarked-upon felicity of the playwright's dialogue, her wonderful ear for the comic nuance of everyday, it flows freely—as William Gibson observed in the Sunday *Times*—in a "range of vibrant rhetoric new in her work and not common on our stage." And it also takes flight into a heightened poetic compression permissible in Ionesco and Beckett but not in popular drama—as in Act III, Scene I, where the disintegration of Sidney's world is paralleled in a disintegration of realistic form.

This stylistic unorthodoxy created certain problems—and ultimate failings—in the production. On stage we tend to consider it enough to *suggest* intellectuals; but too much talk, the actual discussion of ideas, makes us nervous. Heightened speech in an otherwise realistic and comprehensible play, shifts of style, flights of metaphor—are likely to embarrass the actor. The obvious solution is to cut them. And all the more so when we accept the notion, as most of us in the theatre seem to, that there is some inherent, God-given or natural law governing the precise length a play may be—quite as if the fifteen minutes more or less were dictated by some immutable, pre-tested Audience Attention Span Meter, rather than by Stagehands' Union Local #1, and the commuter timetables of the New York Central.

Psychological factors alone are not insurmountable, but

when they are combined with the practical problems of production,* there is seldom time for ideal solutions. Something had to give; and the production on opening night suffered somewhat from both too much cutting and too little. In a few instances themes and character developments arose without adequate grounding in what went before: in Act I, Scene I, Sidney's crucial decision—which gives shape and direction to everything that follows—was not sufficiently established; and, most notably, identification with Iris, his wife, was diminished by the omission of Act II, Scene I. The present edition corrects these omissions—and also includes certain minor additions from the author's original drafts that are interesting in themselves.

Looking back to opening night it is hardly likely, in short, that the critic comfortably settling back with nostalgic reminiscences of *A Raisin in the Sun* could have been prepared for *Sidney Brustein*. Only five years before, at the curtain of what is by now one of the best-loved plays in America, the Younger family had decided to risk all for the new home in the white middle-class neighborhood; now their creator was saying that that house was on fire, the community a disaster area of the soul, and that a great deal of rebuilding would have to be done from the ground up if the neighborhood was to be fit for the Youngers to live in at all. And she was saying it in terms—a style, a frame of reference, a genre—quite different from those the critic might have expected of her.

The fact that all of this was implicit in *Raisin* itself—which was actually no more "naturalistic" than its succes-

* In the case of *Sidney Brustein*, the replacement of our original male star and director two weeks before the opening by Gabriel Dell and Peter Kass, respectively. Mr. Dell's last-minute approach to the role of Sidney—who never once leaves the stage—was the achievement of a fine actor and, in the pitifully short time available to him, the excitement and insight with which Mr. Kass infused the entire company were little short of incredible.

sor; and which did *not* have a "happy ending," only the commitment to new levels of struggle—did not help. For this had quite managed to escape most of the critics at the time, and has eluded them ever since, in the quite understandable rush of their enthusiasm for the new playwright's humor and insight, and the near-ecstatic discovery that she had *not*, praise God, written a play "about Negroes but human beings." As if, apparently, there were some inherent contradiction. (Imagine, if you can, the suggestion that "Tennessee Williams does not write about Americans, he writes about human beings.")

Closer examination might have revealed, of course, the deeper non-naturalistic levels of *Raisin*. Walter Lee Younger's "African" soliloquy, for example, is a speech that could not possibly *literally* be his own—any more than Mavis Parodus could, in life, become Medea, or Gloria so eloquently locate her essence in a Goya etching. The liquor that loosens Walter Lee's tongue releases a language and imagery he could *not* have derived from the books he has never read, nor certainly from the movies that he *has* seen; and language is *not* a quality of the blood. It is the *potential* talking in him, not the actual. It is the stature to which he aspires, not the one he has been permitted. The chauffeur becomes one with African kings—and in poetry's swift illumination we are enabled to grasp, in full pathos, the extent of the disparity: the size of the injustice that has been done him. The moment has nothing whatever to do with naturalism, literalism or "kitchen-sink" drama. It can only be understood as poetic compression, larger than life. (Just as in the Act II curtain the yardstick in Sidney's hand becomes, visibly, the measure of his—and our own—diminishment.)

A closer look might have revealed, too, the philosophical current that is as strong in the Younger living room as in the Brusteins'—if less obvious where the idiom is folk, not Freud; and the allusions are to Tennessee, not Paris.

MAMA

. . . Child, when do you think is the time to love somebody the most . . . it's when he's at his lowest and can't
believe in hisself 'cause the world done whipped him so.
When you starts measuring a man, measure him right,
child, measure him right. Make sure you done taken into
account what hills and valleys he come through before
he got to wherever he is.

Is there any essential difference—except for the language
—between Wally O'Hara in Act III and *this* about Asugai,
the African revolutionist in *Raisin:*

WALTER

You and that boy that was here today. You all want everybody to carry a flag and a spear and sing some marching
songs, huh? You wanna spend your life looking into things
and trying to find the right and the wrong part, huh? Yeah.
You know what's going to happen to that boy someday—
he'll find himself sitting in a dungeon, locked in forever—
and the takers will have the key! Forget it, baby! There
ain't no causes—there ain't nothing but taking in this
world, and he who takes most is smartest—and it don't
make a damn bit of difference *how*.

Or is Sidney Brustein "that boy" *circa* Greenwich Village
in chukka boots and corduroy?

There is a clear line between the plant that sits in Lena
Younger's window and the Sign that hangs in Sidney's. But
*Raisin* had never received that kind of examination. Perhaps because of its author, perhaps because of its hopeful-
ness, perhaps because of its popularity—we do not associate "serious" art with mass success—it was *assumed* to
be simple. The very art by which it concealed its complexity was its critical undoing. Was it likely, then, that the
critic, with all the best intentions in the world, was psychologically prepared to accept from the pen of this engaging
young Negro writer—"hardly more than a girl," as one in-
terviewer described her—what he might have from an author of another milieu or more awesome repute?

It was with many of the above things in mind, but also the prayer that I was far wide of the mark, that I worded my opening-night telegram to Lorraine. Paraphrasing freely from the play, it read in part:

> Witness you ever-burning lights above: we fools are up and at it again: fools who believe that death is waste and love is sweet and people want to be better than they are . . . Whatever the outcome tonight I want you to know:
>
> 1) That it is a great play: a measured, remorseless, dimensional paean to life as no one—no one—has the courage to write these days.
>
> 2) It is a play for people. They come, they laugh, they take sides, they participate; it is their play and it speaks for them—this much is proven already. Let us hope now that the intellectuals surprise us with the depth to rise to their level.
>
> 3) It is not the best production, but it is the very best production we had in us to give.
>
> 4) If the sign hangs long in the window, it is your sign . . . you are tough, Lorraine Hansberry . . . even wracked with pain as now . . . Tougher and stronger and more beautiful than any of us. You are the best that we have. Good health, justice tonight and more to come.

As far as my earlier prayers were concerned, I might as well have saved them for a better purpose. There was justice "to come." But not that night.

Daily reviews are of brief dominion—absolute but without duration. Their hour of ascendance, while it lasts, is awesomely real; their justice swift, final, irrevocable. But good, bad or indifferent, their only life is the life they measure: they seldom survive the run of a play. And when a book appears—when a play is *published*—we know their hour is past. Ordinarily, they would have no relevance here. But in the light of what was to come—and as part of the record—they are worth recalling. It was not that the reviews were negative. Far from it. Among them there were a goodly number of outright "raves." But in the main they so utterly failed to comprehend or evoke the play.

Howard Taubman's notice in *The New York Times* focused on "a scene more searing than anything on Broadway,"—Alton's monologue—"[which] could stand alone as a passionately eloquent sermon for a time when the Rev. Dr. Martin Luther King also wins a Nobel Prize." He spoke of others "that shine with humor, tremble with feeling and summon up a vision of wisdom and integrity." But he also found that "although the stage frequently lights up, it is likely to dim unexpectedly. The trouble is not only in the writing"—which struck him as uneven and in need of tightening—"one has a feeling that the performance has not quite jelled." Walter Kerr in the *Herald Tribune* largely concurred, and Richard Watts in the *New York Post* shared Taubman's reservations. Yet Watts recognized, too, "a courageous, compassionate and warmly human spirit . . . power and insight and . . . forthright integrity" and, above all, "the unsentimental sympathy for the weaknesses of man" which he felt to be "the notable feature of this searching examination of troubled human nature. *The Sign in Sidney Brustein's Window* demonstrates again that Miss Hansberry is a talented and important dramatist." But in the *Journal-American,* John McClain summed up its essence otherwise: "The theme seems to be . . . 'don't pick on the world.' "

A few reviewers, however, had no difficulty with the theme—or what their colleagues complained of being the multifarious themes—and grasped the play in larger dimension. Publications as diverse as *The Journal of Commerce, New Leader, Saturday Review* and *National Guardian* were unstinting in their respect and admiration. But it remained for the *Wall Street Journal*'s Richard P. Cooke, in a straight "rave," to rejoice: "If Broadway has needed a play by someone who can reach into the turbulence of contemporary life and come up with a true report which is also a work of dramatic art, Lorraine Hansberry has accomplished it. . . . The taste left in the mouth after the final curtain is both bitter and good. For the playwright herself has taste, of the best kind."

Richard Gilman's assessment in *Newsweek,* however, was in direct opposition to Cooke's; it was headlined "Borrowed Bitchery" and is worth quoting at length for the sense it gives of the intensity of emotion the play had succeeded in generating. In coming directly to the point, Mr. Gilman did not waste one word on cast or production:

> There was surely a dry agony in Lorraine Hansberry's writing of *The Sign in Sidney Brustein's Window* . . . the play is a vicious sitting in judgment on others. . . .
>
> There is a sort of inverted miracle in the way Miss Hansberry manages to distort so many things—taste, intelligence, craft. . . . Her dragooned themes . . . serve exclusively as containers for her venomous anger: she hates homosexuals, liberals, abstract artists, nonrealistic playwrights, white people unwilling to commit suicide . . . her savage assault on intellectuality brandishes every intellectual catchword. . . .
>
> . . . In turning into a cocktail-party shrew, in shifting her suffering to the backs of others, in using every easy trick to destroy what threatens her, she has betrayed not only the functions of art, but social responsibility, political possibility, her own cause [?] and, most radically, herself.

In his defense of civilization, Richard Gilman was not alone. Others might lack his articulateness, but Martin Gottfried, for one, of *Women's Wear Daily,* was not lacking for courage: he used a bold phrase, the "stinking triviality of it all." Michael Smith, in the *Village Voice,* explained how he "loathed" being forced "to condemn Miss Hansberry's play" and how at first, in fact, he had intended to pay her the tribute of silence: "I would prefer not to cause her further pain. But the play is dreadful, and I am deeply offended at the praise it has received for reasons that are certainly questionable"—the foremost being, he found, "that Lorraine Hansberry, the play's author, is a Negro"— and the next, "the public knowledge of [her] critical illness."

Such comments, however, were the exception. Most reviewers praised the play or its parts in varying degree and combination. But there were strong reservations, too, and an all-too-apparent perplexity about the whole. Where *Raisin* was "warm, simple and direct," *Brustein* was apparently "depressing, diffuse and confusing . . . too many stories . . . too much talk." McClain—who was perhaps typical and who had left in the end "rejoicing"—concluded on a plaintive note: "As I say, I was finally won over—I really came to care—but I wish Miss Hansberry hadn't talked quite so much." A Newark colleague wished she "could have said something *simpler*."

By merely *cataloguing* what she did say—the themes out of the context of flesh and blood; the ideas isolated from the emotions of those who hold them on stage; the problems apart from the complexities out of which they arose; the characters defined only by their most readily apparent aspect—the reviews, even many of the favorable ones, had made *Sidney Brustein* seem *impossible:* a lifeless tract, a potpourri of "wailings and woes." It was like reporting George Bernard Shaw—everything but the humor. A straight-faced inventory of the characters in *You Can't Take It with You*—or a synopsis of *Hamlet*—would have been about as persuasive.

In the light of such reviews the lay theatre-goer might logically assume modest success—and indeed, many of our friends called to offer congratulations. But to anyone who understands the stringent economics of Broadway the contrary was clear. The play was not a "smash." It was not a musical or a comedy and it had no great star. There had been no great advance sale, and no line would form at the box office next morning. There would be no calls from the brokers and theatre-party agents who provide the lifeblood of Broadway but cannot afford to take chances: the next sale depends on the largest number of satisfied purchasers of the last. Furthermore, the play would have no appeal to a not inconsiderable portion of the public: those for whom it does not matter so much *what* they see as long as they can say it was a "hit." And those for whom this is *all* that matters: a pair of "hot tickets" is but the means to an end, a form of currency, not art—or even "entertainment," except as an item for tax deduction. Without these a play cannot run: the drama that is not a "hit" is dead. *Sidney Brustein* cost $20,000 a week just to operate. *It would have to close.*

Serious theatre-lovers who had read the reviews were intrigued, of course, and many certainly planned to see it sooner or later, but that was beside the point: at $7.50 a throw (plus dinner and baby sitter?) to see for oneself is an indulgence; how many of us can afford the luxury of having our own taste? The only way to evaluate a critic is to match him against the play he reviews. Make the comparison often enough, and one begins to get the feel of the man; only then can one know whom, if anyone, to rely upon. But who can afford it? Instead, we are forced to rely on the internal logic of the review itself. If the man writes well enough, we are likely to be persuaded. And if we are persuaded often enough, he becomes a great critic. But how *well* he writes may have nothing whatever to do with the plays he reviews. It is a perfect closed circle (which is perhaps why it is *known* as the Critics' Circle.)

It is only in this context that the New York critic has assumed a power he never sought (and not infrequently protests against—to deaf ears): he is one of the few men with the power to both deliver a verdict—and get rid of the evidence. As Viveca Lindfors was to put it presently: "At the post-mortem there is almost never a corpse." Unless, in short, a large transfusion of money were immediately available, the Sign in our window would have to come down Saturday night. All this was apparent 2 A.M. Thursday when, with wondering eyes, we heard the reviews on the phone.

On Friday we broke the news to Lorraine. She had half expected it. As one who knew the ways of this world only too well, Lorraine Hansberry was always more surprised by success or good news of any kind than the contrary— and thus able to enjoy it the more. Her own earlier triumph; the proper recognition of anyone else's achievement; the plaudits of the tastemakers for work of any kind that was genuinely good—these, to her, were always happy accidents, to be treasured to the full, but never counted on. *"A lot of people 'have it' and they just get trampled to death by the mob trying to get up the same mountain"*—if there was one thing Lorraine Hansberry did *not* believe, it was that talent will "out" in the end.

Still, it was the *immediacy* of the prospect that hurt. *Sidney Brustein* had shared the history common to most plays: the years in the writing, planning, production; the lonely vigils, endless drafts, conferences, crises, battles, debates, casting calls; sessions with actors, directors, designers, up to and down through the rehearsals themselves. *A Raisin in the Sun* had run nineteen months on Broadway. Now to run *not even one week*—can any writer be *prepared* for this?

Some scenes one does not ever forget: Lorraine's always deep, penetrating eyes wide with concern as we talked— what if it were a long time before she could write again? What would she do? How would she live? . . . And in the midst of this, a phone call from Frank and Eleanor Perry, the young couple who had written, produced and directed the film *David and Lisa*. Three days before, they had lent the production $2,500 to be used *only* if the reviews were good and we ran. Now, despite the odds, they were saying:

"Yes, we've read the reviews . . . no, we don't give a damn . . . we know the odds . . . we're calling to say we hope you will use it. . . ."

Twenty-five hundred dollars, though, was like a drop in the bucket, even when supplemented by a like amount from a friend, Victor Rabinowitz, who said he also knew the odds, but would leave the discretion to us. The next day was Saturday, the day for which the closing notice had already been posted. My co-producers (Burt D'Lugoff and J. I. Jahre) and I spent the night on the phones. Trying, as someone said, to "hold back the ocean."

About noon Saturday Lorraine called from the hotel— one of the few occasions I can recall terror in her voice. The numbness, which since yesterday morning she had felt in her legs, had gradually moved up to her chest. If she did not know the full significance of this, we did: cancer had invaded the central nervous system. Burt D'Lugoff, my partner and for many years our dear friend, who shares the dedication of this book, is a doctor. He told Lorraine he would be right over. I stayed on the phones while he and a nurse took her to the hospital for what was to be the last time.

A member of the production called, a by-now familiar voice though we had only met at rehearsals, who at her own insistence must remain anonymous. She had been thinking, she said: over many years she had been associated with many shows, but never one like this . . . "that *mattered* so much . . . it should not be *permitted* to close." She had $8,500 in the bank, would that help? This was not a woman of wealth (though of good earning power), and so I said no, or started to—she would not even hear me out. How dare I say no? It wasn't *my* play . . . in short, she *insisted*. By now we were both laughing and crying at the same time. This was a Mavis Parodus come to life on the other end of the phone. And as *tough*. I thanked her—

wanting to lift my own hands to the gods like Sidney—and got Lorraine on the phone.

"It was like penicillin," Burt later described it, "a radiance, a great beaming smile settled over her face when she heard." For one week at least the Sign would continue to hang in our window. And sometime the next day, alone in her hospital room, she wrote of the play to a friend, in a letter which was never completed. It read in part:

> . . . Yes, a great deal has happened to me since our friendship. In fact, I often feel that everything in the world which can happen has happened to me. But this is nonsense, as a new thing crops up immediately.
>
> . . . I hope that you and Polly get in to see the show. It's ever so much more entertaining than the reviewers try to let on. *And it's very funny.*

The letter stopped there and these were, so far as I know, the last words she put to paper. Characteristically. For it had never ceased to amaze and delight her that the show really *was* so funny—that people could laugh so loud over the lines—just as it never failed to tickle her that these figments of merest fancy, these characters dreamed up out of her own head, could become real to so many; that people could beam and cry, argue and passionately take sides over them—directors storm and fuss and grow furious, actors create whole past histories and inutterably complicated motivations for them and ask the most intricate intimate questions about them; and that, for instance, there never was an audience that did not burst into howls and applause over Mavis' lines about "squares and hipsters" just as they did over Lena Younger's *"It* expresses me!" Lorraine Hansberry was, among other things, a willful little girl playing a prank, as she sometimes said, on a much too sober and pontifical adult world—and never more delighted than to be caught in the act. It was her *funny* lines—the ones that gave people pleasure—of which she was proudest.

In the next week three people came backstage who were to prove instrumental in keeping the Sign in our window: Sidney Kingsley, Shelley Winters and Viveca Lindfors.

The celebrated playwright had come to see Gabriel Dell, whom he had originally discovered and directed as one of the "Dead End Kids" in his perhaps most famous drama. The word he used most frequently in discussing the play afterward, privately and publicly, was "genius"; he made no secret of the fact there were moments he would have treated differently, but overall he had seen nothing to equal its power and beauty in many years. He was outspoken publicly, and behind the scenes worked quietly and effectively in a dozen ways.

Shelley Winters was at once so moved and so profoundly struck by the play's contemporary relevance—"it is not a play *about* our time," she said at a Presidential election rally, "it *is* our time"—that she offered to step into a supporting role at union minimum if this would help. In the weeks to come, Miss Winters, one artist who has never shunned the *responsibility* of public prominence, was to leave no stone unturned in the play's behalf, appearing again and again, in alternation with Miss Lindfors, on radio, television and the public platform, often on a moment's notice.

The Swedish-born star—surely one of the world's most beautiful women and no less an actress and human being —is proudly American now in all respects except one: she still has some difficulty in accepting the dollar as a standard of art. Viveca Lindfors showed up at our office the following morning in a great fur coat and dungarees and at once proceeded to call and write (typing the letters herself until all hours) others in the theatrical community for support. In the months following, I do not recall her ever declining any request for aid, no matter what the hour or inconvenience. The immediate result of her efforts was a meeting scheduled for the following Friday, after show-time, at the Perrys' home.

On the morning of Tuesday, October 20th, Lorraine Hansberry first lost her sight, then went into convulsions: the disease had entered her brain. At midafternoon she lapsed into coma and the doctors informed us it was now only a matter of hours at best. We released the news for the first time that she was critically ill; there was no longer any point in holding it back. My brother stepped in to take my place in the round-the-clock battle of the phones at the office. But she was tough—it is not rhetoric to speak of Lorraine Hansberry's commitment to life; even then, out of the depth of whatever will survived in the darkness that enveloped her, how she clung to it!

Can a person in coma register the world outside? Not once but many times in the next four days I repeated to her the words of a letter from a stranger whom I was later to meet, a young theatre-goer named Howard Bennett, that had arrived at the Longacre that morning. It read in part:

> . . . I would like to thank you for writing *Sidney Brustein.* You have written a beautiful—a painfully beautiful work of art. Please, if *Sidney* fails, please keep writing . . . I don't know why or how it missed being received as one of the modern theatre's greatest achievements. . . .
>
> For my own part, let me tell you that I felt everything that was happening on stage yesterday . . . I believed in everyone, and I hurt—and I saw the beauty in each. Thank you! I hope you will be able to keep carrying a message of hope till the last day of your life. With *Sidney* you helped and touched me as I do not expect to be moved again in the theatre.

Again and again I told Lorraine she would *have* to get better, come back, write again, that there were too many people like this depending on her. Later, when I asked her whether she had heard, she said yes—though I am still not certain of it and do not suppose it really matters now.

Wednesday night we had visitors: William Gibson, whose musical adaptation of *Golden Boy* had opened the night before, and his wife, Margaret. Bill had met Lorraine only on several occasions over the years, yet there was a warm affection between them—she respected his *Miracle Worker,* and she often remarked on one particularly helpful suggestion he had made when *Raisin* was trying out in New Haven. That night was the first opportunity the Gibsons had had to see the new play and they came back to the hospital, late in the night, and he stood for a long time, this tall and somewhat Lincolnesque man, crying by her bed. Afterward, a letter appeared in the Sunday *Times* which, in addition to hailing the play, posed a more general question:

To the Editor:
   It is one of the vexing facts of our theatre that as audience we have so little sense of its cultural continuity.
   At this writing a play by Lorraine Hansberry . . . is struggling to keep open at the Longacre quite as though Miss Hansberry had never in her life written a line to interest anyone. How can it be that, of the hundreds of thousands who roared with pleasure and wept tears at her *Raisin in the Sun,* so few have the intellectual appetancy to hear what her mind has been at work on since? . . .
   . . . Is it a compliment to our culture that one season a writer can be voted best playwright of the year, and another season be ignored like a novice?
                                                William Gibson
Stockbridge, Mass.

By Thursday the doctors gave up predicting: Lorraine Hansberry had quite confounded their charts. And then, beginning on Friday, she returned gradually to life—slowly at first, unable to speak, hardly able to move, but then growing a bit stronger each day, as first sight returned and partial movement, then comprehension and speech, until finally—weeks later—she could eat a little again and converse and even be helped out of bed to sit up in a chair.

There remained some partial loss of memory, and *aphasia:* the mind functioning clearly but not always able to deliver the right words. But in her last months Lorraine was able to follow with considerable relish the events occurring outside.

At the Friday night meeting at the Perrys' on October 23rd, I was thus able to announce a turn for the better—and from that point on no further reference was made to the matter of her health in the course of our campaign. For if the play were worth saving, it had to be saved on its own account and not that of its author—and indeed, most of those who became involved afterward did not know of her condition, or else assumed she was recuperating, since the malignant nature of her illness had never been revealed.

The most lasting impression that night was not made by any of the theatre folk present. These tended to varying degrees of pessimism—not about the play but about the state of our theatre and the resultant implausibility of the effort: it had been tried and failed too many times before; we might eke out a few weeks at most, but "you can't buck the gods of the box-office . . . give up while you're ahead —or else why not try to move the thing off-Broadway?" The off-Broadway "alternative," which Lillian Hellman had put forward earlier and which Shelley Winters echoed, is without doubt the most frequent one heard whenever a serious play is in trouble, reflecting as it does the despair most of our serious artists feel about survival on Broadway. But it also tends to be defeatist and divisive, since on examination it proves to be not an *alternative* at all: the move is *not possible,* and never has been, for a dozen practical reasons, not the least of which are the union requirements (which will not be waived) for a six months' lapse before any play can be reopened off-Broadway—at less than Broadway salaries, that is.

It was easier, too, to go off on tangents, to discuss, with delightfully interlarded anecdotes, all matter of related aspects—publicity columnists, etc.—constructive in themselves but beside the immediate point: survival. It remained for a tall young Negro in overalls, who had seen his *first* play not one year before, to set a different tone for us all.

Louisiana-born Jerome Smith is a CORE field organizer who, at twenty-five, had been jailed, beaten and run out of more towns, from one end of the South to the other, than even the theatrical mind can comfortably imagine. He had come to this meeting because he happened to be in New York at the time and because he knew Lorraine and had seen her play. He spoke softly and haltingly now of the particular relationship between them, and the room fell silent: "Two years ago, I first met Lorraine Hansberry— like many of the young people of the movement, I had come to enlist her support." In a few meetings, he said, she had become one of the "important influences in my life, opening up for me books of all kinds"—and ideas that went beyond the particular parochialisms of the immediate struggle. She had helped to organize a great public meeting in Croton-on-Hudson, New York, which she chaired and at which he spoke. The funds collected there had purchased the station-wagon in which the three civil rights workers, Michael Schwerner, Andrew Goodman and James Chaney, were driving at the time of their abduction and murder. Then, with a groping eloquence new to many in the room, Jerome Smith spoke of a "commitment beyond race . . . the need to reach out and touch each other . . . without which civil rights in themselves don't mean a thing"—and it was *this,* he said, which spoke to him through this play about a Jewish intellectual in Greenwich Village "as through few other experiences in my life." There was silence for a moment, and after that the discussion was brief, sober and to the point.

The following week's *New York Times* carried an ad, signed and paid for by most of those in the room. Titled "An Open Letter: First-Rate Theatre Belongs on Broadway," it read in part:

> The news that Lorraine Hansberry's *The Sign in Sidney Brustein's Window* faces closing should disturb all who love the theatre.
>
> Miss Hansberry's new play is a work of distinction. It contains the humor and insight we associate with the finest traditions of our stage, and it is written with profound respect for the human condition.
>
> *The Sign in Sidney Brustein's Window* is concerned with the turbulent life of our times. It is, in turn, powerful, tender, moving and hilarious.
>
> Whether it survives or closes will be determined this week. . . . We the undersigned, who believe in it enough to pay for this ad, urge you to see it *now*.

The signatories of this first ad were James Baldwin, Paddy Chayefsky, Sammy Davis, Ossie Davis, Ruby Dee, William Gibson, E. Y. Harburg, Julie Harris, Lillian Hellman, Sidney Kingsley, Viveca Lindfors, Frank and Eleanor Perry, Arthur Penn and Shelley Winters. They were joined in subsequent similar ads by Alan Alda, Steve Allen, Kaye Ballard, Anne Bancroft, Theodore Bikel, Marlon Brando, Mel Brooks, Frank Corsaro, Tamara Daykarhanova, Keir Dullea, Arthur Godfrey, June Havoc, Lucille Lortel, Bill Manhoff, Claudia McNeil, Kay Medford, Mike Nichols, Patrick O'Neal, Robert Preston, Lloyd Richards, Diana Sands, Herman Shumlin, Kim Stanley, Joseph Stein, Charles Strouse, George Tabori and Teresa Wright.

Meanwhile things began to happen quite independently of our efforts—and, as a matter of fact, from this point on we were never able to catch up. The play was finding its own voice, generating its own appeal, and the response was rather like the bursting of a dam.

The very day that first ad was going to press we received

a call from Blaine Thompson, the advertising agency. Another producer, one of the most distinguished in the business, with a track record running back a generation and
with *The Deputy* currently on the boards, had seen the
play and, without any knowledge of our ad, had written
one of his own which he wanted to pay for and run—if
that was all right with us. (It was.)

> A FINE PLAY! A MOVING PLAY! A POWERFUL PLAY is on the
> stage of the Longacre Theatre . . . it is maybe even a
> great play. It is sharply witty, beautifully acted and bril-
> liantly illuminated by the author's close touch with today,
> with now. In these days when "to care" is the verb that
> must govern us, such a play is an exciting, enjoyable ex-
> perience.
>                           HERMAN SHUMLIN
> P.S. I would have been proud to produce it myself.

Other noteworthy ads in the weeks that followed carried
a note from Steve Allen:

> THIS WONDERFUL, WARM, FUNNY PLAY made me laugh
> and cry and whistle and stomp. It should run for years.
> *It must! See it!* It's the kind of tough, gutsy yet tender
> drama that the theatre needs.

And there was one ad excerpted from a radio broadcast
which merged Arthur Godfrey's great personal enthusiasm
with his account of an audience which "just went wild with
applause and enthusiasm; people were crying Bravos all
over the place. If we can just get [the play] through these
holidays, then I think it will settle down to a long run—and
well it should."

Wednesday, November 4th, was a most unusual matinee, with some fifty ministers and rabbis—invited by Reverend Donald Harrington, of the Community Church, and
Reverend Eugene Callendar, Moderator of the Presbytery
of New York—in attendance. "At the final curtain," as
one paper reported it, "the mystified audience was invited

to remain . . . and share in one of those rare moments in theatre when actors don their street clothes, sit before the proscenium and talk with the people out front." The cast was joined by Sidney Kingsley, Herman Shumlin, Shelley Winters, Viveca Lindfors and James Baldwin. Mr. Shumlin spoke of the "six men" (critics) who require that a play be perfect: "We must change whatever it is in our social fabric which makes the production of thoughtful plays, serious plays, difficult." He pointed to periods in history when, he said, the theatre was emptied of everything but farces, and then theatre died: "What is needed is the realization that there will be no musicals, no farces, if there are no serious plays. There will be no theatre."

The others on stage delivered what were to us, by now, familiar appreciations of the play. And then, one by one, ministers and rabbis arose to discuss its impact upon and meaning for them. Rev. John Garcia Gensel of Advent Lutheran Church had been to see *Brustein* three times—and was planning to come yet again. That afternoon he had brought his sixteen-year-old daughter: "If I am to preach about life—if she is to *learn* about life, about the evil, the corruption, the fallibility with which she will have to contend—then let it be in *this* context!" Rev. Howard Moody, of Greenwich Village's Judson Memorial Church, called the play a "more moving portrayal of deep moral and spiritual problems than all the mawkish sentimentality of our religious dramas—and far too many of our sermons." But it was the son of a Baptist minister, once "called" as a preacher himself, but long since departed from the faith, who touched the spiritual essence of that meeting.

James Baldwin had cut short his work on a movie scenario on the West Coast in response to our appeal. He arrived late, clambered up over the footlights, and standing there, a short, slight figure in chukka boots, described, with the frankness for which he is famous, his own *negative* reaction to the play on first reading an early draft, and his "troubling ambivalence" after seeing it—". . . until, that is, I realized just what about it was making me so uncomfortable." He continued: "It was the particular quality of commitment in this play. Sidney Brustein believes things that I, that most of us, believed a long time ago . . . in the thirties . . . only Sidney still believes them. And now the poor bastard is a set-up to have his head busted in for it—in the third act he would *have* to. . . . I was *shocked* —and believe me"—he smiled and his eyes crinkled in a great grin—"I am *one* individual I really thought was almost *beyond* shocking—at my own discomfiture . . . at the degree we have, all of us, permitted ourselves to retreat from what we once were . . . at the distance one decade, the era of McCarthy, has driven between us and our own ability to commit ourselves as Sidney is committed." This play was an experience, he concluded, "that caused me to examine more deeply into myself and my own motives than any other in a long, long time. If it cannot survive, then we are in trouble . . . because it is about nothing less than our responsibility to ourselves and to each other."

Out of this meeting came a statement drawn and signed by the clergy in attendance:

> *The Sign in Sidney Brustein's Window* presents almost too poignantly the whole range of the dilemmas and confusion of contemporary man. If it does not contain the answer it presents the challenge. Organized religion cannot ignore this cry for help as well as hope, and it will have to respond with more than a reiteration of time-worn platitudes. . . .

The statement thanked the author for her "humane, wise and deeply perceptive challenge" and on subsequent weekends *Sidney Brustein* was the subject of not a few sermons.

It now became possible to introduce certain of Lorraine's revisions which there had not been time to incorporate prior to the opening. These were not so extensive as has since been supposed. They involved about ten minutes at most—a cut of three pages of quite extraneous dialogue at the very beginning, which I had foolishly resisted earlier; some minor cuts; and the transposition into Act I of a speech from the omitted Act II, Scene I, which clarified Iris' character. But they did tighten and speed the action somewhat, and on this basis we invited the critics back for a second viewing, and one of them actually availed himself of the opportunity.

Norman Nadel of the *New York World Telegram and Sun* had written by far the most negative of the original daily reviews. It was headlined " 'THE SIGN' IS MUCH TOO SORDID" and had concluded: "I think an audience is willing to forgive most on-stage sin—and in this play it ranges from plain and fancy lying through plain and fancy illicit sex, including voyeurism. But when the sin becomes oppressive . . . it cancels out caring for the people involved. This play sinks under its own sordid substance."

The new review took a quite different tone and in the light of the original is worth quoting at length:

> Nothing in this world remains the same, with the possible exception of faith, nowhere is this better illustrated than in the living theatre. For evidence, turn to the creation, metamorphosis and rebirth of Lorraine Hansberry's new play. . . .

After filling in the background to the new changes, Mr. Nadel said he was "glad" to report that "the play has discovered its own eloquence":

> The first act . . . is [now] a spirited, and even quite tender exposition of a troubled, though not entirely hopeless marriage. . . . Before, it sweated social consciousness. Now, the shrewdly worded truths come forth with far less conspicuous labor. The new spontaneity and conciseness of that first act are worth their weight in gold . . . which could mean box-office gold as the word gets around.

And the improvement in the first act is most significant;
it tends to clarify and coordinate all that follows. . . .

Gabriel Dell as Brustein, Rita Moreno as his wife, Alice
Ghostley as the suburban sister, and all the cast have en-
riched and enlivened their roles.

I wasn't alone in my reaction last night. The audience
embraced this play, laughed at it, and understood why
everyone on stage felt and behaved as he did. The changes
are working, and the play has found its voice.

Perhaps it was the tightening to which Mr. Nadel referred.
Perhaps it was the greater security the actors had achieved
in an additional two weeks on stage. Perhaps it was a different frame of mind or—as I believe—the greater perspective
a second viewing allowed. But, in any event, in the long an-
nals of the daily review, a reassessment of this kind is almost unique.

One rainy Sunday I received a message from the answering service that "a Mr. John Brynn" had left a number.
"John Brynn" turned out to be *the* John *Braine,* the celebrated British novelist, who was passing through town on
a lecture tour and had happened into the play the night
before. Late that Sunday night we talked into the early
hours at Downey's. The author of *A Room at the Top* had
known nothing of the play, our battle, or indeed its author
(other than that she had written *A Raisin in the Sun*), only
that it was one of the few plays for which you could buy a
Saturday-night ticket. For a "long dreadful moment at the
end of the play," as he said, he had feared that she was
"giving in" and would come up with no more than the
despair that is the fashion in England almost as much as in
our own country. "But no—she had gone out facing the
guns" as he had hoped she would. His reactions were published as a personal communication in the *Village Voice.*

The events which in rapid succession followed my meeting with Braine were initiated at a midnight session at the

home of Anne Bancroft and Mel Brooks, which was strikingly—and sympathetically—reported by the not infrequently acerbic Lillian Ross in *The New Yorker*. Titled "Strategy Meeting," her piece began:

> Five beautiful movie and stage actresses, one librettist of a current hit musical, one composer of another current hit musical, one writer of a new hit comedy, one busy and flourishing writer-comedian, and two young producers of an economically foundering play got together on a recent Saturday for a midnight meeting to work out some strategy for keeping the young producers' play running. . . . They were all serious, determined, and ready to fight, and were all concentrating on the play, *The Sign in Sidney Brustein's Window*, by Lorraine Hansberry.

Miss Ross quickly revealed that, in addition to Miss Bancroft, the actresses at the meeting were Viveca Lindfors, and Diana Sands (then appearing in *The Owl and the Pussycat*), who had first been seen on Broadway as Beneatha in *Raisin*, and our costars, Rita Moreno and Alice Ghostley.* The librettist was Joseph Stein (*Fiddler on the Roof*), the composer Charles Strouse (*Golden Boy*), the writer Bill Manhoff (*The Owl and the Pussycat*), and the writer-comedian Mel Brooks, our host. The meeting was typical of many in numerous living rooms in the last months of 1964, and out of it came, among other things, a noteworthy letter by Miss Bancroft and Mr. Brooks—an invitation to a special Sunday matinee performance for the theatrical community. It was addressed "To Our Friends in the Theatre," and was posted on the backstage bulletin boards of all theatres. It opened:

---

* These two, together with Gabriel Dell and our entire cast, were in fact the unsung heroes of the whole drama, performing not only on stage but off—yet seldom even knowing for certain whether or not they would be in or out of a job the next week. (Miss Ghostley's brilliant performance as Mavis was ultimately to win her the Tony Award for "Best Supporting Actress," 1964-1965.)

The show must go on . . . *my show,* baby, not yours!

This is the selfish truth as we in show business too often have come to know it. But once in a blue moon, a phenomenon occurs. Actors, directors, producers, playwrights, gently lay aside their megalomania and join hands in a common cause. . . .

Last week we saw that play. We had joined the cause originally out of respect for Lorraine Hansberry, but on the way to the theatre we secretly figured it was a bomb. It must be a bomb; Kerr didn't rave, Chapman didn't like it, and Hadassah hadn't bought a single theatre party. Actually we went more out of obligation than anticipation.

We were shocked.

It was a *wonderful* play.·

We laughed, we cried, we *thought.* In our opinion . . . *Brustein* . . . is a more mature and compelling work than Miss Hansberry's award-winning *A Raisin in the Sun.*

If there is in you one single filament of curiosity that glows to know what is happening in our theatre today, see it! Now!

The "selfish truth" of which the writers spoke was certainly not in evidence, or in any event predominant, in some circles along Broadway as the year 1964 drew toward a close. In the closing moments of *Sidney Brustein* there is a line to the effect that "people want to be better than they are," and in a small corner of our lives one might have thought the line was coming to life. There is traditionally, of course, a goodly amount of "sentiment" in show business—a performer falls ill for a performance and a dozen stars come forward to leap into his shoes—but this is good for one night, perhaps, and a headline next morning; a movement sustained as this one became can only be understood as the expression of something deeper. Again and again on radio or TV, a star would spend more time talking about the Sign in our window than his own show (half the time we would not even know he was scheduled—the report would filter back later). A Kay Medford would suddenly show up with $100 for an ad, or Teresa Wright would appear and spend days on the phone calling friends "just to see it." June Havoc devoted her entire television show to it one night, and "the Randi Show" turned over five hours on WOR-Radio, from midnight til dawn, to it. The actors in our own company petitioned the union to permit pay cuts and even the traditionally inexorable Shubert Office took a fraction less in rental each week than our contract provided. The cast of *The Subject Was Roses*, with the cooperation of the author, Frank Gilroy, and the producers, started curtain speeches to tell the audience about "the 'other' drama worth seeing in town." And soon Sammy Davis, too, was stopping the applause at the Majestic each night to urge a trip to the Longacre. Other shows—*Any Wednesday, How To Succeed in Business*—stuffed flyers in their programs.

The momentum was not limited to theatre folk. Most significantly, it embraced the audience itself. People would troop backstage every night to ask what could they do, how could they help. Volunteer workers flooded the office, captained by Judy Hankin, Marguerite Kisseloff and Jean Lindgren. Student contingents arrived from outlying colleges and others distributed flyers nightly in Shubert Alley. Larry Butler, a part-time usher and candy-hawker, delivered messages. Mary Ann Mantell, who owns Cædmon Records, taped interviews for radio. Herb Saltzman, marketing director for RKO-General, placed them, and, with Bea Wilson, a public relations expert, and Merle Debuskey, the show's ever-willing but overworked press agent—who had never seen anything like this—concentrated on the mass media generally. Novelist John O. Killens, his wife Grace and members of the Harlem Writers Guild sent out mailings in the thousands.

Charles Belous, Deputy County Attorney of Nassau County, who many years before had been a leader of the La Guardia-Fusion movement, saw in the play a "great new affirmation" of independent reform city politics and circularized former leaders of the party—Newbold Morris, Charles McGoldrick—for support. Three hundred women met with Viveca Lindfors in Wantagh, Long Island, to consider "the crisis on Broadway" and to garner support. A nursery school director in Great Neck personally called and channelled some four hundred souls to the box office. People called friends. Friends called other friends. And at least one party—Bell Telephone—showed a profit on the show.

A minister at one after-curtain discussion summed it up: this was *"living* theatre, as significant as anything occurring on stage . . . for audiences were reaching out of—beyond —their own lives to become *involved* again, committed, engaged to something larger . . . which can only make us all the larger for it." Irish audiences at the Abbey Theatre in another era might show their passion by rioting; here involvement took another, far less dramatic form, but in its own small way it was no less real.

For all this momentum, however, we still were not out of the woods. The Sign hung, but precariously. Each week attendance continued to grow—not overwhelmingly, but appreciably—and on one matinee day I remember rushing over to the theatre to see a line actually formed halfway down the block. Thanksgiving climaxed our best week yet: we actually broke even. But ahead lay the economic "deep freeze" that comes before Christmas, traditionally the theatre's worst time of the year. These are the doldrum days given over to Christmas shopping and close budgeting in anticipation of the big splurge to come; the nights when all along Broadway you get the feeling that nine million New Yorkers blithely got up that morning and decided, in concert, "Tonight I am *not* going to a show!" Attendance at all shows plummets, and only the big ones—those sold out well in advance by mail and theatre party, or cushioned with a substantial reserve—can survive.

It was with these things in mind, weighing the facts and deciding, for once, to be "realistic," that we agreed we would finally have to close. Unless somehow an additional five to ten thousand dollars could be scared up in loans to meet our anticipated deficit—by now we had run out of names to call and a frantic week on the phones had not turned up any new ones—Sunday matinee, November 29th, would bring down the curtain.

Only—because we had gone so far already that there was nothing to lose—we would "go down fighting." That last performance would be followed by a public "open hearing" —right in the theatre. A telegram, drafted at 4 A.M. at the Brooks' home and signed by 28 of those who had sponsored our ads, was dispatched to Governor Rockefeller, Mayor Wagner, Senators Javits and Kennedy, and Roger L. Stevens, head of the President's Commission on the Arts:

> Undersigned urgently request your attendance next Sunday, Longacre Theatre, open hearing re: *Sidney Brustein* and crisis in our theatre.
>
> After endless talk, theatre community now beginning to act. We can no longer permit our finest plays to die. Have joined hands to save a play. We are making it our focus because what threatens it threatens the heart of American Theatre. If plays of such quality, humor, wisdom cannot survive in nation's cultural center, then all of us must seriously question our future in theatre.
>
> Today only 27 shows running on Broadway. Only five dramas—and of these, three have posted closing notices. If theatre continues to shrink, what happens to New York business, hotels, restaurants, trade? What else draws millions here?
>
> It is time cultural and governmental leaders joined forces on behalf American theatre as they have other vital issues. . . . Your presence and participation will un-

derline for all the crucial importance of maintaining first-rate theatre.

The "crisis" to which this telegram referred was in no sense an exaggeration. The three dramas that closed that weekend were *The Physicists* by Friedrich Duerrenmatt, one of the giants of the modern stage, after successive triumphs throughout Europe and in England (three weeks on Broadway); *Poor Bitos* by Jean Anouilh, a great success in London (three weeks on Broadway); and Rolf Hochhuth's *The Deputy,* the only one of the three to enjoy a substantial (though not entirely financially successful) run. *Sidney Brustein* was to be number four—leaving only *The Subject Was Roses* which, with "rave" reviews, a tenacious effort, a cast of three and an exceedingly low break-even point, had managed to last. (The following week *Slow Dance on the Killing Ground,* by William Hanley, opened to raves; it survived for 88 performances.)

That Sunday morning I awoke, for the first time that I can recall in all the weeks before or after, with the *physical* feeling of defeat in the pit of my stomach. This was really it: we had run out of miracles. We had tried but failed—and to *know* you have tried may distract the mind, but it does not lessen the fact of failure. A telegram that morning from Senator and Mrs. Javits "regretfully" expressed great respect for the play (which they had seen) and admiration for our effort—but they would be unable to attend. Another from Governor Rockefeller wished us success: "I share your concern for the future of the theatre and applaud the initiative the theatre community itself is now taking"—but also declined. A third from Senator Kennedy, which he subsequently permitted us to use as an ad—"I urge all friends of the theatre to come to the aid of this play. I earnestly hope that contributions from them will preserve this play for the public and for us all"—brought the same news of commitment elsewhere. The press, which was by now somewhat bored with the whole affair, generally indicated their disinclination to turn out on a Sunday. Only the artists, the audience and Robert Dowling, the Mayor's cultural emissary, would be present.

Nonetheless, at 5:30, when the curtain came down, Ossie Davis—playwright, actor and always one of the theatre's most public-spirited citizens—stepped forward in the midst of an, as usual, sustained ovation, to open the hearing. He spoke briefly, then introduced me, indicating that the crisis in the theatre was "too general an abstraction: let us first devote a moment to the crisis at hand." What followed is perhaps best described in the report carried the next morning by *Newsday,* one of the few papers present:

> New York—In a highly improbably but dramatically superb performance yesterday, the audience at the Longacre Theatre took to the stage to save the play.
> . . . When the final curtain fell yesterday, co-producer Robert Nemiroff . . . [announced] sorrowfully, "You have been present at the final performance of *The Sign in Sidney Brustein's Window* . . . unless something happens this afternoon."
>
> The theatre buzzed with excitement . . .
>
> "If there is an individual that has the means to help," Nemiroff said, "we'll take a minute or two. . ." And he waited. No big voice spoke up but someone suggested a collection. Nemiroff hesitated. Another audience voice spoke: ". . . We want to save this thing. We want to give money. Take it . . ." But Davis said no, if not enough was collected, how would it be returned?

Yet the more we onstage said no, that it could not be done, that this was "commercial theatre," where you cannot take up collections, it just isn't *done*—and that it could not help anyway because too much was needed—the more the audience, one person after another standing up in his seat, argued back until, finally in effect, they had shouted us down and it was agreed that we would accept loans. By now there was bedlam in the house—but this was a "mob scene" unlike any other, as the audience rose from their seats, found their own leaders and literally took charge—formed lines, marched down the aisles *and up onto the stage itself* . . . while Ossie Davis read out the names and amounts and I sat down—some say, collapsed—on the Brustein staircase, looking on for the next hour in bemused, if gratified, wonder. *Newsday* concluded:

> . . . A collection desk was set up on stage, in the middle of the set of Sidney Brustein's living room. As the audience filed forward, actress Madeline Sherwood . . . shouted from the stage: "This is the most exciting thing I've seen in New York."
>
> After an accountant was found in the audience, tabulation began. It totalled exactly $5,000, with $2,500 being given by one anonymous individual. Nemiroff, standing with his cast, actress Anne Bancroft, and Davis, seemed overcome as he announced the play would continue.

That "anonymous individual" was the Mayor's representative, Mr. Dowling, acting as a private citizen on behalf of his own firm. After this, what?

We tried to express the gratitude and the jubilation we felt in our next ad, and it was even possible now to look at the lighter side:

> WE HAVE TRIED REPEATEDLY TO CLOSE THE SHOW, AND THEY JUST WON'T LET US!
>
> We have tried again and again and again—but every time a Shelley Winters, a Herman Shumlin, an Anne Bancroft, three Pulitzer Prize playwrights, or fifty ministers and rabbis in concert say, "You must be out of your mind —it's a *great* show! You *can't* close it!"
>
> Last Sunday we tried again. We announced this had been the last performance. The audience shouted us down . . . [and] raised their own $5,000 to continue the show another week.
>
> There must be something there. Not just that *The Sign in Sidney Brustein's Window* is "important," "the most talked about play of the year," or one of the only two

dramas to survive this season. But that people seem to love this play. . . .

Next Sunday we will try again to close the show. So if you want to be *sure* to see it, you will have to catch it this week. On the other hand, you'll be taking a chance: in this business there are no guarantees—and, who knows, we may *never* succeed in closing it.

As a matter of fact, we now discovered to our amazement that we had entered the charmed circle: the *New York Daily News'* "golden dozen"—*Sidney Brustein* was one of the longest running shows of the year on Broadway! (Look down, ye gods, and weep.)

In this fashion we survived the pre-Christmas lull . . . and staggered forward to the next crisis, which was already prefigured, as described in a column by Dorothy Kilgallen:

> The entire company of *The Sign in Sidney Brustein's Window*, still bravely trying to keep the play running, is campaigning to raise another $5,000. An anonymous friend has agreed to donate that amount if only they can match it, and that would mean they could move to another theatre. Box office receipts have been going up, in spite of the usual pre-Christmas slump, but they have to vacate the Longacre Theatre next week, no matter how good business gets—and they have no money to move. . . .

Since late October another show had been booked into the Longacre, its tenure to begin just before the twelve days of Christmas—the best time of the year. The simple act of dismembering and moving a set from one Broadway theatre to another would cost us $7,000, plus a new marquee, new posters, new signs, publicity—but there is no point in further painful detail here. Necessity simply produced a new set of heroes: Mr. and Mrs. Stan Frank, Richard Rodgers, Abe Weisburd, Gardner Cowles, Imre Rosenthal, Alan Jay Lerner. On Tuesday, December 22nd, our Sign hung in a new window.

The curtain rose at Henry Miller's Theatre to a jam-packed house—and came down to a thunderous standing ovation. And two days later, on Christmas Eve, we were able—at last, and publicly—to express some measure of what we had felt and experienced. In appropriately seasonal type our ad was headlined: "AND A MERRY CHRISTMAS TO ALL OUR FRIENDS who have made it a happy Christmas for us." There followed simply a list of names. Many have figured already in the telling of this story. Others I have neglected to mention thus far: Charles Taubman, Art D'Lugoff, Jane Lander, Renée Kaplan, Joel Dein, Albert Maher, Marcia Schlather, Peter Mumford, Lillian Gruber, Abbot Simon, Bev Landau, Mrs. Burton Lane, Stephen Silverman, Cora Weiss, Mr. and Mrs. William vanden Heuvels, Theodora Peck, Ruth Nichols, Fran Bennett, Clarence and Ann Jones, Fran Damon, Maurice Gruber, and still others, whose omission must be forgiven me, in immeasurable ways made our continuance possible.

It was not that the appearance of each new friend could be said to have "saved the show" (although in more than one instance that was precisely the case). It was that without them all—together—*The Sign in Sidney Brustein's Window* could never have persisted. For each, at some crucial moment when spirits were lowest, had come forward to provide whatever spark, or inspiration, or money was needed until another could step into the breach and carry on from there.

*Not* closing, however, did not mean successfully *running*. *Sidney Brustein,* in its first run, was not a financial success —ever. The balcony and mezzanine might be sold out, as frequently they were now, but on Broadway it is the 500-odd *orchestra* seats ($6.90 weekdays, $7.50 weekends) that count—and it was precisely here that we were the weakest. There was good reason for this. The brokers, business firms, theatre party agents, who together account for the bulk of these seats, cannot, as noted earlier, afford to take chances on anything less than a hit. But to be a "hit" in New York you have got to *act* like a hit. And to act like a hit you must hold the price line, make no concessions, advertise freely that you are a hit (our budget did not even permit us to appear in the alphabetical listings of some papers, and consequently readers assumed we were closed) and have what it takes to back up the claim. You have to place your tickets on sale far in advance—which means *not* having to depend on a maximum sale in the current week— and *know* that you will *be* there when the date comes round. To sell a theatre party, for example, you must guarantee the agent's commission on the promised date (it is still painful to recall how many parties we had, literally, to *turn down* for just this reason!). And above all, you have to be *sold out* when somebody calls or comes to the window—or else why should they bother to buy in advance? The show that depends on its nightly sale is not only *not* a hit—it cannot become one.

Also, there was that about our entire effort which, measured strictly in terms of box-office return, was psychologically self-defeating. In *The New Yorker* we might be "the talk of the town"—and indeed, from what I am told, there were not a few homes that winter in which eyes turned first to the morning headlines over coffee, and then directly to the theatrical page for our latest ad, or adventure. But to be *too* much talked about is not an unmixed blessing. In the theatre as in any other business there is no greater virtue than in a certain amount of safe *non*-distinction. It is the better part of valor to be part of the crowd and there is nothing so reassuring to the buyer as a good *conservative* old-fashioned hit; if he doesn't have the greatest evening in the world, at least it won't be the worst.

To appeal for help from the stage is thus automatically to reduce your *natural* appeal; it may carry you through the week but it could cost you the month. It may generate *intensity* of support but, by the same token, vitiate numbers. It is to sacrifice long-run possibility for short-run necessity. For we do not go to plays as a duty or to help others, but to *enjoy ourselves*. And the bolder the campaign, the more precedents overturned, the more some proclaim the values of a play—the more suspect it must seem to others; not *entertainment* but a "cause," edifying perhaps and "good for the soul"—but who wants to spend a night out on his soul?

Nor is there anything mystifying or especially guarded or secret about this knowledge: all that it takes to act upon it is money. If at any one moment we had had the money—*enough* money to proclaim *Sidney Brustein* a hit and *act* like a hit, to be less newsworthy and more safely, securely, conservative there is little doubt in my mind, to judge from the nightly response of those who did see the show and kept it running week after week, that in short order *Sidney Brustein* would have become just that.

Whether financial success is the only, or the main, criterion of success is another matter, of course, although more and more in our theatre we have come to act and *think* as if it were. In the introduction to his collected essays, *Lies Like Truth,* Harold Clurman draws a careful distinction: "What must be sharply emphasized . . . is that excellence and box-office success or profit are separate things, and must never be equated or interrelated in our thoughts." Noting, however, that Elia Kazan, his onetime co-worker, was quoted in *The New York Times,* as saying, "I equate good plays with successful plays," Clurman offers a further comment, to which we had more than one occasion to refer in this period:

> If this is taken literally, we are preparing for the burial of our theatre as an institution devoted to significant expression. Contrary to popular legend, the plays of Ibsen, Shaw, Chekhov were not immediately successful in their

own countries in their own day . . . in fact, I doubt whether, except for certain off-Broadway productions, Chekhov has even actually made money in America. Is he therefore a bad playwright?

Box-office success, which nobody in the theatre of any country at any time has ever been averse to, is contingent on a number of factors of which only a few are related to the intrinsic merit of the plays presented. Most of us admired Arthur Miller's *Death of a Salesman* (directed by Kazan), but its profits were not nearly so great as those of *Tea and Sympathy* (Kazan's, too) or *The Bad Seed*. Are success and excellence then commensurate? . . . is *The Threepenny Opera*, a dismal flop in New York in the early thirties, less valuable a musical than *Happy Hunting*?

On Broadway today the simple fact is that the play that does not *make* money is a "failure." Not just a *financial* failure but an unmodified failure—one that requires no further qualification. *Sidney Brustein* played to 80,000 people—more than if it had run two years off-Broadway; more than saw *"Mourning Becomes Electra"* or *"The Iceman Cometh"* on Broadway, or *Juno and the Paycock* in Dublin or New York; more perhaps than saw *Hamlet* in Shakespeare's London. But in the parlance of Broadway, not just of accountants—in the minds of serious theatre people and even many artists themselves and in the press—80,000 people do not an audience make. As one reporter lamented, with no irony intended, there was "no public" for the play.

As it was, between 7:45 and 8:30 each night we might do one of the busiest window sales in town—and indeed between those hours on a Saturday night we more than once racked up $3,000—but this very fact was our undoing; it left us totally to the caprice of the elements and the mood of the hour. No one was committed *in advance*. A simple shower or snowstorm could throw us deeper in debt. An extended weekend blizzard could wipe us out—as indeed one finally did.

For Christmas, 1964, I bought Lorraine a necklace of delicate gold and amber; of the kind that in years past would have set off the dark coals of her eyes and—magnificently—the brown richness of her skin. Yet seeing it, she was suddenly distressed: "Do you *really* think so? Oh God, if it could only be true—that I could *wear* it!" But she was too wise to play the game of deception and she often talked now of "something horrible" that she felt was going to happen.

Lorraine Hansberry was never so enamored of life that she would clutch it at any price. But neither for one moment was she one to let it go gently, or gracefully, or with anything less than protest unremitting. What was happening to her I can only describe as indecent, unjust, infuriatingly beyond reason, knowing even as I write that the very words have no relevance—one cannot expect justice or reason of a universe where these are only glorious concepts the living *impose— as Lorraine always insisted.* She would have none of the platitudes that might soften her own strong sense of truth or provide easy cover for others. I spent New Year's Eve by her bed and at midnight toasted a "Happy New Year." She made a face harsh with annoyance, and dismissed this utterly, wanting to know what was "happy" about it? She was *not* reconciled.

On the morning of January 12th, she was, I am told, smiling and talkative and then, at about 8:30, she grew suddenly weaker and lapsed into unconsciousness. Just before 9:00 I received the phone call that Lorraine Hansberry was no more.

After that it might perhaps have been possible—with a new sustained effort—to raise the curtain on her play again, but for the moment the heart had gone out of us. *"That is*

*the first thing . . . to let ourselves feel again. . . . Then
tomorrow, we shall make something strong of this
sorrow. . . ."*

Five years before, at the turn of the decade, a young and
healthy Lorraine Hansberry, who had just been awarded the
greatest honor our theatre can bestow, had been asked by
*Mademoiselle* magazine what she wished for the New Year
and the coming decade. She had wished for peace in the
world; for plenty for all the people of these United States;
for an end to racism, and "a new spirit . . . in the ranks of
Negro Leadership. . . ." Her article had concluded with a
wish for the arts:

> In the next ten years I hope that serious American art
> will rediscover the world around it, that our finest painters
> and writers will dismiss the vogue of unmodified despair in
> order to pick up the heritage of a nobler art. In spite of
> some awe-inspiring talents involved in recent writing, the
> appointment of sinister universality to Ego in settings of
> timeless torture has been a virtual abdication of the mean-
> ing of history, which has been resplendent with what may
> most certainly be called progress. I hope American cre-
> ative artists will look again and see that Ego, like every-
> thing else, exists in time and context, and that the results
> of the lives of Abraham Lincoln and Adolf Hitler are
> hardly comparable, regardless of the common properties
> of that abstraction, the Ego. Nor is this a call, Heaven
> forbid, to happy endings or clichés of affirmation. For the
> supreme test of technical skill and creative imagination is
> the depth of art it requires to render the infinite varieties
> of the human spirit—which invariably hangs *between*
> despair and joy.

*Sidney Brustein* was that kind of play. The degree to
which it succeeded I leave to the reader; but its author was
never one to lay down prescriptions she did not herself
strive to fulfill. The lines I treasure most from it are the ones
which precede this story. They will be inscribed on the

author's tombstone in Croton-on-Hudson. They are the essence of her work, her life, and for three months they intruded themselves upon, became part of the lives of a great many others who came to "care," if not "about it all," then at least about something more than they had perhaps permitted themselves to care about for some time.

It wasn't much: for one hundred and one performances we had joined to keep a Sign in a window. But before it came down, *The Sign in Sidney Brustein's Window* had been recognized by thousands for the play it is. As I write that Sign is going up in other windows across the country. And in the years to come it will hang in windows all over the world. But for me, as I suspect for not a few others, it will always hang there at the Longacre Theatre, where, with her own penetrating eyes, Lorraine Hansberry first saw it raised. For there, in spite of ourselves and all our vaunted sophistication, for one brief moment she had helped us each to become—what she always was—"an insurgent again."

April, 1965

# POSTSCRIPT

When the Random House edition of *Sidney Brustein* was published, I sent copies to the many friends who had stood by during the struggle of that difficult winter.

At the suggestion of our good friend, George Tabori, some copies had gone to people abroad who might share our feelings about the play. One of these was the noted French actress Simone Signoret. This was in June 1965.

On a September afternoon I was called out of rehearsals for another play. "Paris on the line!" The familiar tones of a voice recalled from a dozen movies—low, vibrant, with only enough of an accent to augment the eloquence of the message:

"I have just finished reading it, *The Sign in Sidney Brustein's Window*, for the fourth time. First, *before* reading what you wrote about the play . . . and then, again and again and again. And I am afraid I have taken a liberty. I have already translated half the first act. It is available? I had to know, I had to reach you at once . . . May I finish the translation and undertake to arrange a Paris production?"

In the letter that followed, Mme. Signoret indicated her feeling that . . . "it's a play which deals with so many problems which, though they *seem* to be only typically American ones, are not—anyway not any more . . ."

Knowing of her beautiful rendering into French of a number of important plays, I did not hesitate. And it was with much delight and gratification that I read in a subsequent letter that

> I finished completely the adaptation, and I am very happy with it. In fact I was enjoying so much their company, that the last day, I was typing very slowly, in order to live with them all a little longer, and I even had actually, tears in my eyes, while typing the last lines, for both the reasons that they are heart-breaking, and that *that* was it.
> . . . I have been reading, incidentally, quite a lot of American and English "hits" [She enumerates a few of the biggest] . . . Every time I finish one of these "hits," I go back to Iris, Sidney, Alton, Mavis, and the others, and I am so proud to realize they have so much to tell, so much of us, of today, of the world, whether *they* are going to like it or not—"hit" or "no hit."

Mme. Signoret's version, incidentally, will follow the author's original conception of Act Three, Scene One, and incorporate several dozen lines from that scene not used on Broadway or included in the Random House edition.

R. N.                                                                 May, 1966

THE SIGN IN SIDNEY BRUSTEIN'S WINDOW *was first presented by Burt C. D'Lugoff, Robert Nemiroff and J. I. Jahre at the Longacre Theatre, New York City, N.Y., on October 15, 1964, with the following cast:*

| | |
|---|---|
| SIDNEY BRUSTEIN | Gabriel Dell |
| ALTON SCALES | Ben Aliza |
| IRIS PARODUS BRUSTEIN | Rita Moreno |
| WALLY O'HARA | Frank Schofield |
| MAX | Dolph Sweet |
| MAVIS PARODUS BRYSON | Alice Ghostley |
| DAVID RAGIN | John Alderman |
| GLORIA PARODUS | Cynthia O'Neal |
| DETECTIVE | Josip Elic |

*Directed by* Peter Kass
*Scenery by* Jack Blackman
*Lighting by* Jules Fisher
*Costumes by* Fred Voelpel

"The Wally O'Hara Campaign Song" *by* Ernie Sheldon
*Production Associate:* Alan Heyman
*Associate to the Producers:* Beverly Landau

The action of the play takes place in the BRUSTEIN apartment and adjoining courtyard, in Greenwich Village, New
York City.

### Act I

Scene One:  Time: This very present. Early evening, the
            late spring.
Scene Two:  Dusk. The following week.

### Act II

Scene One:   Just before daybreak. The following day.
Scene Two:   Evening. Late summer.
Scene Three: Election Night. Early fall.

### Act III

Scene One:  Several hours later.
Scene Two:  Early the next morning.

# ACT I

## SCENE ONE

*The setting is Greenwich Village, New York City—the preferred habitat of many who fancy revolt, or at least, detachment from the social order that surrounds us.*

*At the rear are all the recognizable sight symbols of the great city. They are, however, in the murk of distance and dominated by a proscenium foreground which is made up of jutting façades. These are the representative bits and pieces of architecture which seem almost inevitably to set the character of those communities where the arts and bohemia try to reside in isolation—before the fact of their presence tends to attract those others who wish to be in bohemia if not of it—and whose presence, in turn, paradoxically tends to drive the rents beyond the reach of the former. Tenements of commonplace and unglamorized misery huddle together with cherished relics of the beginning days of a civilization; the priceless and the unworthy leaning indiscriminately together in both arty pretentiousness and genuine picturesque assertiveness.*

*Thus, here is a renovation of a "Dutch farmhouse"; there, a stable reputed to have, housed some early governor's horses; and here the baroque chambers of some famed and eccentric actor. And leading off, one or two narrow and twisty little streets with squared-off panes of glass that do, in midwinter, with their frosted corners, actually succeed in reminding of Dickensian London. The studio apartment of the* BRUSTEINS, *at left, is the ground floor of a converted brownstone, which—like a few other brownstones in the Village—has an old-fashioned, wrought-iron outside staircase arching over a tiny patio where city-type vegetation miraculously and doggedly grows. Beneath the staircase landing is the* BRUSTEINS' *private entrance. Nearby, downstage right, is a tree.*

*In the cut-away interior of the apartment the walls are painted, after the current fashion in this district, the starkest white. To arrest the eye—because those who live here think much of such things—the colors which have been set against it are soft yellows and warm browns and, strikingly, touches of orange, vivid sharp orange, and that lovely blue associated with Navajo culture. We can see at once that the people who live here would not, even if they did have a great deal of money—which they certainly do not—spend it on expensive furnishings. They prefer by pocket book and taste—to the point of snobbery, perhaps—to scrounge about the Salvation Army bargain outlets; almost never the "Early American" shops which are largely if not entirely priced for the tourist trade. In any case, a few years ago most things would have been discernably "do-it-yourself" modern in these rooms; but that mood is past now and there is not a single sling chair or low, sharply angled table. "Country things" have come with all their knocked-about air and utilitarian comfort. But there remain, still, crafted ceramic pots of massive rhododendrons in various corners and, everywhere, stacks of last year's magazines and a goodly number of newspapers. The result is that—while it is not a dirty place—clutter amounts almost to a motif. Prints range through reproductions of both the most obscure and the most celebrated art of human history, and* *these, without exception, are superbly and fittingly framed. And there is a sole expensive item: a well-arranged hi-fidelity unit, and, therefore, whole walls of long-playing records, and not one of them at an angle. Fighting them for supremacy of the walls, however, are hundreds and hundreds of books. And on one wall—*SIDNEY's *banjo.*

*In fine, it is to the eye and spirit an attractive place. Its carelessness does not make it less so. And, indeed, one might lounge here more easily than in some other contemporary rooms—and, perhaps, think more easily. Upstage center is the bedroom door. To its right, the bathroom. Downstage left is part of the kitchen area, which disappears offstage. And, dominating all, upstage left, the large irregularly shaped bay window, angled out from the building wall in a skylight effect, in which will presently hang—the* Sign *in* SIDNEY BRUSTEIN's *window.*

*Time: This very present. Early evening, the late spring.*

*At rise:* SIDNEY BRUSTEIN *and* ALTON SCALES *enter, each burdened down with armloads, two or three each, of those wire racks of glasses such as are found in restaurants. They are heavy and the two men have carried them several blocks. They are very much out of breath and speak haltingly as they struggle with the loads.* SIDNEY BRUSTEIN *is in his late thirties and inclined to no category of dress whatsoever—that is to say, unlike his associates, who tend to the toggle-coated, woven, mustardy, corduroy appearance of the post-war generation of intellectuals in Europe and America. This has escaped* SIDNEY: *he wears white dress shirts as often as not, usually for some reason or other open at the cuffs—but not rolled; old college shoes; and whichever pair of trousers he has happened to put on with whichever jacket he has happened to reach for that morning; and they will be more likely mismated suit parts than sports outfits. It is not an affectation; he does not care. He is of medium build, vague carriage, tending to shuffle a bit, except when in a fit*

*of excitement. And his eyes are wider and more childish
than the sort generally associated with the romance of the
intellectual. His sole attractive feature perhaps is a mat of
tight willful dark curls atop his head. He does not wear
glasses.* ALTON SCALES *is a youth of about twenty-seven or
so; lithe, dark, with close-cropped hair. Unlike his friend,
he is dressed in the mustard, corduroy and sweatered manner of his milieu.*

SIDNEY    Never mind the kid's mother, for Christ's sake.
And never mind the "great swelling crests of water" in
his girl's eyes. Don't bleed it. Write it like you figure we
already *care* without you sending up organ music. Follow?
(*He puts down his load and fumbles for his key;*
ALTON *leans against the staircase railing*)

ALTON (*Stiffly*)    I hear what you are saying.

SIDNEY    But *compassion* is consuming your heart and you
want us to *know it*, don't you? The old uptown sob sister
credo: "*In the beginning was the tear.*"
(*He picks up the glasses and they go into the apartment. As the lights come up on the interior,* SIDNEY
*deposits his load on the living-room floor*)

ALTON    He may die. Mrs. Peretti said Sal could still die.
(*He racks his glasses up on top of* SIDNEY'S *and
reels away with fatigue to the couch, where he
drops down, spent*)

SIDNEY (*Snatches out the page of newspaper copy to which
he has been referring*)    And this is going to save him?
He needs *this?* Look, baby, from now on, when we write,
let's forget we *absolutely love* mankind. Don't venerate,
don't celebrate, don't hallow what you take to be—(*Facing out to the audience with a bit of a smile*)—the human
spirit. Keep your conscience to yourself. Readers don't
want it—they feel pretty damn sure that they can't afford

it. That's why Harvey had to unload the paper. And that's why I am now the proud owner, editor, publisher, guiding light. (*With a flourish, returning the copy to* ALTON) Presume no commitment, disavow all engagement, mock all great expectations. (*His eyes are now only for the audience; scanning our reaction with a wet-lipped savoring*) And above all else, avoid the impulse to correct: all movements, causes, clubs and anti-clubs. It's the only form of compassion left. (*He lights a cigarette and wanders back to the glasses, where he suddenly confronts them with a mock funereal gravity, to the point of making the sign of the cross*) So—there they are: the last remains of the Silver Dagger.

ALTON   You're better off. What the hell did you know about running a night club, man?

SIDNEY   It wasn't *supposed* to be a night club.

ALTON   That's right. It wasn't a night club and it wasn't a coffee house or anything else that anybody ever heard of.

SIDNEY   I thought it was something people wanted. A place to listen to good folk music. Without hoked-up come-ons. (*Puzzled, rubbing his face*) I thought there'd be an audience for it. For people like myself. There gotta be people like me somewhere, don't there?

ALTON   There are. And they don't go to night spots—of whatever kind—just like you don't.

SIDNEY   (*Moving toward the glasses again*) You know what those glasses really are, Alt? They're a testament to the release of Manny. He's free, now, my brother Manny. Free of Sidney. Finally. Let's drink to it. Drink to Manny's absolution.

> (*He crosses downstage left to the counter. It is a combination bar and kitchen surface, on either side of which stand two unfinished wooden stools*)

ALTON   Bourbon for me.

SIDNEY   You can have vodka *with* ice or vodka without
ice. (*Pouring*) Good old absolved Manny. (*Crossing
with a glass for* ALTON *and then turning and saluting the
racks of glasses once again*) The day he put up the
money for the Silver Dagger he sat there with "End of
Obligation" written all over him. An expression on his
face which read: "This thing will be a failure. But having done this I will have done all I can for Sidney. After
that I can call it quits in good conscience. You can do
so much and then—well, that's it." So here's to you,
Manny, you Prince of Philistines. Sidney the Kook has
set you free! To hell with that. (*He puts down his glass,
abruptly hauls out a huge pad of tracing paper and a big
marking crayon, and sits down at his drafting table,
which is framed by the window; it is angled almost hori-
zontally to serve as his desk*) Let's talk about the paper.
   (*With broad strokes he marks off apportionments of
space on the sheets*)

ALTON   (*Idle curiosity—that is not so idle*)   Ahh—Sidney . . . Does Iris know you've *bought*—and I use the
term loosely—the paper yet?

SIDNEY   No.

ALTON   Well, don't you think she oughta know?

SIDNEY   Yes, I'll tell her.

ALTON   When? It's been two weeks already.

SIDNEY   (*Trapped, therefore evasively*)   When I get a
chance, I'll tell her.

ALTON   She's going to have a lot of opinions about it.

SIDNEY   She always has opinions. If I paid them any attention I'd never accomplish anything. (*He looks back to*

*his sheets*) You know what? I think I'd like to try the next issue in reverse. You know, white on black. What's with this black on white jazz all the time? People get in ruts.

> (IRIS, *his wife, enters with an armful of groceries. She has not yet reached thirty, is of ordinary prettiness of the sort one does not notice at a distance; but she is quick with a gamin vivacity that charms utterly the moment she speaks or one looks in her very large eyes. And true to a great number of the girls of the locale, she possesses vast quantities of long, long hair, presently done up in a French twist. It is dark brown. Life has already made* IRIS *too nervous and slightly inclined to hunch. But whatever her accomplishments on stage, she is an actress, given to playful mimicry, and, at least with* SIDNEY, *she feels free to play this to the hilt. Between them, though this is not at all their actual relationship in years, there is more than a little of the adolescent girl showing off for father, seeking his approval, testing the limits of his knowledge and authority; and, especially of late, more than a little chafing at the bonds. He has been her lover, father, universe, god. But the man has feet of clay and, coupled with increasing dissatisfaction with her own state, there is the insistent, though as yet unidentified, need to break free. The tension between them bubbles freely to the surface; yet, save in their sharpest exchanges, there is still the element of banter and fun. At the click of the lock,* SIDNEY *thrusts his pad aside. She crosses to the bar, nodding to* ALTON; *stops momentarily at the glasses; throws a look at* SIDNEY; *deposits her groceries; stops again at the glasses; and takes off the raincoat she is wearing to reveal one of those hideous yel-*

*low and white uniforms of the kind that are invariably inflicted on counter waitresses in luncheonettes)*

IRIS (*From the glasses to* SIDNEY)    I don't want them in my living room.

SIDNEY    Where else can I put them?

IRIS    We're not going to have the residue of all your failures in the living room.

SIDNEY    Look. Don't start. It's all over. Isn't that enough? (*He crosses to the phonograph and puts a record on*)

ALTON    I just remembered a very pressing engagement someplace.

SIDNEY (*"Don't desert me"*)    Where?

ALTON    I don't know, I'll think of it later. (*He exits*)

IRIS    It was all over *before* it started, if you ask me. (SID-NEY *does not rise to this; she goes into the kitchen. The music comes up. It is a white blues out of the Southland; a lyrical lament whose melody probably started somewhere in the British Isles more than one century ago and has crossed the ocean to be touched by the throb of black folk blues and then, finally, by the soul of back-country crackers. It is, in a word, old, haunting, American, and infinitely beautiful; and, mingled with the voice of Joan Baez, it is a statement which does not allow embarrassment for its soaring and curiously ascendant melancholy.* SIDNEY *busies himself at the drawing board, with an occasional side glance toward* IRIS. *The song, "Babe, I'm Gonna Leave You," dominates utterly. Suddenly* IRIS *changes the subject*) Ben Asch was in for lunch.

SIDNEY So?

IRIS (*Turns off the phonograph*)   He said they're doing a tent production of *South Pacific* out on the island this summer. Casting now. And guess who's doing it? Harry Maxton! Sidney, *Harry Maxton*. Remember, he *loved* me when I read for him that time!
> (*She is up and at the mirror whipping through a few of the hand gestures which signified "Happy Talk" in the original production. Her husband looks up at this for a few seconds, sobers, and looks away*)
> "Happy talk, keep talkin' happy talk
> Talk about things you like to do . . ."
> (*Wheeling and facing him exuberantly*)
Remember—he really flipped for my Liat!

SIDNEY   And he hired somebody else. And you know perfectly well you won't show up for the audition.
> (*He is immediately sorry*)

IRIS (*Frozen in the Liat pose*)   You rotten, cruel, sadistic, self-satisfying son of a bitch!
> (*She exits into the bedroom*)

SIDNEY   I'm sorry. I don't know why I do that.

IRIS   Then why don't you find out and give us both a break?
> (*He fans that away dispiritedly*)

SIDNEY   Does Steiner really tell you to go around drumming up business for him like that?

IRIS   I have *not* mentioned Dr. Steiner. And I am *not* going to! I am not *ever* going to mention Dr. Steiner in this house again. *Or* my analysis. You don't understand it. You can't—

SIDNEY *and* IRIS (*Together, he wearily with her*)   "Unless you've been through it yourself!"

IRIS (*Re-entering from bedroom. She has changed into tight high-water pants and a sweater*)     That happens to be true!

SIDNEY     Iris, honey, you've been in analysis for two years and the only difference is that before you used to cry all the time and now you *scream* before you cry.

IRIS     *You don't get better overnight, Sidney, but it is helping me!* Do you think that I would have been able to say the things I just said if I weren't going through a *tremendous* change?

SIDNEY (*Genuinely*)     What things?

IRIS     I just called you a sadistic, self-satisfying, cruel son of a bitch to your face instead of just thinking it. Don't you remember when I couldn't say things like that? Just think them and feel them—but not *say* them?

SIDNEY     Which amounts to you paying that quack twenty dollars a session to teach you how to swear! Lots of luck!

IRIS     That's not the point!

SIDNEY     I'm sorry. Swear *out loud.*

IRIS (*Through her teeth*)     For someone who thinks that they are the great intellect of all times, the top-heaviest son of a bitch that ever lived—

SIDNEY (*Dryly*)     Another step toward mental health—

IRIS     For someone who thinks that they've got the most *open* mind that was ever opened—you are the most narrow-minded, provincial—

SIDNEY     —"insular and parochial—"

IRIS     —insular and parochial bastard alive! And I'll tell you this: I may be whacked up, sweetie, but I really would hate to see the inside of *your* stomach. *Oh-ho,* I really would! St. John of the Twelve Agonies, I'll tell you.

SIDNEY   I am not agonized.

IRIS   *Everyone* is agonized!

SIDNEY   How do you know this, Iris?

IRIS   *Everyone* knows it. *Der (She hesitates and mispro-nounces it) Angst* is Everywhere. And I'll tell you this— if I had all your hostilities—

SIDNEY   Look, Iris, three years ago you practically tore up our marriage looking for a sex problem, because one fine day you decided we *had* to have one. We even *invented* one for six months because you *knew* we had to have one —because *everybody* did. Well, I promise you this time we are not going to embark on the search for my *(Correcting her) Angst!*

IRIS   *(Darkly. Sitting beside him on couch and teasing)*   I happen to know some things about you *in bed* that you don't know.

SIDNEY   *(False and weary patience—but reaching out for her: he loves this girl)*   Then tell me about them so we can discuss them.

IRIS   *(An air of the holy)   Oh no!* No siree. Get thyself to a professional. You're not going to catch *me* engaging in parlor analysis!

SIDNEY   There was no psychiatric mystery about it! It was almost purely technical. There were just some things in bed I wished you *wouldn't* do—*(Huskily)*—and some I wished you would.
   *(He holds her in his arms)*

IRIS   *(In the sway of the moment)*   That just shows you: nothing about *sex* is *just* technical. *(Sitting up)*   And, I notice, *I'm* not the one around here with an ulcer. And

I must say that for a *contented* man, who just *happens* to have an ulcer, you drink one hell of a lot!

SIDNEY    It's *my* ulcer! Moreover, I remember a time when, between the agonized and the contented, there was a *whole spectrum* of humanity.

IRIS    (*Rather by rote*)    Basically you are an ambivalent personality. You can't admit to disorder of any sort because that symbolizes weakness to you, and you can't admit to health either because you associate that with superficiality . . .

SIDNEY    Oh shut the hell up! I can't stand it when you're on this jag!
    (*Reaching for her again: this precious foolishness is all a game he dearly loves*)

IRIS    (*Shouting*)    Then why didn't you marry somebody you did like to talk to then!
    (*It hangs a second, is absorbed with minor melancholy by the husband, who, to rise above it, offers a parodied Elizabethan flourish*)

SIDNEY    Because—(*Lifting a drink like Cyrano*) "what did please the morning's academic ear did seem indeed —(*Bringing the hand down defeatedly*) to repel the evening's sensuous touch. Think this poor poet not cruel to say it; but—(*Concluding the flourish*) gentle Sid, be but a mortal thing."

IRIS    (*Feminine cruelty*)    Awwww, is that what you told poor Evie when she proposed?

SIDNEY    She didn't propose. Cut it out.

IRIS    You once told me she did.

SIDNEY    Bedroom boasts. You don't pretend to believe mine and I won't pretend to believe yours. (*Holding her;*

*in a quieter tone*) What you were supposed to say was, "In such regard and diluted esteem doth my master hold his own sweet Iris—"

IRIS (*Looking up*)  I don't know the piece. What is it?

SIDNEY (*Dully, staring off*)  Nothing.

IRIS  What?

SIDNEY  Plutarch or some damn body! What difference does it make *what* it's from?

IRIS  Well, whatever it's from, it said that you really do think I'm stupid!

SIDNEY (*Hardly to her at all*)  "My pardon on it, I will get me gone." (*A pause, then to her*) It said: I love you. It said I do not counsel reason or quarrel with my nature. It said, girl, that I love my wife. Curious thing. (*Stops her lips with a kiss*)

IRIS  Meaning frivolous mind and all.

SIDNEY  You make a silly fishwife. Stop it.

IRIS  Can't I say *anything?*

SIDNEY  Not in this mood, it's driving me crazy! (*He gets up agitatedly and goes to the window and looks out at the street*)

IRIS (*Resolute anger*)  And one thing is clear: You prefer picking at me to talking to me.

SIDNEY (*Shouting*)  I do not! And tell that Steiner to take his love-hate obsession and shove it!

IRIS  It is not something *you* can know about, Sid. I am talking about *unconscious* motivation.

SIDNEY  If it is all that *"un"* then you don't know about it either!

IRIS (*Puzzled; caught*)  I meant "sub." A *sub*conscious motivation.

IRIS (*Sore spot*)  Sidney, why can't you understand about to go to the audition.

IRIS (*Sore spot*)  Sidney, why can't you understand about the blocks that people have?

SIDNEY (*Seated at his drawing board*)  I do understand about them and I know that if they are nurtured enough they get bigger and bigger and bigger.

IRIS (*In kind, through her teeth*)  All right, so I haven't worked out my life so good. Have you? Or are those glasses there a mere mirage I see before me?

SIDNEY  Aw, what do you know about it?

IRIS (*Undulating away with triumph*)  I know that there is no great wisdom in opening a folk-singing establishment where there are something like twenty of such establishments in a radius of four blocks square. I know that, darling-pie! And what the hell did you know about running a night club anyway?
    (*She crosses into the bathroom to brush her teeth*)

SIDNEY (*Painfully: old refrain, lost cause*)  It wasn't *supposed* to be a night club. (*A beat*) It *would* have done okay if Bruno had done a better job on the publicity.

IRIS (*Closes the bathroom door, and comes back*)  He thought he should be paid.

SIDNEY  I offered him a quarter of the place!

IRIS  Who wants a quarter of a nonprofit night club?

SIDNEY  *It wasn't a night club!*

IRIS  And what are you going to do with all those glasses?

SIDNEY   How do I know right now? There have to be other enterprises that need a hundred and fifty sturdy restaurant glasses, don't there?

IRIS   When they *audit* the place they're going to think it's awfully funny that there're no glasses. What are you going to say happened to them?

SIDNEY   How come I should know what happened to them? Why should I know every little detail. Maybe somebody broke in and took them or something.

IRIS   Auditors like to know about the details, Sid. They specialize in the details.

SIDNEY   And what are you worrying about that for? You oughta be glad I at least salvaged something out of it— that I had the get-up to go over there and get *something* out of there *before* they audit. Why can't you ever look at things that way? From the point of view of the things I do that have foresight. How come you gotta play wife-harpic all the time?

   (IRIS *turns back the tracing paper on* SIDNEY'S *board to reveal the masthead on which he had been working*)

IRIS (*Picking it up*)   So now what? You're going to be an artist? This is *aw-ful.*
   (*A fit of appropriate giggling*)

SIDNEY   It's not supposed to be a drawing. It's the layout for the—
   (*He halts, not having meant to get into this just this way*)

IRIS (*Already expecting almost anything*)   For the *what,* Sidney?

SIDNEY (*He exhales heavily*)   Harvey Wyatt met some chick—

IRIS  Yes, *and*—

SIDNEY  —he decided to go live in Majorca. I mean forget the whole scene and just like that go live in Majorca . . .

IRIS  (*Sitting, one hand over her lips*)  Oh, my God, no . . . Sidney—*no*.

SIDNEY  (*Shrugging*)  So he *had* to unload the paper.

IRIS  No. God, don't let it be true. Unload it on—*whom?* Oh, Sidney, you haven't . . . ?

SIDNEY  I know it's hard for you, Iris. To understand what I'm all about—

IRIS  (*Slumping where she is*)  I don't believe this. I don't believe that you could come out of—of *that*—(*Gesturing to the glasses*) and get into *this*. Aside from anything else at the moment, what did you conceivably tell Harvey that you were going to pay him?

SIDNEY  We made an arrangement. Don't worry about it.

IRIS  What kind of arrangement, Sidney?

SIDNEY  *An arrangement*. That's all. I know what I arranged. I tell you, don't worry about it, that's all.

IRIS  Where in the name of God are you going to get the money to pay for a newspaper?

SIDNEY  It's a *small* newspaper. A weekly.

IRIS  Sidney, you can't afford a *yearly leaflet!*

SIDNEY  (*Quietly*)  Why isn't it ever enough for me to tell you that I know what I'm doing? The money was not the important part of the deal one way or the other. This is a real rich babe Harvey's hooked up with so he's not worried about the money. Just yet.

IRIS   And when he is——? Where are you going to get it? That's what little old Iris is standing here with her bare-faced everyday-self wondering about.

SIDNEY   I'll raise it. That's all. I'll raise it. Period. Didn't I raise it for the Silver Dagger? Well, I'll raise it for this. In order to *do* things you have to *do* things. That's all.
    (*During the above* WALLY O'HARA *and* ALTON SCALES *have approached; the former is a conventionally dressed man, in his early forties, with rust-colored thinning hair; he carries several cardboard placards. For a moment the two stand in animated conversation, as if planning their next move. Now* ALTON *beats on the door.* IRIS *throws up her hands in disgust and admits them*)

ALTON   (*Kissing her broadly. Gesturing toward* WALLY) Hey, look who I ran into.

WALLY   (*Shows a campaign poster to* SID *and* IRIS. *It reads:* VOTE O'HARA FOR REFORM) Hey, Sid.

SIDNEY   (*Standing stock-still, resolutely*)   The answer is no.

ALTON   (*Yelling at him*)   Don't be a clown! At least hear what the man has to say!

WALLY   Iris.
    (*He kisses her. She goes into the kitchen to make a salad*)

SIDNEY   I know what he has to say and I don't want to hear it. I'm out of it. Period. My little artsy-craftsy news-paper is going to stay clear of politics. *Any* kind of politics. Politics are for people who have those kinds of interests, that's all. I don't happen to have them any more.

WALLY (*As if he expected that; making himself comfortable*)  Yes, I know. You've made yourself clear in the past: "Politics are a blight on the natural spirit of man. Politics are a cancer of the soul. Politics are dirty, fetid, compromise-ridden exercises in futility." Et cetera, et cetera, et cetera. (*Wandering over to the glass racks and picking up a glass*) A bunch of big drinkers here? (*Pouring a drink, then turning a knowing, skilled gaze on the editor*) Nonetheless, Sidney—I've finally faced up to something that you've got to face up to; there is work to be done and someone has got to do it. Now, I'm taking time out from a busy law practice which is just beginning to build. I'm sticking my neck out to run, and all I'm asking from you is a little legwork, and the endorsement of —what I take it is now—your paper.

SIDNEY  Not even for you, Wally. My readers can do as they please. In my paper—no endorsements. And no editorials.

ALTON (*To* WALLY, *agitatedly*)  You see! There it is, man! We are confronted with the great disease of the modern bourgeois intellectual: *ostrich*-ism. I've been watching it happen to this one; the great sad withdrawal from the affairs of men. (*With bitter facetiousness, pounding his breast—he pins up the poster on the bookshelves*) It sort of gets me, *here.*

SIDNEY  Alton, do you know that it is an absolute fact that the one infallible way that one can always, and I mean *always,* tell an ex-Communist from ordinary human beings is by the sheer volume of his use of the word *bourgeois?*

ALTON   And do you know how one can always, infallibly, no matter what, tell a card-carrying phony? By the minuteness of the pretext on which he will manage to change the subject, *if* the subject is even remotely important.

WALLY (*Laughing smoothly*)   Why do you boys hang out together?

SIDNEY (*Turning in kind on* ALTON)   Yes, I suppose I *have* lost the pretensions of the campus revolutionary, Alton. I do admit that I no longer have the energy, the purity or the comprehension to—"save the world." (*Takes down* WALLY's *poster. Looking at them with an internalized smile working the corners of his mouth*) As a matter of fact, to get *real* big about it, I no longer even believe that spring must necessarily come at all. Or, that if it does, that it will bring forth anything more poetic or insurgent than—(*With a flourish*) the winter's dormant ulcers.

WALLY (*Getting up, crossing to* SIDNEY. *There is a pervasive assurance about him*)   We're not talking about the world, we're talking about this community. It's like getting on the wagon, the way they tell you in the AA: Don't think about all the drinks you've got to give up, just concentrate on the next one. That's the trick, Sid. Don't think about the ailing world for the time being, just think about your own little ailing neighborhood, that's the point.

SIDNEY (*Wandering away from him*)   That's very impressive. (*Hands the poster back to* WALLY) But the truth of the matter is, dear friends, I am afraid that I have experienced the *death* of the exclamation point. It has died in me. I no longer want to exhort anybody about anything. It's the final end of boyhood. (*Grinning wryly at his friends*) Now, I admit that this is something that doesn't happen to everyone. Take old Alton here: one *long* exclamation point!

ALTON (*Loftily*)   Capitulation has one smell, one shape, one sound.

SIDNEY (*In kind*)   Look, I'm not a neophyte. You wanna see my scrapbooks? Since I was eighteen I've belonged to every committee To Save, To Abolish, Prohibit, Preserve, Reserve and Conserve that ever was. And the result—(*With an almost rollicking flippancy*) is that the mere thought of a "movement" to do *anything* chills my bones. I simply can no longer bear the spectacle of the hatchetry of power-driven insurgents trying at all costs to gain control—(*The coup de grâce*) of the refreshment committee!
     (*He crosses into the bathroom for a bottle of pills*)

WALLY (*Smiling easily*)   I told you: Think only of not taking the next drink.

SIDNEY (*Crossing back to the drawing board to take his pill with a drink*)   You mean diddle around with the *little* things since we can't do anything about the *big* ones? Like the fact that I was born of a father who was maimed in one war, did some fighting of my own in another and have survived into the clear and present danger of a third? Forget about all that jazz, huh, and worry about—reforms in the traffic court or something?

WALLY (*Putting his drink down, with vigor*)   Christ, man, this is the second largest narcotics drop in the city, the outpost of every racket known to man! The syndicate thinks it owns this neighborhood, and there sits the regular machine—

SIDNEY   You kid yourself if you want to, Wally. *Do things* if it makes you happy. Just don't bug me about it. Iris, beer!

IRIS (*Coming out from the kitchen*)   All I've got to say, Sidney, is just mean what you say, that's all, just *mean* what you say.

WALLY (*Strictly in jest*)   All of which goes to prove that a woman's place is in the oven.

ALTON (*Mugging*)   *With* the door closed.

WALLY   I'm wondering, Sidney. In the clear and present danger—
　　　(*The phone is ringing*)

IRIS   Jesus, that'll be Mavis. I don't feel like Mavis tonight. Sid, you get it.

SIDNEY   I never feel like Mavis. You get it. (*Iris goes to answer*) That Mavis, boy—I *still* swear she is something Sinclair Lewis made up which has escaped the book! (*Looking at* ALTON *soberly*) Speaking of Iris' sisters, I gather you've been seeing a lot of Gloria when she's in town.
　　　(IRIS *at the phone, throws a swift pregnant glance at her husband*)

ALTON (*Mugging heavily and smacking his lips*) Yeaaahhhh.

SIDNEY   Yeah, well, take it from me and beware of the daughters of the House of Atreus.
　　　(IRIS *looks daggers*)

ALTON (*Glibly, unaware of the by-play*)   I'll take my chances. (*To* WALLY) You should *see* this one, man!
　　　(*Waving his fingers for the heat*)

WALLY (*Smiling*) I'd like to. (*Back to the attack*) Sidney, if you can't function—

ALTON Only there's no point in your meeting her *now*, man. Like *I* have come into her vision and I am filling it out *entirely!*

WALLY So where is this perfection? Why doesn't she drop by and help restore Sidney's vision?

IRIS (*Cutting in, one hand cupping the receiver*) She's in Los Angeles. Travels a lot. She's a high-fashion model. (ALTON *passes a photo of* GLORIA *to* SID *and* WALLY) I *am* listening to you, love. I don't care, Mav, that's all. Good-bye! (*As she hangs up the phone and wanders back to a position near her husband*) Poor old Mavis. But you've got to admit that she doesn't give up. She's been trying to civilize me for years. Now she's got some dress for me.

SIDNEY Dear old Mav, Mother of the Philistines. My brother is the Prince, but your sister is the Mother of them all!

> (*He suddenly pulls the pins out of his wife's hair, causing it to fall down all over her. She is infuriated by this habit of his*)

IRIS Oh, damn it, Sid! Don't start that, I'm telling you! I mean it!

ALTON (*To* WALLY) If he had his way he'd have her running barefoot in a gingham dress with all that hair flying around. (*To* SIDNEY) What are you, some kind of arrested rustic?

WALLY I've often wondered how such a "nice middle-class Jewish boy" got so hung up on such a tired old Anglo-Saxon myth.

SIDNEY (*Western drawl*)  I reckon my particular Jewish psyche was less discriminating than most.

WALLY (*Pressing forward*)  Sidney, if you can't function in one little community, then how—

SIDNEY (*Escaping again*)  Hey, honey, you know what I feel like? I am suddenly suffering from an all-consuming desire to take my books, my cameras, my records, and— my wife—and go—

IRIS, ALTON *and* WALLY (*Together, in unison*)  —up to the woods!
> (*She, without appreciation, starts working at her hair, trying to get it back up*)

SIDNEY (*Painfully*)  Yes. And stay . . . (*Pulling her head back hard and looking into her eyes*) Forever.
> (*She sighs*)

ALTON (*To* WALLY)  Man, you see what we are up against here? This clown is not only committed to the symbolic mountain tops. He goes in for the *whole real live physical thing.*

SIDNEY (*Changing the subject; to* ALTON)  By the way, I made an appointment with Mickey Dafoe for you. He expects you in his office at noon. Wear a tie and your best Establishment Ass-kissing Manner or something so you won't make him nervous.

ALTON  What do you mean you made an appointment for me? For what? What do I want to see Mickey Dafoe for?

SIDNEY  Gotta be you. Nobody else to go.

ALTON  Well, there's not me, I have nothing to say to people like Mickey Dafoe.

SIDNEY  You're right, you're wrong for it. Absolutely the wrong man to send. The Trade and Commerce Association is only responsible for like half of the advertising in the paper. We need somebody—(*Moving "aimlessly" toward* WALLY *so that at the last word they are face to face.* WALLY *is already shaking his head "no"*) smoo-ooooth.

WALLY   Don't look at me.

SIDNEY   Why not, you fat cat you—?

WALLY   What makes you think you can always ask, ask, ask for things, Sid—and never give?

SIDNEY (*Throwing up his hands*)   Because before I am through my little artsy-craftsy newspaper i⸱ going—

IRIS   Oh, Sidney, newspaper, newspaper, newspaper! How long do you think that you're going to *have* a newspaper!
        (*She disappears into the bedroom, putting her hair up*)

ALTON   What's the matter with her lately?

SIDNEY (*A shrug*)   Who knows? Maybe she's changing life.

WALLY   Come on, it's the Greek in her. You should know that. The triumph of the innate tragedy in her soul.

SIDNEY (*This entire exchange is for* IRIS *to hear*)   She's only half Greek, so she should be only half tragic. Hey, Iris, when you come back out, turn up just one side of your face.

IRIS   Boy, are you fellows fun-nee!
        (*A wild cackle of sardonic laughter*)

WALLY   Hey, what is the other half?

SIDNEY   Irish 'n' Cherokee. I'm married to the only Greco-Gaelic-Indian hillbilly in captivity. If one can really think of Iris as being in captivity . . . Do your dance, honey.

(*She snakes out promptly, hissing, in the dance steps of the Greek Miserlou—which turns into a jig and then into the usual stereotyped notion of some Indian war dance, concluding with a Marilyn Monroe freeze. Then she backs out*) I taught her everything she knows! You should hear my mother on Iris. (*The inevitable*) "*Not* that I have anything against the *goyim*, Sidney, she's a nice girl, but the rice is too greasy. And *lamb* fat? For the *stomach?* With hominy grits? *Like a lump it sits.*"

WALLY (*Nodding toward where* IRIS *is*)   Any shows coming up?

SIDNEY (*Softly, hand up to discourage the subject*)   Don't bring it up.

ALTON (*Who has been flipping the pages of a book on the coffee table in front of him*)   One of your troubles is, Sid, that you admire the wrong parts of Thoreau.

SIDNEY (*Who is deep in the chair; his back to* ALTON, *hand behind his head*)   How do you know what parts of Thoreau I do or don't admire?

ALTON   You mark passages—(*He promptly starts to read aloud, while roaming the room, meaning in the beginning to inflict the facetious taunt on it, trilling his r's, but ultimately finding some difficulty in it, perhaps as the words have appeal even to him. As he reads we are aware of certain familiar colorings and inflections in his speech though we cannot presently place them*) ". . . In the coldest and bleakest places, the warmest charities still maintain a foothold. A cold and searching wind drives away all contagion, and nothing can withstand it but what has virtue in it. Whatever we meet in cold and bleak places, as the tops of mountains—" See! Always looking for them *mountain tops!* ". . . we respect for a sort of sturdy innocence. . . . It is invigorating to breathe the cleansèd air . . . and we fain would stay out long and late, that the gales may sigh through us, too, as through the lifeless trees, and fit us for the winter:—as if we hoped so to borrow some pure and steadfast virtue which will stead us in all seasons."

(SIDNEY *takes the book from him thoughtfully and a little defiantly, snaps it shut and returns it to its place on the shelf, then sits looking off.* IRIS *reappears in the bedroom doorway*)

WALLY    All right—how's about the rest of Thoreau, Sidney boy? How's about the Thoreau of sublime social consciousness, the Thoreau who was standing in jail one day when that holy of holies, Mr. Ralph Waldo Emerson, comes strolling by and asks, "Well, Henry, what are you doing in there?" And Thoreau, who was "in there" for protesting the evils of his day, looked out at him and said—"The question is, Ralph, what are you doing (*New England old-timer inflection*) out *thay-ah?*"

(IRIS *knowing* SIDNEY *only too well and sensing the drift, starts humming "The Battle Hymn of the Republic" as she crosses into the kitchen*)

SIDNEY    Cut it out.

(IRIS *enters with salad bowl and stands slicing vegetables at counter*)

ALTON (*Coolly plunging in for the kill*)    Why, Sid? She's right . . . Wally, stop that foolishness! Cool it, man. You're "venerating"! You're "celebrating the human spirit"! Your *"conscience* is showing"! Don't you know, Wally, "Readers—(*Indicating* IRIS) don't want it." The great untutored public—(*Indicating the window*) doesn't want it. And what's more, the exhausted insurgent—

(*Indicating* SIDNEY) cannot afford it. 'S no use, Wally:
the man's in mourning for his boyhood. Let's go before
he sells you one hundred and fifty restaurant glasses.
(*He gets up*)

SIDNEY (*Stung*)   Well, hooray the hell for you! . . . John
the Baptist! (*He throws himself onto his knees and with
outstretched arms offers a slow and very precise salaam*)
God bless your Saviour-type soul!
(*Hands fluttering holy-roller style, he begins a wailing chant, which peters out as* ALTON *stands over
him, relentless*)

ALTON   Look out, man, you're getting overinvolved. Too
emotional; you might *shed a tear*. After all, what is it?
Only one kid. One lousy junkie, all of seventeen. (*Bru-
tally offhand*) What'd he do, sweep for you at the Silver
Dagger, whatever his name is?

SIDNEY (*Softly*)   Sal Peretti . . .

ALTON   Oh yeah—Sal Peretti.

SIDNEY   I did what I could—

IRIS (*Furious, pleading to hold back the inevitable*)   Sidney, you gave him a job—you can't be responsible for
*every strange kid that walks in off the street!*

SIDNEY   I tried to help.

ALTON   Let's go, Wally, we're wasting time.
(*Pulling* WALLY *after him*)

WALLY (*At the door*)   I'm counting on you, Sid.

SIDNEY   *Don't.*

(*They exit. There is a long, pregnant beat as* SIDNEY
*stands looking after them.* IRIS'S *eyes are immedi-*

*ately riveted to him from the counter, where she
continues slicing salad—and they do not leave him,
not for one instant, for the balance of the scene.*
SIDNEY *stirs, wanders deep in thought about the
room, back and forth, round and about. He takes
up the poster, puts it on the coffee table, sits looking at it. He flops on the couch. Sits up. Flops
back down again, looking off unseeing, then sits
up and—at last—turns tentatively to* IRIS)

IRIS (*as their eyes meet*)  Sidney, I swear to heaven—
I'll poison you!

*Blackout*

*Time: Dusk. The following week. In the darkness before
the lights come up, once again the quarrelsome voices are
heard.*

MAX  (*Round, juicy, gravel-voiced*)  Sca-rrew Michelangelo! You and Michelangelo all the time! Christ! Not
again . . .

ALTON  Yes, again. The *larger* statement has to say it *all*—
(*The lights come up.* ALTON *and* MAX *are in the
apartment. The latter's free-form paintings, laid out
for inspection about the place, have inspired the
present violent discussion.* MAX *is by all odds an
original: middle-aged, gravel-voiced, squat, his salt-
and-pepper short hair brushed dead forward; he
wears sandals, stained jeans, a black turtleneck and
a pained expression*)

MAX  Your main trouble is that you are a literalist. You
were born a literalist and you will die a literalist.

ALTON  And all I am saying is that decay is *not* the deepest
damn thing going, you know? It's sick—so, like, it's supposed to be pro*found?* Too easy, baby. Death is too
damn easy. Chaos is easier. And when you pretend that
*that* is the scale of existence—

MAX  (*Gesture of the streets*)  Go the hell away, Alton.
You don't know a damn thing except *poster* art.

ALTON  What old poster art! Is Leonardo poster art?

MAX  (*Slamming down something with outrage*)  I knew
it, here we go again: back to the frigging Renaissance!
(SIDNEY *enters carrying a large banner*)

SIDNEY   I got it.

ALTON   Great. Let's put it up, I've already got the nails in. (SIDNEY *flings one end to* ALTON *and they hold it, for a moment unfurled. It reads:*

---

## CLEAN UP COMMUNITY POLITICS

Wipe Out Bossism

## VOTE REFORM

---

*(They stride to the window—where, presently, it hangs, face out to the street)*

SIDNEY   All right, let's go to work. (*He sits at his board,* ALTON *at his side.* MAX *sits benignly apart: the "man of the hour," awaiting the call*) Now, with a new masthead, the front page will stay pretty much as it is. Page two, some jumps and lesser items . . . page three, interviews, you know. Page four, letters to the editor and some weekly artwork.

ALTON (*Winks—the victor*)   *And* the editorials.

SIDNEY (*Toss-off—who ever denied it? Then laughs*) And the editorials. Five and six: theatre, dance and movie reviews. By the way, I want to get rid of Dan Wallace and get Paul Russo. He's good.

ALTON   If you like obscurity, he's the best.

SIDNEY   Sure, Russo gets a little fuzzy, but you've got to admit the man knows films. (*As if this were somehow relevant*) He's a very gentle man. Do you know he wanders around with little bits and pieces of paper in his pocket on which he writes down every single thing that moves him, good or bad, in a day?

ALTON  And at the end of the week he puts them in a hat and stirs them—and that's his movie review for the week!

SIDNEY  Oh, Alton, knock off! Where's the masthead, Max?

> (MAX *rises and crosses ceremoniously with his port-folio; he opens it and places the masthead before them. Then, with a flourish, he flips off the tracing paper to unveil it, and stands back*)

MAX (*Modestly*)  Here. It's a rough idea, you know.

> (SIDNEY *and* ALTON *squint at it hard, look at each other, puzzled; the two turn it sidewise and upside down.* MAX *restores it rightside up. The two squint again. Finally,* ALTON *points to the bottom of the page*)

SIDNEY  Three-point type for the nameplate of a news-paper? At the bottom of the page? Who's going to see it?

MAX (*Columbus Incarnate, Galileo, Copernicus, the Wright Brothers and Frank Lloyd, in one*)  That's the whole point. You put it far right and low on the big field—and the eye *has* to follow. (*Professor to slow pupil, guides their eyes down and around the page with a finger. The other two men are silent;* MAX *is offended and starts to gather his things*)

SIDNEY  Max, I like it—it just occurred to me—I like it!

MAX (*Petulant, undeterred*)  Look, I thought it was some-thing different, something fresh.

> (*He starts out*)

SIDNEY  But, Max—

MAX  It's always that way. You revolutionaries are all the same. You start out full of fire and end up full of . . . shit!

> (*He stamps out the door.* SIDNEY *rises to follow*)

ALTON    Oh, Sidney! I'm telling you, it looks like a bunch of art majors from Music and Art designed that page.

SIDNEY    Alton, will you please! (*Follows* MAX *out—takes the masthead from* MAX, *studies it*) Max, you've done it again!

MAX (*One more moment of immovable glory; then relents*) As a matter of fact, Sid, let's change it every week. (SID-NEY *and* MAX *re-enter and cross to the board*) You know, a different type—Old English, Gothic, Bodoni. However we feel the day we're making it up.

SIDNEY    Max—you're so creative!

MAX    And in a different place! Locate it on a different place on the sheet every week!

ALTON (*Suddenly shouting*)    It's a newspaper! It's a god-damned newspaper—not an avant-garde toy!

MAX    He doesn't change, does he? You know, once you've had that Marxist monkey on your back you're hooked for life. To Alton—a newspaper's not an aesthetic adven-ture, it's—(*He tightens his face and balls his fist in a mock-serious gesture*) a weapon! (*Carried away by his idea, he leaps on the couch with an imaginary banner and sings*)
"    'Tis the final conflict
Let each stand in his place—
The Internationale—"

ALTON    Aw, go to hell.

MAX (*Sings*)    "Unites the human race!"
(IRIS *enters and halts at the sight. She is in her uniform, carrying paella in a brown paper bag*)

IRIS (*Violent facetiousness*)    Well, *company*. And who have I invited to supper tonight?
(*She has their attention at last*)

ALTON  Paella?
> (*She nods "yes," with eyes closed, knowing that he will stay now. He puts his hand in the air to deliberately affect the class-room mannerism of a small child*)

IRIS  Max?

MAX  (*Still on the couch*) Paella. Like crazy. (*Rubbing his head, stomach and consulting his watch, genuinely conflicted*) But the problem is . . . there's this chick I was *supposed* to have met in the Black Knight—Jesus, an hour ago . . .

SIDNEY  There it is: the primeval decision, food or sex.
> (MAX *closes his eyes to imagine a little of each presumably, caught in the pose of the true primitive*)

ALTON  (*Going and leaning under* MAX *more or less to study the decision*)  And let us watch *primitive* man decide—
> (MAX *opens his eyes, steps down from the couch and begins to gather up his things in order to make the prior date.* IRIS *exits into the bedroom*)

ALTON  The *loins* triumph! See, Max, you're *not* a true primitive or you would have put *food* first! You only *paint* like a savage. (*Pursuing* MAX *to the door*) And—where the hell did you get that outfit, man? You look just like a put-up job for *Life*-Magazine-Visits-the-Left-Bank-and-all. Where's your goatee?

MAX  (*Staring him down—a squelch*)  That's the difference between me and you, Alton: I have finally become a truly free man. I have even stopped worrying about *not* trying to look like a nonconformist *not* nonconforming. Dig?
> (*He exits, giving* ALTON *one last baby chuck on the chin.* IRIS *re-enters from bedroom in jeans and a sweater, with mail*)

IRIS   Hey, I got a letter from Gloria.

ALTON   How is life in the pancake world, Iris, my light?

IRIS   (*Reading her mail*)   Be still, I gotta read my mail. (ALTON *takes the banjo down, crosses to the rocker, begins to pick the banjo* . . . IRIS *looks up from the letter slowly, with astonishment and many confusions in her face*) Why, Alton Scales . . . Gloria says that you asked her to marry you.

ALTON   (*Affecting the bashful teenager*)   Yup.

SIDNEY   (*Looks up at him and then at his wife, and then back to his friend*)   Are you for real?

ALTON   (Ibid.)   Yup.

SIDNEY   You're that gone on her?

ALTON   (*Sudden lover's hoarse sincerity*)   In fact, I figure that if that babe doesn't hurry up and get herself back here—like I could flip.

SIDNEY   I'll be damned. (*To his wife*) You never know.

IRIS   (*In astonishment*)   You never know.

SIDNEY   What did she say: "yes" or "no"?

ALTON   She didn't. She said she'd think about it while she was away—(*Strumming out an accompaniment on the banjo for emphasis*)—and like I have been *living* with tension for two weeks! (*Abruptly, his strum breaks into "The Midnight Special!" and he sings. After a few lines he stops. As the silence dawns on him—tensely*) What's the matter? (*The other two avoid replying in an awkward moment of misunderstood discomfort.* SIDNEY *reconcentrates on his board;* IRIS *just sits, not knowing what to say.* ALTON, *tightly, with mounting anger, speaks directly to* SIDNEY, *crossing to him and standing fully in*

*front of him; angrily*) I said what's the matter, god-
damnit! Come on, let's have it out, my little gray friends!
This is like the moment of truth, old babies! Yeah, come
on! Let's get to the nitty gritty, as it were! Let's blast all
the crap away—

IRIS   Oh, Alton!

SIDNEY (*Simply*)   Why don't you take that damn tree off
your shoulder, Alton? Frankly, it's embarrassing.
(*They glare at one another;* ALTON *softens to a different kind of embarrassment*)

ALTON   Well, don't expect me to apologize . . . I have a
right to think anything I want. In *this* world. Even of *you*
—Sid.

SIDNEY   There are some misunderstandings that cost more
than others, Alton.

IRIS   Besides, the point is—well for crying out loud—
who'd expect that you two? Well, you know what I
mean: You're so Paul P. Proletarian and all, and she's
the Living Spirit of Madison Avenue.

ALTON   Well, hell, opposites attract and all, to coin a
phrase. Besides, like—(*Slowly, real slow*) I dig her!

SIDNEY (*With great sobriety*)   That much?

ALTON (*A lover*)   *That* much!

SIDNEY (*Russian accent*)   Another bolshevik bites the
dust.

IRIS (*Her eyes on him intently*)   And that's all that we
have to say about it, isn't it, Sidney?

SIDNEY (*Considering swiftly and accepting this judgment*)
That's all.

IRIS   Where's my *Variety?*

SIDNEY (*Back with his board*)   Under the apples.

IRIS (*A long afterthought*)   And I don't like that expression, come to think of it.

SIDNEY   What expression?

IRIS (*Shaking her finger, not serious*)   About biting the dust. I know where that came from. And on behalf of my Cherokee grandfather, I protest.

ALTON   I got your point, so knock it off.

IRIS (*Turning on him*)   You knock it off, sometimes, Alton! It's a bore. You and the causes all the time. It's phony as hell!

ALTON (*Sharply, back at her*)   I was born with *this* cause.

IRIS   That's what I mean! Fun with illusion and reality: white boy playing black boy all the time.

ALTON   I *am* a black boy. I didn't make up the game, and as long as a lot of people think there is something wrong with the fact that I *am* a Negro—I am going to make a point out of being one. Follow!

IRIS (*Pragmatic bohemia*)   But that's what makes it so phony. The country is full of people who dropped it when they could—what makes you so ever-loving different?

ALTON   It's something you either understand or don't understand.
     (*He shrugs*)

IRIS   Well, I guess everybody has to do *something* with their guilts.

ALTON (*Flaring*)   Guilt's got nothing to do with it . . .

SIDNEY   Come on, this is a stupid conversation. Be a Martian if you wanna.

IRIS (*Settling down with her* Variety. *Whistling it out*) Heroes, heroes, everywhere—and not a battle won! (ALTON *rises, abruptly—quickly crosses to the door*) Alton?

ALTON (*Turning at the door—gruff, indirect apology*) I'm going out for some wine for my contribution to the feed. Want something? Cigarettes?

SIDNEY (*Grinning*) Nope.

ALTON How about you, Laughing Tomahawk? (*He exits*)

IRIS Flowers. For the table. (*Follows him out the door— calls after him*) If you're going to be a brother-in-law you should try to get in with me. I know *plenty* about being a sister-in-law. Bring me flowers every day . . . (*At the top of her lungs*) Lumumba. (*She ducks as the paperback he has been reading comes crashing against the door frame. She comes back in, closing the door. At once to her husband, sharply, wife-ishly*) You just keep your mouth shut about Gloria, you hear!

SIDNEY Did I say anything?

IRIS No, but you sat there looking like death. Let them work it out, see! Let them work it out. Keep your mouth off it, I'm telling you.

SIDNEY (*Almost screaming, as the point has been made*) Did I say anything, did I say anything, *shrew*?

IRIS (*Turning back to her paper*) No, but I know you— the world's biggest busybody. (SIDNEY *rises, crosses, hands her the new masthead and, like the cat that swallowed the canary, unveils it with the same proud flourish as* MAX. IRIS *sits blankly, squints, looks at* SIDNEY, *turns it sidewise and upside down; finally he rights it and guides her eye in almost exact repetition of the prior sequence*) You keeping it a secret? Looks arty.

SIDNEY (*Furious*)   All right—so it looks arty. What does that mean, do you know?

IRIS   Do I know what?

SIDNEY   Do you know what "arty" means? Or is it just some little capsule phrase thrown out to try to diminish me, since you have nothing genuinely analytical or even observant to say?
(*He is staring at her hard, angrily*)

IRIS   I wasn't trying to be analytical. I was saying what I thought, which is that it looks arty.

SIDNEY   You mean that it looks different from other publications.

IRIS   No, I mean it looks different from other publications in a self-conscious sort of way. *Arty.*

SIDNEY   Iris, where did you get the idea you know enough about these things to pass judgment on them?

IRIS   From the same place you got the idea that you were an editor.

SIDNEY   Which happens at least to be more reasonable than the idea that you are anybody's actress.

IRIS (*Putting down her paper, slowly, hurtfully*)   Why don't you just hit me with your fists sometimes, Sid.
(*Exits into the bathroom. Sobs are heard*)

SIDNEY   I didn't mean that, baby. Come on. Do *South Pacific*. I'll hold the book for you.

IRIS   No.
(*More sobs*)

SIDNEY  Iris, honey, come on.
(*He opens the door—she pulls it shut. After a moment he tries again and she, clutching the inner knob, is tugged half into the room*)

IRIS  (*Flaring irrationally, crossing out and down*)  Why should I go through all of that to read for something that I know I won't get in the first place. They don't want actresses, they just want easy lays, that's all. (*Snarling*) That Harry Maxton, *please!* He's the biggest lech of them all. You want to know something, you really want to hear something I hope will burn your little ears off? That's why I didn't get the part before. I said "no"!
(SIDNEY *has halted and is standing, half turned from her, letting it pour out of her as he has many, many times before*)

SIDNEY  (*Turning quietly, almost gently*)  Iris, everybody knows that Harry Maxton is one of the most famous fags in America.

IRIS  All right, then. So everything goes with him! He just puts on the fag bit to cover up what he really is—

SIDNEY  (*With proper incredulity*)  You mean a lech?

IRIS  (*With a wild, cornered gesture*)  Sure, that's how twisted up they are in show business, you just don't know!

SIDNEY  (*Helplessly*)  Even in show business—*that* twisted they're not. And making up sordid excuses to yourself is not the solution to your problem, so come off it!

IRIS  Leave me alone, Sidney. I don't want the part.
(*She has curled into a tight sulking ball*)

SIDNEY  (*Continuing on, getting the book and then crossing back to her and kneeling in front of her*)  Oh, Iris, Iris,

Iris . . . (*He puts his head wearily on her knee*) I want to help . . . so much . . . I'm on your side.

IRIS  I just don't have it. They say if you really have it—you stick with it no matter what—and that—that you'll do anything—

SIDNEY  That is one of the great romantic and cruel ideas of our civilization. A lot of people "have it" and they just get trampled to death by the mob trying to get up the same mountain.

IRIS  Oh—please, Sidney, don't start blaming everything on society. Sooner or later a person learns to hold *himself* accountable—that's what maturity is. If I haven't learned anything else in analysis I've sure learned that.

SIDNEY  Thank you, Dr. Steiner! Look, Iris, the world's finest swimmer cannot swim the Atlantic Ocean—even if analysis *does* prove it was his mother's fault!

IRIS  That's not an analogy. *Nobody* can swim the Atlantic Ocean—but some people *do* make it in the theatre. (*She smiles at him and puts her hand on his head and he settles at her feet*) You make the lousiest analogies. Just like you can't add. I couldn't believe that at first.

SIDNEY  What?

IRIS  About your arithmetic. When I first met you I thought you were putting me on. You know, anybody all *that* brilliant who couldn't *add.* God, at home almost *nobody* could read—but *everybody* could add. (*Looking at him and playing with his hair a little*) What's seven and seven—?

SIDNEY  Fourteen, naturally.

IRIS (*Quickly*)  And fourteen and fourteen?

SIDNEY (*Hesitates. She giggles and he nestles playfully against her legs*)  Twenty-eight.

IRIS  And twenty-eight and twenty-eight?

SIDNEY  (*Abruptly lost*)  Oh, c'mon. That's calculus . . .
(*Both laugh; he comes into her arms*)

IRIS  You don't know what it's like though—(*She is looking off, moving her fingers through his hair*) God, to
walk through those agency doors . . . There's always
some gal sitting on the other side, at a desk, you know,
with a stack of pictures practically up to the ceiling in
front of her. And they're always sort of bored, you know.
Even the polite ones, the nice ones, I mean, they can't
help it. They've seen five million and two like you and
by the time you come through that door they are *bored*.
And when you get past them, into the waiting room,
there they are—the five million and two sitting there,
waiting to be seen, and they look scared and mean and
as competitive as you do. And so you all sit there, and
you don't know anything: how you look, how you feel,
anything. And least of all do you know how they *want*
you to read. And when you get inside, you know less.
There are just those faces, Christ, half the time you almost wish that someone *would* make a pass or something;
you could deal with that, you know—that's from *life*.
You can deal with that and take your chances, but that almost never happens, at least not to me. All I ever see are
those blank director-producer-writer faces just staring
at you like a piece of unfinished wood, waiting for you
to show them something that will excite them, get them
to arguing about you . . . And you just stand there
knowing that you *can't*, no matter what, *do* it the way
you *did* it at home in front of the mirror, the brilliant
imaginative way you did it the night before. No matter
what. All you can think is: What the hell am I doing
standing here in front of these strangers, reading these
silly words and jumping around for that fairy like some
kind of nut . . . ? (*Looking up at him*) Sidney, I wish

I had it in me to—be *tougher*. (*Gently*) Like—like Gloria, I guess.

SIDNEY  Gloria wasn't tough *enough*, but let's not get into that.

IRIS  No, let's not! Anyhow, this is all a waste of time. You know and I know that I will never show up for that audition. I just don't want to see those faces again—Jesus, do I ever feel *twenty-nine!*

SIDNEY  Take down your hair for me, Iris . . .

IRIS (*Hoarsely, but not angrily*)  Christ, you're still so hooked on my hair . . . (*Laughter through tears*) It's spooky to be loved for your hair, don't you know that?

SIDNEY  Take down your hair . . . (*He reaches up behind and pulls the pins and it falls and there really is a great deal of it which almost covers her. Then he gets up and crosses to the phonograph, puts on a record and turns and waits; in a second or two a stinging mountain banjo hoe-down cuts into the silence. It swells and races: louder, swifter, filling room and theatre, this untamed music of the Bluegrass; in all the world there is none more vibrant*) Dance for me, Iris Parodus . . . Come down out of the hills and dance for me, Mountain Girl.

IRIS (*Lifting up her eyes to him from behind the hair*)  I just don't feel Appalachian tonight, Sid. It just won't work tonight—(*They look at one another a long moment. The music continues. During the above,* MAVIS BRYSON, IRIS' *older sister, has crossed to the door. She is a heavier, red-headed version of* IRIS, *more uptown and fashionable. She knocks and* IRIS *gets up and opens the door—then, as swiftly, shuts and bars it with her outstretched body. Meaning the dress box which her sister is carrying:*) I don't want it, I don't need it and I won't take it.

MAVIS   Just try it on. That's all I ask. (IRIS *reluctantly opens the door to admit her*) Hello, Sid, darling.

SIDNEY   Hello, Mav.

MAVIS   (*Blithely opens the box*)   Could you conceivably have the hootenanny at another time?
(*She turns off the phonograph*)

IRIS   We don't go to cocktail parties, Mavis. At least the kind where you dress like *that*. I want to tell you from the top, Mavis. This is not a good time. I am in no mood for the big sister-little sister hassle today—that's all—
(MAVIS *crosses and maternally stops* IRIS' *mouth in mid-speech with one hand*)

MAVIS   Just slip it on; I had it taken up for you. You'll look stunning in it. (*Confidentially, as she zips and buttons*) What's that awful sign? Iris, it looks so vulgar to have writing in your window. (IRIS *points to* SID *as the culprit*) What have you heard from Gloria?

IRIS   Not a word.

MAVIS   Here, let me smooth it down on you. Now, really, I can't tell a thing with those sticking out. (IRIS *pulls up her jeans as far as possible under the dress*) It's stunning! (*As, in fact, it is, because, whatever else,* MAVIS' *taste is simple and elegant and the dress* will *be handsome on* IRIS) Now, all you'll need for Easter is a new pair of sneakers.

SIDNEY   (*Appreciatively*)   You're coming along, Mavis, you're coming along. How about a drink?
(*He goes to the bar*)

MAVIS   You know, you're drinking a lot lately, Sidney. (*To* IRIS) I thought you always said that the Jews didn't drink.

SIDNEY (*Crossing from the bar*)   Mavis, I'm assimilated!

MAVIS   Where was Gloria when you heard from her?

IRIS   Miami Beach. (*Then, angry with herself*) And you're turning into a pure sneak—when it comes to digging.

MAVIS   And you weren't going to tell me. (*To* SIDNEY) Why can't she tell me? Miami Beach, my God! (*A beat*) Is she—?

IRIS   Of course she is, what do you think!

MAVIS (*Covering her eyes*)   The poor baby. All I can think of is that I am so glad Papa didn't live to—

IRIS   Look, Mavis, don't start. I just don't want the Gloria problem tonight. No matter what else—she is living *her* life and we are living *ours*. (*A beat*) So to speak.
(*She exits into the bedroom*)

MAVIS   Is she coming any time soon?

IRIS   She didn't say.
(*She enters again*)

MAVIS   When?

IRIS   Why can't you leave it alone, Mav? She won't see you when she does come. I guess she just can't take all those lectures any more.

MAVIS   And you don't lecture her—do you?

IRIS (*Pouring a drink*)   Mavis, if you weren't the world's greatest living anti-Semite you really should have married Sidney so that the two of you could have minded the world's business together. Jees!

MAVIS   That's not funny and I am not, for the four thousandth time, on anti-Semite. (*Swiftly*) You don't think that about me, do you, Sid? Why?

IRIS  Now, come on: you nearly had a heart attack when we got married. In fact, that's when you went into analysis. Now either you were madly in love with *me* or you hate the Jews—*pick!*

MAVIS  (*Glaring at her*)  Sometimes, Iris . . . (*A beat*) Did she say if she needs anything?

IRIS  Now, what could *she* need? She's the successful one. As a matter of fact—(*Winks*) I plan to put the old touch on her when she comes back.

MAVIS  Iris, you've gotten to be just plain dirty-minded.

IRIS  Look, I happen to have a sister who is a fancy call girl, a big-time, high-fashion whore. And I say so what? She's racking up thousands of tax-free dollars a year and it's her life so—who's to say?
      (*Having done with responsibility, she shrugs with confidence*)

MAVIS  (*Plaintively*)  It's your baby sister—how can you talk like that?

IRIS  Look, Mav, you're all hung up in the puritan ethic and all. That's not my problem.

MAVIS  (*Gazing at her*)  Is anything?

IRIS  Frankly, it's an anti-sex society—

SIDNEY  (*Exploding: enough is enough*)  Oh, shut up! I can't stand it when you start prattling every lame-brained libertarian slogan that comes along, without knowing what the hell you're talking about.

IRIS  (*With great indignation*)  I am entitled to my opinion, Sid-nee!

SIDNEY  (*Riding over her*)  You are *not!* Not so long as your opinion is based on stylish ignorance!

IRIS   Oh shut up, Sidney. On this subject you are the last of the Victorians.

SIDNEY   Not at all. You give old Victoria too much credit. If there was anything Victorians believed in it was that there *was* a place for the whore in society. The Victorians, sweet, were not against "sin," they were opposed to its *visibility*.

IRIS   All I know is this is an anti-sex soci—

SIDNEY   Look, Iris love—(*He grabs his head with frustration, wanting to make himself understood*) how can I put it to you, in front of Mavis, so that you get it? (MAVIS *rolls her eyes offendedly*) Victoria is dead so—like—it's just not that hard to *have* it, if you know what I mean, with your own girl friend. Dig? The guys running to the call girls are not pushing the sex revolution you think you are cheer-leading—they are indulging in a medieval notion of its disrespectability! Aside from which, there ought to be some human relationships on which commerce cannot put its grisly paws, doncha think?

MAVIS   The *things* you *think* you have to talk about!

IRIS   Who cares? My whole point is that I just don't care.

MAVIS   Sidney, Gloria is a very sick girl. She's not bad. She's very, very sick.

IRIS   Well, she's in analysis, for crying out loud! (*Both turn and look at her,* MAVIS *blankly,* SIDNEY *triumphant*) Well, she *says* he's helping her . . .

SIDNEY (*Eyeing* MAVIS; *to* IRIS—*cat and mouse*)   Oh, Iris, why don't you tell her the new development?

MAVIS (*To* SIDNEY)   What?

IRIS (*To* SIDNEY)   Fat mouth.

MAVIS (*Wheeling to her sister*)   What—?

IRIS (*To* MAVIS, *after another beat*) There's somebody we know who wants to marry her.

MAVIS (*Closing her eyes and leaning back as if some particular prayer has been answered at exactly this moment*) Praise his name! (*Opening her eyes*) Who? (*Anxiously —to* SIDNEY) One of your friends? (*He nods "yes." To* IRIS) What does he do?

SIDNEY (*Almost laughing*)   Well, as a matter of fact, he works in a bookstore.

MAVIS   In a *what?*

SIDNEY   He works in a bookstore. Part time. (*Almost breaking up now*) And as a matter of fact he used to be a Communist. (*His sister-in-law just stares at him with an open mouth and then looks to her sister; she then exhales a breath to demonstrate she feels that anything is possible here*) But it's all right, Mav. He's strictly an NMSH-type Red.

MAVIS   What kind is that?

SIDNEY (*Mugging*)   "No-more-since-Hungary."

MAVIS   Does he know what—ah . . .

SIDNEY   Does he know what Gloria does for a living? No. She told him the model bit.

MAVIS (*Hopefully*)   Listen, people like that, I mean Communists and things—they're supposed to be very *radical* . . . about things . . . well . . . (*Pathetically*) Well, aren't they?

SIDNEY   Who can say? There's "people like that" and "people like that."

MAVIS   Is he good-looking? What about Gloria? What does she . . . ?

SIDNEY (*Deliberately playing it*)    Uh, Mavis—

MAVIS    I knew this nightmare would have to end . . . It was just something that happened. It's the way the world is . . .

SIDNEY    He's also a Negro one, Mavis.

MAVIS    . . . these days. People don't know what to do with—(*Deep, guttural*) A *Negro what*—?

SIDNEY (*Still deliberately*)    A Negro Communist. That is to say, that he's not a Communist any more—but he's still a Negro.

MAVIS (*Looking from one to the other in open-mouthed silence*) Are you—(*A beat, as she turns her head back and forth again*) Are you—(*Finally, composing herself, she crosses to* SIDNEY) sitting there talking about . . . a *colored* boy?

SIDNEY (*Rapidly, wagging his finger*)    1964, Mavis, 1964! "Uncommitted Nations," "Free World!" Don't say it, honey, don't say it! We'll think you're not chic!

MAVIS    I don't think you're funny worth a damn! (*Looking from one to the other*) What do you think Gloria *is?!* (*The question hangs*) If this is your idea of some kind of bohemian joke I just don't think it's cute or clever or *anything*. I would rather see her—

SIDNEY (*Finishing it for her*)    —go on shacking up with any poor sick bastard in the world with a hundred bucks for a convention weekend!
    (*They glare at one another*)

MAVIS    Well now, listen, there are other men in the world! The last time I looked around me there were still some white men left in this world. Some fine ordinary upstanding plain decent very white men who were still looking to marry very white women . . .

(*During the above* DAVID RAGIN *has descended the stairway from his apartment overhead; now he pushes open the door and saunters in. An intense, slim, studied young man, of the latest fashionably casual dress and style, his mannerisms intend to suggest the entirely unmannered—but by choice. He is not in the least—"swish"*)

IRIS  Why hello, David, this is my sister, Mrs. Bryson.

MAVIS  How do you do.
(*He sits*)

IRIS  (*Facetiously, to him*)  I wouldn't bother, but she is from uptown where people knock on doors and all that jazz.

DAVID  (*He ignores* MAVIS *completely—wearily*)  You have any paper?

IRIS  The desk in the bedroom. (DAVID *exits into the bedroom*) David is a playwright who lives upstairs. And we are the government—and we subsidize him.
(MAVIS *nods and turns to* SIDNEY)

MAVIS  Well, *he's* sort of cute. Is he married?

SIDNEY  (*Simply*)  David's gay. (MAVIS *doesn't get it*) Queer. (*Still doesn't*) Homosexual. (*Gets it, drawing back*) Utterly.

MAVIS  Oh. (*Afterthought*)  Well, maybe she would want a rest . . . (DAVID *re-enters, crosses to the bar for a drink.* MAVIS *gathers up her things*) Well, I should get on. I've got to meet Fred. Did I tell you the news, Iris? Fred's been put in charge of the Folk River Dam Project. Now, what do you think of that?
(SIDNEY *is struck by this*)

IRIS   I think we are a talented family, obviously. Success in whatever we put our— (*Holding—to outrage the sister*) hands to.

MAVIS   Iris, not in front of people.

IRIS   David isn't people. He's a writer. And he worships prostitutes. He says they are the only *real* women—the core of life, as it were. Don't you, David?

MAVIS   The only thing about your flippancies, Iris, is that they don't solve any problems.

SIDNEY   (*Who has remained preoccupied by the earlier remark*) So old Fred is really doing all right for himself, huh?
         (IRIS *lifts her eyes at this knowingly*)

IRIS   Look out, Mavis, you're about to be tapped—

SIDNEY   You!

MAVIS   (*Pleasantly*)   Now Sidney, you know Fred won't invest in a night club.

IRIS   The night club is dead. Long live the newspaper.

SIDNEY   (*To* IRIS)   It wasn't a *night club*.

MAVIS   A newspaper? (*Great intake of breath and, immediately, maternal exhalation*) Oh, Sidney, Sidney, Sidney! You're thirty-seven years old. When are you going to grow up. (*Shaking her head*) A *newspaper*.

SIDNEY   (*Tightly*)   And what would a really "grown-up man" be doing with himself—in your enlightened opinion, Mavis?

MAVIS   Well, now, I know for a fact that your brother Manny has offered any number of times to get you a place in his firm. You're very lucky to have a brother in that kind of position, Sidney. A man like Fred had to do it all the hard way. I mean the *hard* way.

SIDNEY  And what will happen, Mavis, if I try, knowing better before I even open my mouth, to explain to you— that I consider my brother Manny a failure? I consider Fred a failure. I consider them to be men who accepted the alternatives that circumscribed them when they were born. I don't! I have a different set of alternatives—alternatives that I create! I either want to run my newspaper or—or go be an ambulance driver in Angola. I do not, for any reason, want to become part of Emmanuel Brustein, Inc.

MAVIS  (*Blinking, having heard nothing after "Angola"*) Be an ambulance driver—*where*, dear?

IRIS  But, Sidney, you can hardly drive . . .

SIDNEY  Oh, forget it!

IRIS  (*Hands on hips—to* DAVID) Talk about *bad* Hemingway.

MAVIS  Well, I really must go. (*To her sister, softly*) You *will* let me know when Gloria is coming?

IRIS (*A great sigh*)  Mavis—sooner or later you are going to have to learn that Gloria is living her life and doesn't want you to play Mama. Live and let live, that's all.

MAVIS  That's just a shoddy little way of trying to avoid responsibility in the world.

SIDNEY  Mavis—please go. It makes me *nervous* to be on your side! (*Bellowing*)

MAVIS  (*To* DAVID, *as she pulls on her gloves*) What are you writing, young man?

DAVID  Nothing you'd be interested in.

SIDNEY  Go on and tell her about your play, David. There is nothing else she can hear that's shocking today.

DAVID  Cool it, Sidney.

SIDNEY  David is engaged in the supreme effort of trying to wrest the theatre from the stranglehold of Ibsenesque naturalism, are you not, David? (DAVID *just stares indifferently at both of them. He is above, he feels, such repartee*) As a matter of fact he has a play in production right now.

MAVIS  Oh, how nice! Is there something in it for Iris?

IRIS  You're not supposed to do that, Mavis.

SIDNEY  Besides, there are only two characters in David's play and they are both male and married to each other and the entire action takes place in a refrigerator.

MAVIS (*Eyeing* DAVID *coolly and edging off a little*)    I see.

DAVID  *I* didn't try to tell you what it was about. (*He has wandered to the sign. He studies it and turns to* SIDNEY, *shaking his head*) And what have you got against the "machine" this week?

SIDNEY  Didn't you ever read *Huckleberry Finn*, David?

IRIS (*Setting out the supper dishes; indicating her husband*) He's Huck this week.

SIDNEY (*Shouting: raspy-voiced, affecting Hal Holbrook affecting the garrulous old man of conscience*)    And therefore "continually happy"! It's a machine, David! With a boss! A highly entrenched boss. Don't believe in bosses. Believe in independent men, like old Huckleberry!

DAVID (*Shaking his head*)    That's what I thought. Sidney, don't you know yet "the good guys" and "the bad guys" went out with World War Two?

MAVIS  Well, sure. When you come right down to it, one politician *is* just like another.

SIDNEY  (*Rocking with his hands in prayerful fashion*) And a new religion is upon the West and it has only one hymn: (*Intoning a mock Mass*) "We are all guilty . . . Father Camus, we are all guilty . . . *Ipso facto,* all guilt is equal . . . Therefore we shall in clear conscience abstain from the social act . . . and even the social thought . . ."

DAVID  (*Glaring at him*)  Go ahead: kid it. It's easier to kid it than face the pain in it.

SIDNEY  (*Possessed by an all-consuming vision of the omnipotent catchword*)  Ah, *"Pain!"* "Pain" in recognizing those dark tunnels which lead back to our primate souls, groveling about—(*He rises to a half-stoop, arms dangling; and ape-like throughout this speech, he crosses to, and up onto, the coffee table and then the sofa*) in caves of sloth. The savage soul of man from whence sprang, in the first place, the Lord of the Flies, Beelzebub himself! (*Rather shouting*) Man, dark gutted creature of ancestral—(*Leaping over the back of the sofa and lifting his hands in Bela Lugosi style*) cannibalism and mysterious all-consuming eeevil! Ahhhhhh. (*Through the bars of the rocking chair he snarls and claws at all of them to burlesque this philosophy*) Yahhhh! The Shadow knows.

MAVIS  I just said to Fred this morning: "Say what you like, it's always something different down at Iris and Sid's."

DAVID  (*A little roused finally*)  Well, what is the virtue of getting one boss out and putting another one in?

SIDNEY   The virtue—the virtue, my dear boy, if you will pardon the rhetoric, is to participate in some expression of the people about the way things are, that's all.

DAVID (*Waving around, with derision*)   Well, hel-lo, out there! (*He shakes his head*) Well, that's what comes from reading too much Shaw.

SIDNEY (*Angry*)   Yah, well. Speaking of the drama, David, what *is* your play about?

DAVID   You read it. You tell me.

SIDNEY   No, you tell *me*.

DAVID   It's not for me to say.

SIDNEY (*For him*)   ". . . each person will get from it what he brings to it?" Right?

DAVID (*As befits the present circumstance*)   To be real simple-minded about it—yes.

SIDNEY   Then tell me this: What makes *you* the artist and the *audience* the consumer if they have to write your play for you?

DAVID   I know what it's about. (SIDNEY *merely looks at him—querulously*) I told you, my plays have to speak for themselves.

SIDNEY   But to *whom?* For *whom?* For whom are they written, and, above all, *why* are they written?

DAVID (*Getting up; his host is beyond belief*)   You hate my kind of writing because it goes beyond the walls of Ibsen's prisons and Shaw's lectures—that's *your* problem, Sid.

MAVIS (*Who has been turning from one to the other throughout, fascinated, incredulous, and trying all the while to get a word in edgewise herself*)   I just don't know whatever happened to simple people with simple problems in literature.

SIDNEY (*Riding right over her. To* DAVID, *grandiosely*) Oh come now, don't just choose the members of my team that you feel are most vulnerable. Go for my stars, too, David. Or are you afraid to tackle the masks of Euripedes and the shadows and hymns of Shakespeare? (*They are almost toe to toe*)

DAVID Are you retreating from Ibsen and Shaw?

SIDNEY *Not* on your life! But are you retreating before Euripedes and Shakespeare!

IRIS I get so tired of this endless chess game!

DAVID (*Heading for the door*) All I can say is that I write because I have to and what I have to. You don't know anything about it. Whatever you think of it, Sidney, I write. I squeeze out my own juices and offer them up. I may be afraid, but *I* write. (ALTON *re-enters with paper bags and the flowers*) Well, Dr. Castro, I presume.

ALTON (*In kind*) Jean Genet, as I live and breathe. (*They shake hands*)

SIDNEY (*Taking the beer*) Did you bottle it yourself?

IRIS (*Taking her flowers, and exchanging glances with her husband about what they are setting up*) David, are you going to stay to eat?

DAVID Why not?

IRIS (*As they sit down to eat*) Mav?

MAVIS No—dear! I've got to meet Fred. (*Reluctantly; her matchmaker eyes have not left* ALTON *since his entrance*)

IRIS  Alton, I'd like you to meet my sister Mavis. Mavis, this is Alton Scales.

MAVIS  How do you do.

ALTON  How do you do.
(*As he crosses, she stands admiring him*)

MAVIS (*To* SIDNEY)  Is *he* married?

SIDNEY  No.

MAVIS  He isn't—ahhh—(*Meaning homosexual*)

SIDNEY  We're not sure yet!

MAVIS (*A trill in her voice*)  Good night, Mr. Scales.

ALTON  Good night.

SIDNEY (*With deliberate casualness*)  Oh, Mavis, this is the chap we were just telling you about. (*She looks blank*) From the bookstore.
(*There is silence; all except* DAVID *know the meaning of the moment for* MAVIS. *They variously concentrate on the food and exchange superior and rather childish glances; letting her live through the moment of discomfort. She turns slowly around to face the youth again. It is a contemporary confrontation for which nothing in her life has prepared her. There is silence and much deliberate chewing and eye-rolling. For his part,* ALTON *is prepared for virtually anything—to smile and kiss and be kissed, to scream or be screamed at, or to be struck and strike back. He is silent. Presently, this woman of conformist helplessness does the only thing she can, under these circumstances, she gags on her words so that they are hardly audible and repeats what she has already said*)

MAVIS  Oh. How do you do.

ALTON  (*Raising his eyes evenly*)  How do you do.
    (*He turns and reaches for the food.* MAVIS *stands
    thoughtfully, watching this table in bohemia, the
    random art of the setting: a huge leafy salad, a bot-
    tle of wine, some candles, thick European bread; a
    portrait of diners who would sit down together only
    here: the taciturn young homosexual, the young
    Negro who is to be a kinsman, her sister, hair
    down, seemingly at home here; her brother-in-law,
    who presides*)

SIDNEY  (*Swiftly, with open-hearted malice as she heads for
    the door*)  Well, Alton, now you have met Mavis.
    There she is: the Bulwark of the Republic. The Mother
    Middleclass itself standing there revealed in all its tow-
    ering courage. (*There are snickers of delight from the
    diners; he has even perhaps lifted his wine glass to her
    for these insults. Dismissal*)  Mavis, go or stay—but
    we're eating. (*Slapping at* ALTON'S *paws*)  One to a man.
    One to a man!
      (MAVIS *halts and turns to face them*)

MAVIS  (*She is silent so long that they look up at her, still
    with varying degrees of amusement; then—*)  I am
    standing here and I am thinking: how smug it is in bo-
    hemia. I was taught to believe that—(*Near tears*) crea-
    tivity and great intelligence ought to make one expansive
    and understanding. That if ordinary people, among
    whom I have the sense at least to count myself, could
    not expect understanding from artists and—whatever it
    is that *you* are, Sidney—then where indeed might we
    look for it at all—in this quite dreadful world. (*She al-
    most starts out, but thinks of the cap*)  Since you have all
    so busily got rid of God for us.
      (*She turns and exits*)

IRIS (*At once, unaffected by this eloquence, although* SID-
NEY *is somewhat*)  So—(*Knocking him in the ribs*)
put that in your pipe and smoke it, old dear!

DAVID (*Also unaffected*)  Some day I really must look
into what it is that makes the majority so oppressively
defensive under certain circumstances.

ALTON (*The most affected*)  Oh quit it!

DAVID (*Turning on him*)  And now the gentle heart of the
oppressed will also admonish us.

ALTON  Turn off, Fag Face!

DAVID (*Glaring at him*)  Isn't it marvelous, some people
have their Altons and some have their Davids. You
should be grateful to the Davids of the world, Alton: we
at least provide a distraction from the cross you so nobly
and (*Bitterly*) so *deliberately* bear.
(ALTON *jumps up and heads for the door*)

IRIS  Where are you going—?

ALTON  I'm sorry if it makes me unsophisticated in your
eyes; but after a while, hanging out with queers gets on
my nerves!
(ALTON *slams out of the house.* DAVID *puts down
his fork slowly and sits quietly.* IRIS *notices and
suddenly reaches out and touches him gently on the
hand*)

IRIS  Eat your supper, David. Alton's a big kid. You
know.

DAVID (*Turning his eyes on her slowly, steadily. A trap,
casually*)  *You* accept queers, don't you, Iris . . . ?

IRIS (*An innocent shrug*)  Sure.

DAVID  Yes, because you accept *anything*. But—I am not

*anything.* I hope he never has to explore the *why* of his discomfort.

SIDNEY (*Winding up big*)  Oh no· . . . Come on, David! Don't start that jazz with me tonight. Is that the best you can do? I mean it! Is that really it? Anybody who attacks one—*is* one? Can it, boy!

IRIS (*A whine*)  Sidney. Can't you be still sometimes . . . ?

SIDNEY (*Raising his hand in a definite "stop" sign*)  Oh no! I mean it. I have had it with that bit. I am bored with the syndrome.

IRIS  Who cares!

SIDNEY (*Shouting at* IRIS)  Is that all you can ever say? Who cares, who cares? Let the damn bomb fall, if somebody wants to drop it, 'tis the last days of Rome, so rejoice ye Romans and swill ye these last sick hours away! Well, I admit it: I *care!* I care about it all. It takes too much energy *not* to care. Yesterday I counted twenty-six gray hairs in the top of my head—all from trying *not* to care. And you, David, you have now written fourteen plays about not caring, about the isolation of the soul of man, the alienation of the human spirit, the desolation of all love, all possible communication. When what you really want to say is that you are ravaged by a society that will not sanctify your particular sexuality!

DAVID  It seems to have conveniently escaped your attention that *I* am the insulted party here.

SIDNEY  If somebody insults you—sock 'em in the jaw. If you don't like the sex laws, attack 'em, I think they're silly. You wanna get up a petition? I'll sign one. Love little fishes if you want. *But,* David, please get over the notion that your particular "thing" is something that only the deepest, saddest, the most nobly tortured can know about. It ain't—(*Spearing into the salad*) it's just one kind of sex—that's all. And, in my opinion—(*Revolving his fork*) the universe turns regardless.

    (DAVID *looks at him for a long time, and then goes to the door*)

IRIS (*Going after* DAVID) What's the matter with everybody? David, come on, eat your supper.

DAVID If you don't mind, I really can't stand the proud sociological oversimplifications which are beginning to abound—(*He nods to the sign in the window*) in this house. I would rather eat alone.

    (*He exits abruptly*)

IRIS (*Closing the door*) Well, that was some dinner party, thank you. What's with you lately, Sidney? Why do you have to pick at everybody? Where did you get the idea it was up to you to improve everybody? Leave people the hell alone!

SIDNEY (*In a fierce mood*) I don't try to improve people. Or, at least, you can't tell it by you.

IRIS (*Properly hurt*) All right, Sid, one of these days you've got to decide who you want—Margaret Mead or Barbry Allen! I won't play both! As a matter of fact it's getting pretty clear—that I've got to decide too. (*Under her breath, to herself*) God, have I got to decide!

SIDNEY The least excuse and you haul up the old self-pitying introspection bit.

IRIS (*Through her teeth*) What makes you think anybody can live with your insults?

SIDNEY The world needs insults!

IRIS (*The last straw*) Sweet Heaven.
    (*She starts to clear the table*)

SIDNEY (*Turning and noticing her exasperation with him*) I'm sorry. (*He moves to help; she rejects this. Several beats*) There's a rally. You wanna go?

IRIS  I told you, don't expect me to get involved with that stuff!

SIDNEY  All right, all right. You wanna go over to the Black Knight and have a couple of beers?

IRIS  No, I don't want to go over to the Black Knight and have a couple of beers.

SIDNEY  Well then, suppose *you* just come up with *something, anything* that you would like to do. It will be your first achievement in this entire marriage.

IRIS  What does it do for you, Sid? Picking at me like that. Look, why don't you just go to your rally? And leave poor old Iris alone.
　　(*She turns on the phonograph*)

SIDNEY (*Grabs his jacket and heads for the door; then halts, hand on the knob, flings his jacket to the floor— helpless. More to himself than her:*) Leave "poor old Iris alone"—and watch her turn quietly and willingly into a vegetable.
　　(IRIS *sits on the window seat, looking off, into the street—as a haunting guitar cuts the silence*)

IRIS (*Softly, fighting back tears*)  It's getting different, Sidney, our fighting. Something's either gone out of it or come into it. I don't know which. But it's something that keeps me from wanting to make up with you a few hours later. That's bad, isn't it?

SIDNEY  Yeah, that's bad.
　　(*He turns and looks at his wife; she is crying—then picks up his jacket and starts out*)

IRIS (*Crying out*)  Then let's put up a fight for it, Sidney!
I mean it—let's fight like hell for it.

> (*He halts at the outer staircase and stands clutch-ing the rail and looking back toward the room where his wife sits looking after him, as the light fades on all but the two of them and the voice of Joan Baez, singing "All My Trials," fills the dark-ening stage*)

*Curtain*

# ACT II

## SCENE ONE

*Time: Just before daybreak. The following day.*

*At rise: Only the faint light of pre-dawn illumines the outside staircase landing over the* BRUSTEIN *doorway; here* SIDNEY *lies, on his back, arms underhead, one leg doubled up and the other resting on his knee. New York at this hour is a world known to few of its inhabitants, and the silence of the great sleeping city is only accentuated by its few familiar sounds: the occasional moan of a foghorn on the Hudson or, now and then, the whirr of tires or clatter of a milk truck. The apartment is dark.*

*Presently* SIDNEY *sits up, picks up his banjo and, legs dangling over the patio, begins to pick it. The melody seems surely drawn from that other world which ever beckons him, a wistful, throbbing mountain blues. As he plays the lighting shifts magically, and nonrealistically, to create the mountain of his dreams. Gone is even the distant foghorn; he is no longer in the city. After several phrases of this, the music soars and quickens into a vibrant, stinging hoedown and the* IRIS-*of-his-Mind appears, barefooted, with flowing hair and mountain dress, and mounts the steps. She*

273

*embraces him and then, as by the lore of hill people, is possessed by these rhythms, and dances in the shadows before him. The dance is a moving montage of all the bits and pieces of dance Americana: the dip for the oyster, the grand right and left.* SIDNEY'S *banjo drives her on until both these spirits are exhausted and the mountain nymph gives him a final kiss and flees. He sits on, spent, plucks idly at the instrument. Now a light appears in the apartment's bedroom doorway and his wife enters through it, belting her robe, yawning, rubbing her eyes.*

IRIS   Sid—? (*He does not reply or even hear her*) Sidney? (*She switches on the lamp. For a moment stands blankly, then goes to the door and leans out*)   What are you doing up there? You'll wake the neighbors.

SIDNEY (*In the same unbroken reverie*)   They can't hear me, Iris.

IRIS (*At the foot of the steps*)   Oh, Sidney, you're a nut. C'mon down, I'll make you some coffee.
   (*She fishes out her cigarettes and lights one*)

SIDNEY (*Shakes his head*)   Listen! Do you hear the brook? There is nothing like clear brook water at daybreak. And when you drink, it gives back your own image.

IRIS (*Charmed in spite of herself*)   You'll catch cold, Sidney. It's too early for games. Come to bed.

SIDNEY   No, Iris. Come up. (*She does, as he speaks; and, finally, kneels beside him*) Look at the pines—look at the goddamn pines. You can taste and feel the scent of them. And if you look down, down through the mist, you will make out the thin line of dawn far distant. There's not another soul for miles, and if you listen, *really* listen —you might almost hear yourself think.

IRIS (*Surveying the realm, gently laughing*)   This is some mountain.

SIDNEY (*Playful proprietary pride*)  It's a small mountain
—but it's ours.

IRIS  Sidney . . . how much is fourteen and fourteen?
(*She smiles and touches his face—and, for the moment, enters fully into his dream*)

SIDNEY (*Fondling her hair*)  "Nymph in . . . all . . .
my Orisons remembered."

IRIS (*Looking up at him thoughtfully*)  It really gets to
you, doesn't it? Being here. You really are happy? You'd
like to live right here, in the woods, wouldn't you?

SIDNEY  Yes. Yes. I would.

IRIS  And you're afraid to ask me to do something like
that, aren't you? (*No answer*) Afraid I'll look around at
the woods and the brook and say, *"Here? Live?"* (*They
both laugh at her mugging of her own attitude*) And the
worst of it is you'd be right. I would say exactly that. I
wouldn't want to live here. (*Drooping her head a bit*)
I'm sorry. The truth is that I am cold and bored. I feel
like watching television. I feel like having a swinging argument. I feel like sitting in a stupid movie or, or even a
night club, a real stupid night club with dirty jokes and
bad dancers. (*Looking at him*) I've changed on you,
haven't I, Sid? This particular mountain girl has been
turning into an urban wastelander. (*Rather sweetly, still
looking at him*) Sorry. (*Several beats, she has been
thinking of this*) Most of all, I hate my hair. (*A beat*)
The things you don't know about me! (*A little laugh*)
Did you know, for instance, that you're the reason I
wear it like this in the first place? (*Shaking her head with
the little laugh again*) There's a different style of "man
trap" in every kind of woman. When I first came here,
you know, I was working, dancing in this funny little old
nothing of a sawed-off club, you know. And like I

thought that the men who came there were not the ones that I came to the (*Charade-style quote marks*) big city —to meet. I mean they were the kind that you could meet back home. So one of the girls who worked there and knew all the this-and-that listened to me and she said, "Well, honey, if that's what you're looking for, you've gotta go down to the Black Knight Tavern and sit." (*Smiling*) "Let your hair grow and go down to the Black Knight Tavern." Sounds like a folk song. Well, anyhow, the fourth time I went there, remember, it was about to . . . here. (*Marking off the shorter place*) And there you were, just like that, sitting in that corner booth with—(*Remembering*) Marty and Alt, wasn't it? Yes, it was Marty and Alt. And there you were sitting there, "holding forth." And I said to m'self: There's the one. After that I started eating vitamins to make m'hair grow faster. (*He laughs a soft, delighted "Oh, Iris!"*) So, s'help me! It's true! This same girl who told me everything, she got these vitamins for me too. And, well—*something* worked.

SIDNEY    I'm charmed.

IRIS    Women are a mess, aren't they? I mean they get these *fantastic* IDEAS about things, I mean life and all, when they're like three, you know. And nothing, I mean nothing gets it out of you. When I got off that train from Trenersville ten years ago I knew one thing in this world: I wanted to meet men who were as—as different from Papa as—as possible.

SIDNEY    (*Taking her hand*)    Listen, Iris. Listen to the woods. Let's go for a walk.

IRIS    (*Huddling close*)    It's too cold. And dark. And the woods frighten me.

SIDNEY    All right then, let's just go into the cabin and I'll make us a bang-up fire and some of the hottest coffee ever brewed. (*She just looks at him*) You just want to go back to the city, don't you?

IRIS  Yes.

SIDNEY  You really hate it here in the woods?

IRIS  Yes. (*The tears come; tears of frustration, as she does not know exactly why. Gesturing around*) I was born in country like this, you know, the real thing. I mean you didn't drive out anywhere to sort of *see* it. You just sat down on the back porch and—there it was. Something to run from; something to get the hell away from as fast as you could. All of us felt like that, me, Mav— Gloria.

SIDNEY  Then you've always hated coming up here. I didn't know that.

IRIS  (*Sort of a painful whine born of the effort to really make him finally understand*)  No, I didn't *always* hate it . . . the first couple of years I just wanted to do what you wanted to do, be where you were—you know, sort of wild and romantic the way it was supposed to be—(*A great burst of frustration*) I mean, I thought it was going to be different. Papa was so crude and stupid . . . You know, I never heard my father make an abstract thought in his life; and, well, he had plenty of time to think, if you know what I mean. Didn't work that steady. And each of us; I think we've sort of grown up wanting some part of Papa that we thought was the thing missing in him. I wanted somebody who could, well, think; Mavis wanted somebody steady and ordinary. And Gloria, well, you know—rich men. Lots of them. (*Lifting up her hand anticipating*) I know you're going to tell me that's parlor analysis, and it is, but—

SIDNEY   I'm not saying anything, Iris. I'm listening. I really am. I am listening to you.

IRIS   And now something is happening to me, changing me. Since we've been married. Sometimes, Sidney, I think if—if I hear any more talk from Alton and Max and David and—you—I'll shrivel up and die from it. You know what I want, Sidney? I am twenty-nine and I want to begin to know that when I die more than ten or a hundred people will know the difference. I want to *make* it, Sid. *Whatever* that means and *however* it means it: That's what I want. (*He is nodding; he genuinely understands and is deeply pained by it*) Anyhow, what does it do for you, Sid? To come up here and talk to your— what do you call them—

SIDNEY (*Smilingly*)   My trolls.

IRIS   Yeah. 'Cause I tried having a few words with 'em and like what they had to say to me was nothing.

SIDNEY (*Looking around*)   Coming here makes me believe that the planet is mine again. In the primeval sense. Man and earth and earth and man and all that. You know. That we have just been born, the earth and me, and are just starting out. There is no pollution, no hurt; just me and this ball of minerals and gases suddenly shot together out of the cosmos.

IRIS (*Looking at him, head tilted puppy style, mouth ajar*)   Jeees.

SIDNEY   I love you very much.
       (*They are quiet; he leans over gently and kisses her. After a long beat:*)

IRIS   Take me back to the city, please, Sid.
       (*He gets up and puts his banjo over his shoulder and takes her hand and they start down the steps—*

*while at the same time the magic that is* SIDNEY'S *World fades and the lighting returns to normal. A passing truck guns its motor and day breaks on the city)*

IRIS (*At the foot of the steps. Remembering*)    Sidney, it's Tuesday: you've got to move the car!
     (*They start to go in*)

*Dimout*

## SCENE TWO

*Time: Early evening in late summer.*

*In the darkness—and in sharp contrast to the prior mood —a soundtruck loudspeaker blares out the buoyant, bois- terous strains of "The Wally O'Hara Campaign Song"— sung by a folk group to the accompaniment of booming guitars and the occasional cheers and comments of the crowd, which joins in on the chorus.*

## THE WALLY O'HARA CAMPAIGN SONG

Sing out the old, sing in the new,
It's your ballot and it's got a lot of work to do;
Sing out the old, sing in the new,
Wally O'Hara is the man for you!

CHORUS Wally O'Hara, Wally O'Hara
    Wally O'Hara is the man—for—you!

Sweep out the old, sweep in the new,
We've got a lot of sweeping to do;
Sweep out the old, sweep in the new,
Wally O'Hara is the man for you!

CHORUS (*Repeats*)
    Who knows the people, every one?
    (Wally! Wally!)
    Who knows the job that must be done?
    (Wally! Wally!)
    Who is the man to beat the machine?
    Who'll clean up this district and keep it clean?
    (Wally! Wal-ly O'Hara!)

Vote out the old, vote in the new,
It's your ballot and it's got a lot of work to do;
Vote out the old, vote in the new,
Wally O'Hara is the man for you!

CHORUS (*Repeats*)

*The song is not performed for its own sake, but rather
as it might be by local talent from a touring vehicle in the
campaign's heat; and, inevitably too, the speaker system is
overworked, with resultant static and crackle from time to
time. Still, what is lacking in polish is more than made up
in fervor, and the tone is festive. The song should not be
heard in its entirety, but gained in and out as indicated at
appropriate moments. As the lights come up* SIDNEY *and*
WALLY *come on from the right in animated conversation.
Each carries an armload of leaflets, and* SIDNEY, *a rolled-up
flag.* WALLY *has his free arm about* SIDNEY'S *shoulder and
is agitated, moist-eyed.* SIDNEY *is more bemused. The
soundtruck music moves off in the distance.*

WALLY (*With self-absorbed wonder*)  No, Sid, I mean it.
You can feel it in the air. There's a difference this time, a
rumbling in the streets. My God, did you see the reception we got on Christopher Street? I tell you we really
have underestimated the whole thing. (*Looking out at
the audience*) I mean it, we are going to win. Sidney,
baby, we are going to win this thing, *I am going to win!*
(*He slaps* SIDNEY *on the back, crosses and exits
with the flag*)

SIDNEY (*With disbelieving eyes. To the audience*) It's a
disease. We are at that point in a campaign which ushers
in the dementia of the dark horse. Now comes the delu-
sion, as ancient as elections themselves, which takes over
the soul of the candidate. There is nothing to be done
about it: it is in the nature of the type. He really thinks
he is going to win. (*Whistling the campaign song, he*

*balances his leaflets in the doorway and fishes for his keys
—as* DAVID *enters, reading a newspaper and carrying a
batch of others. To* DAVID) So?

DAVID (*Dryly, as if above self-appreciation*)　"A complete
unqualified hit."
　　　(*He hands* SIDNEY *the paper*)

SIDNEY　I'll be damned. Well, congratulations. Come on,
I'll give you a drink.
　　　(*They enter*)

IRIS (*Menacingly, from the bedroom*)　Sid? Did you say
it was all right for Alton to leave the loudspeaker system
in the *bathtub*?

SIDNEY　That clown. (*The phone rings. He picks it up*)
No, no, no . . . (*Finding it on a wall map of the Village*) You're in the Eighth Election District. (*He hangs
up*)

IRIS (*Over part of the above—in a tizzy*)　And *who* gave
this number as the *canvassing* headquarters? (*Shouting*)
I haven't been off the phone all afternoon!

SIDNEY (*To* IRIS, *changing the subject*)　Did you see the
reviews? We don't have to put on any more. We *know* a
celebrity.

DAVID　Will you cut it out.

SIDNEY　Just listen—(*He reads aloud*) ". . . Mr. Ragin
has found a device which transcends language itself. In
his work all façade fades, all panaceas dissolve, and the
ultimate questions are finally asked of existence itself . . ." (*The obvious joke on himself*) See. Just like I
always said. (SIDNEY *gives him his drink. They toast.*
SIDNEY *looks about the room for something. Then to*
IRIS, *ever so sweetly, afraid of rousing the dead*) Oh,

Iris, did they leave the mailing piece? We've got all those envelopes to stuff.

IRIS (*Shrieking, a veritable avenging Fury by now*)   Sidney, if you don't get that trash out of here *today*, I'm going to *burn* the apartment down!!!
>    (SIDNEY *finds the enclosures, stacks them on the table and begins stuffing envelopes, whistling as he does—all but ignoring* DAVID)

DAVID   By your recent antics I take it you believe there is something to be accomplished by all this? Presumably for the good?

SIDNEY (*Not taking the bait, gaily*)   C'mon, David. There is work to be done. Lend a hand. (*The phone rings. He answers*) Yes? No, it's *not* a mistake . . . Fourth Street *does* cross Eleventh Street.
>    (*He hangs up, goes back to work*)

DAVID (*Studying him as a specimen*)   Well, I don't attack you for it. I know it is something most men, even thinking men, resist long after they know better.

SIDNEY (*Between envelopes, not even raising his eyes*)   You mean that Zarathustra has spoken—and God is dead?

DAVID   Yes.

SIDNEY   "Progress" is an illusion and the only reality is—nothing?

DAVID   You surprise me. Can one debate it?

SIDNEY (*Finally sitting back for this; he feels himself in fine fettle*)   One can observe that it is the debate which is, for all human purposes, beside the point. The *debate* which is absurd. The "why" of why we are here is an intrigue for adolescents; the "how" is what must command the living. Which is why I have lately become an insurgent again.

> (*Back to work. The phone rings again—and this
> time* IRIS *comes shrieking out of the bedroom: one
> more call and she* will *burn the apartment down!
> She wears the dress* MAVIS *bought*)

IRIS    *Sid-nee*—(*Noticing* DAVID *for the first time*) David. (*Genuinely*) My God, those reviews! It's marvelous. How do you feel?

SIDNEY (*On the phone*)    You don't say? Right . . . right . . . right.

DAVID (*To* IRIS. *Embarrassed by her display*)    Please. Well, I've got to go to work.

IRIS    Work? Already? Aren't you just going to bask awhile or something?

DAVID (*Sadly*)    Doing what? See you.
> (*Exits*)

SIDNEY (*Hangs up*)    You know what, the craziest thing is happening to Wally . . . that clown is actually—(*As the fact of* MAVIS' *dress dawns on him*) Well, get you!

IRIS    I look pretty all right in this—huh, Sid?

SIDNEY    Sure, if you like the type. I like you in other things better.

IRIS    I know. I'm going out tonight, Sidney.

SIDNEY    Yeah? Where? (*Not thinking about that too much*) You know not one, not one of the entire collection I've surrounded myself with . . .

IRIS    I talked to Lucille Terry today. She's having a cocktail party.

SIDNEY    Lucille Terry? *Lucille Terry!* Where in the name

of God did she pop up from? I didn't know that you still saw each other.

IRIS   We haven't in years. But, you know, just like that people suddenly call each other up. So just like that she called me up last week about this party she was having.

SIDNEY   (*His hand on the phone; he couldn't care less*) How is Lucy? Lemme see now, gotta call Mickey Dafoe, put on the old Establishment voice. "Hello, Mr. Dafoe, well, how are you, sir—" Fix me a drink, why doncha, honey?

IRIS   (*Crossing to the pantry; in a muted voice*)   Lucy didn't call me, Sid. I called *her*.

SIDNEY   (*Still thinking more about the call he has to make*) Yeah? You know I really hate to give fuel to Alton's narrow view of the world, but there is turning out to be a surprising amount of validity to his notions of base and superstructure. Two banks, a restaurant and three real estate firms have already canceled ads since we've come out for Wally . . .

IRIS   (*Disinterested, bringing him his drink*)   Oh, really— (*The phone rings*) Interesting.

SIDNEY   (*Picking it up*)   Yes, Renee . . . She says what? . . . *Sure*, O'Hara could be an Italian name . . . Or his *mother's* Italian. (*Hangs up, to* IRIS) Well, she *could* be. (*Noticing her standing there, finally just looking at him quietly*) Aw, I'm sorry, honey, I really am, but I just don't feel like going to any party tonight. Especially the uptown scene. Not tonight. (*He is taking the entire situation lightly*) Tell Lucy we love her but no.

IRIS   (*Starkly, staring down at him*)   I wasn't asking you to come with me, Sidney.
         (*He drinks, slowly absorbs this last remark and, for*

*the first time, reacts with some sense of the porten-
tousness of the moment*)

SIDNEY    Oh?

IRIS    That's sort of the point. I—I am going alone.

SIDNEY    Oh. (*They are both quiet; neither looking at the
other; the awkwardness shouts*) Well, hell, so you're going to a party. Great. You should do things alone sometimes. Everybody should. What are we acting so funny
about it for?

IRIS    Because we know it isn't just *a* party. It's the fact that
I want to go. That I called Lucy.

SIDNEY (*Very worried*)    Well, don't worry about it. It's
okay. Just have a nice time, that's all.

IRIS (*Sadly*)    Would you—would you like me to make you
some supper before I go?

SIDNEY (*Rising and crossing away not to face her*)    Uh—
no. No. Thanks. Wally and I are due on MacDougal
Street in an hour. We'll go out with the kids after or
something.

IRIS    You could have them here. There's—there's a lot of
stuff in the box and—plenty of beer.

SIDNEY (*Getting it fully*)    Is there?

IRIS    Yes. I'm sorry, Sid.

SIDNEY    You're planning on being late, aren't you?

IRIS    I think it'll be kind of late.

SIDNEY (*Finally*)    Who's going to be at this party, Iris?

IRIS    How do I know who's going to be there? Lucy's
friends.

SIDNEY  Lucy's friends. The "would-be" set, as I recall it.

IRIS  Huh?

SIDNEY  The "would-be" set, would-be actresses, would-be producers. The would-bes tend to collect around Lucy a lot.

IRIS  Some of her friends are pretty successful.

SIDNEY  Like Ben Asch?
    (*She wheels and they exchange a violent conversation without words*)

IRIS  (*Getting into her shoes*) · Look, Sid; let's make an agreement based on the recognition of reality. The reality being that the big thaw has set in with us and that we don't know what that means yet. So let's make some real civilized kind of agreement that until—well—until we know just what we feel, I mean about everything—let's not ask each other a whole lot of slimy questions.

SIDNEY  I'll ask all the slimy questions I want! Listen, Iris, have you been seeing this clown or something?

IRIS  Only once—after the time I told you.

SIDNEY  Once is all it takes.

IRIS  He thinks he can help me.

SIDNEY  Do what?

IRIS  Break in, that's what!

SIDNEY  Then why didn't he see *us?*

IRIS  I don't know, Sidney. I guess he was under the impression that I was a big girl now.

SIDNEY  I'll bet!

IRIS    But none of this is the main point, Sid. The main
point is that I feel I want to do something else with my
life. Other than—

SIDNEY    Other than what?

IRIS    Other than—this. Other than conversation about the
Reformation; other than conversations about Albert
Camus. Other than scraping together enough pancake
money to study with every has-been actor who's teaching
now because he can't work any more. There has to be
another way.

SIDNEY    From the has-beens to the would-bes. I'll admit
there is a progression there!

IRIS    Ben knows some extremely influential people. People who have been around—people who *do* the things
they mean to do.

SIDNEY    Where?

IRIS    In the theatre and in politics too! Especially in politics. People who are not just talkers—but doers. Who
do not take on a newspaper they cannot even afford and
run it into the ground for a hopeless campaign. And for
what? For Wally? If even half of what they say about
Wally is true—

SIDNEY    Oh? And just what do "they" say?
    (*He waits, knowing as he does, there is nothing
    she can say*)

IRIS (*Trapped*)    Well, I don't know about any of this, but
Lucy thinks—

SIDNEY (*Holding up one hand; the issue is closed*)    Right
the first time, Iris! You *don't* know.

IRIS    Sidney, this is not the Silver Dagger you're getting
into. These people are sharks.

SIDNEY (*With finality; father knows best*) Look, Iris, I'll make a deal with you: You let me fight City Hall and I'll stay out of Shubert Alley.

IRIS (*Quietly; she has had it*)   All right, Sidney.

SIDNEY   And stop ducking the main point: What is this glorious doer Ben Asch going to do for you?

IRIS   As a matter of fact he's already got me some work.

SIDNEY   Oh—why haven't you mentioned it? What show?

IRIS (*Defensively*)   It isn't exactly a show—but it *is* acting. Sort of. (*He stares at her*) It's a TV commercial . . .

SIDNEY (*Laughing*)   Oh, Iris, Iris.

IRIS (*Hotly*)   Oh, aren't we better than everybody, Sidney Brustein! Aren't we above it! Well, I have news: If he gets me that job, I am going to take it. And when I'm doing it—I'll know that it beats hell out of slinging hash while I wait for "pure art" to come along.

SIDNEY   Iris, it's not just *what* you're getting into—it's *how*. You've got no business hanging out with Lucy and that crowd. How can it be that after five years of life with me you don't know better than this?
   (*He has taken hold of her*)

IRIS (*Exploding, near tears*)   I have learned *a lot* after five years of life with you, Sidney! When I met you I thought Kant was a stilted way of saying cannot; I thought Puccini was a kind of spaghetti; I thought the louder an actor yelled and fell out on the floor the greater he was. But you taught me to look deeper and harder. At everything: from Japanese painting to acting. Including, Sidney, my *own* acting. Thanks to you, I now know something I wouldn't have learned if it hadn't been for you. The fact . . . the *fact* that I am probably the world's *lousiest* actress . . . (*He releases her*) So, there it is, the trouble with looking at ourselves honestly, Sidney, is that we come up with the truth. And, baby, the truth is a bitch.

(*Iris goes out the door*)

SIDNEY (*Going after her*)   Iris, Iris, just listen—

IRIS (*Facing him. Resolutely; she will not be stopped*)  All I know is that, from now on, I just want something to happen in my life. I don't much care *what*. Just something.

SIDNEY   I just want you to know that—whatever happens—you've been one of the few things in my life that made me happy.

IRIS (*An anguished voice—for both of them*)   Oh, Sid, "happy." (*She reaches up, to touch his face a moment*) Whoever started that anyhow? What little bastard was it? Teaching little kids there was such a thing?
(*She exits.* SIDNEY *goes back inside, sits, goes to the drawing board, then leaves that and picks up his banjo and then, with resolution, steps to the door and throws it open*)

SIDNEY   Hey—David . . . David! Can you come down a sec—
(*But* DAVID *is right there, on his way out—rather sheepish, more boyish, genuine than in his prior scenes*)

DAVID (*A grin*)   Oh, you caught me. Waaaal, I decided to go out after all. Maybe I owe myself, under the circumstances, at least one night off. (*He continues, halts, comes back.* SIDNEY *hardly hears him; he is thinking of something intently*) I'll tell you the truth . . . It—it seemed emptier than usual up there. I swore I wouldn't, you know—(*Embarrassed at the humanity of his present feelings*) sort of go out and strut around . . . But by God, it's almost like I *have* to. Do you know what I mean? I mean—(*He laughs freely and drops his hands*) I mean I *feel pretty good.*

SIDNEY (*Half steering, half pushing him inside*) Well, why not! Who wouldn't? . . . C'mon in a sec . . .

DAVID (*Suddenly, not aware that he is mainly talking to himself under the circumstances*) Don't make fun of me, Sidney! The truth is, today is not yesterday. Nothing could have made me believe this yesterday— But I am somebody else today. Inside. It's in my rooms upstairs, it's in my coat . . . it's in my skin. Christ, Sid—(*Pure unadulterated wonder*) I'm famous. (*A grin*) I have to go outside and find out what it's like to wear it in the streets. (*Sobering*) As if I can't guess. Everybody will just be more self-conscious, phonier than they would have been yesterday. Just because my picture was in the papers. It's crazy. The phone keeps on ringing. For years I made fun of people who had unlisted numbers. First thing Monday—I'll have to get one. (*Final smile*) G'night, Sid.

SIDNEY No, wait a minute. Please. I'd like to talk to you. You want a drink?

DAVID What do you want, Sidney? I'm in a hurry!

SIDNEY (*Not looking at him*) Hey—David . . . it's as good as on, isn't it?

DAVID (*Turning*) What—?

SIDNEY (*A little madly*) Your next play. It's as good as on—isn't it? Every producer in town will be looking for it, won't they?

DAVID (*Annoyed to talk about this; a modest person in the true sense*) Well . . . my agent said there've been some

calls already—(*A sigh about producers*) First you can't
get into their offices—

SIDNEY   You're very talented, David.

DAVID   I have to go.
   (*He turns on his heels to leave*)

SIDNEY   No. Look, remember we went once, together, to
   see that thing that Iris was in a couple of years ago?

DAVID   Yes?

SIDNEY   Well, you thought she was pretty good. Even
   better than I thought she was, didn't you? You said so.

DAVID   Those were my polite years. When I still cared
   what people thought about me.

SIDNEY   No, come on, you said that you thought what she
   did was pretty good.

DAVID   When she just danced. When she spoke, when she
   had lines, it was horrible.

SIDNEY   Well, now, *not horrible.* Just average.

DAVID   What do you want, Sidney?

SIDNEY   She's a hung-up kid, David. She needs something
   to happen for her, before she gets all turned around
   sideways.

DAVID (*Unrelentingly*)   What is it that you want, Sidney?

SIDNEY (*Sitting and turning away from the other man*)
   Write her into your play, David. Something for her.
   Something simple that she can do. With dancing.

DAVID (*Absorbing it; pressing his lips together with sadness
   and pulling his collar up about his ears*)   I have to go
   now, Sid.

SIDNEY  It wouldn't have to be a big part, for Christ's sake! Look, she *needs* something to happen for her, don't you understand?

DAVID  You solve your marriage problems any way you have to, Sidney. I won't judge you, but don't bring them to me.

SIDNEY  I'll do the review—
  (*Catching* DAVID *in the door,* SIDNEY *stops himself, amazed at the thought*)

DAVID (*Turning slowly back to him*)  What did you say? (SIDNEY *is quiet, knowing the enormity of his error*) Okay, I'll pretend I never heard you. I am going out now, Sidney. I don't need to experience the other part of this scene. The recovery of Morality and all that. That's *up*town drama. I can't stand those. I'll go and let you have this one all by yourself.
  (*He starts out again, fast.* SIDNEY *grabs him*)

SIDNEY  What's so awful about it? Can't you write about more than two characters at a time? How could it hurt?

DAVID  Just in case you don't understand me at all, Sidney, I'll tell you something. Prostitutes interest me clinically; I've not the least intention of ever becoming one. (*Crossing close to* SIDNEY *so that they are face to face*) Now I'll tell you something else. Look into this cynic's eyes, Sidney. Go ahead, look! And finally understand what these pools of implacable cynicism stand for! It's integrity, Sidney.

SIDNEY (*In profound humiliation*)  Don't feel so holy about it, David. I asked and you refused. Let's forget it. It was such a little—such a tiny little act on the part of a slightly desperate man.

DAVID  Such a tiny little corruption. Not three people in the whole world would ever really care whether or not

my little insignificant play did or did not have its unities
stretched to just happen to include a part for your wife in
trade for a patch of glowing praise in your paper. Not
three people in the whole world. That's the magic of
the tiny corruptions, isn't it, Sidney? Their insignificance
makes them so appealing.

SIDNEY (*Profoundly embarrassed*)    All right. I asked and
you refused. Let's forget it.

DAVID (*All warmth has receded; his voice is tight, harsh
and cold*)    Well, thanks for something, anyway. I was
really too mellow to go out in this world. Too vulnerable.
I would have been torn to pieces. But you've fixed that.
I'm ready for it now.
(WALLY *has crossed outside and enters in high
jubilance, doing minstrel kicks, wiggling his hat
above his head*)

WALLY (*Singing, clowning*)
"When the red, red, robin
Comes bob, bob, bobbin' along—!"

DAVID (*Dryly*)    Enter, the future.

WALLY (*Halting the clowning; to* DAVID)    Could be, could
be. (*Facetiously, flippantly in high spirits*)    Allow me
to offer the grim Past a leaflet. (*To* SIDNEY)    You should
have seen the crowd on Hudson Street. Sidney, there is
something *happening!*

DAVID (*Demonstratively crumpling the leaflet and letting it
fall to the floor*)    It is my fondest hope and greatest expectation that one of these days the hoods will just get
tired of you children and wrap you up in sacks and drop
you in the river as in the old days.

WALLY    Well now—(*Nodding up and down, as if to encourage. Facetiously*)    There is an utterance from the

very bowels of disenchantment. The only problem is, young man, you wear it badly. Those French intellectuals you aim to be imitating have a few things weighing on them that you don't know very much about. Including two world wars and the loss of an empire. What's weighing *you* down, David? As far as I have ever been able to make out from your writings—some problem or other about your mother?

DAVID  Your friend—(*Angry, but not wishing to show it*) is very clever, isn't he, Sidney? (*To* SIDNEY *alone*) Put his remarks alongside the little proposition you just made me and see what you think of my disgust with both of you. (*He turns and exits*)

WALLY  (*Limp-wristedly*)  "Well, I hope yew got that!"

SIDNEY  Cut it out. He's not swish. (*Dully*) Aside from which, he's right.

WALLY  Ah me, ah me: pessimism is weighing heavily on the land. I wonder why. How's Iris?

SIDNEY  Fine.

WALLY  What's happening?

SIDNEY  What do you mean what's happening?

WALLY  She seems to be spending a lot of time lately with the girl friend of one of my poker-playing buddies, that's all.

SIDNEY  If you were married, you'd understand. Things get a little strained . . .

WALLY  Seems like a funny crowd for Iris. (*Noticing suddenly that* SIDNEY *is doubled over with pain*) What's the matter?

SIDNEY  My ulcer is having a rock-and-roll party.

WALLY   Where's your medicine? I'll get it for you.

SIDNEY   In the bathroom. The brown bottle. (*Bitterly*) They're tranquilizers.

WALLY (*Reading from the bottle*)   Says you're supposed to take one every morning. Didn't you take it?

SIDNEY   No.

WALLY   Why not?

SIDNEY   Because I hate them.

WALLY   Don't be such a nut. You should take them. It keeps you from getting upset about every little thing. That's the point of them.
>      (*He hands the pills to* SIDNEY, *who is sitting in the rocker*)

SIDNEY (*Turning his head slowly to his friend*)   "Every little thing," huh, Wally? (*Reaching out and taking the pill and the water and setting them carefully in front of him on the table*) Yes, by all means hand me the chloroform of my passions; the sweetening of my conscience; the balm of my glands. (*Lifting the pills like Poor Yorick's skull*) Oh blessèd age! That has provided that I need never live again in the full temper of my rage. (*Rising and crossing to drawing board, he picks up a yardstick, which, in his hand, becomes the "sword" of the speech*) In the ancient times, the good men among my ancestors, when they heard of evil, strapped a sword to their loins and strode into the desert; and when they found it, they cut it down—or were cut down and bloodied the earth with purifying death. But how does one confront these thousand nameless faceless vapors that are the evil of our time? Could a sword pierce it? (*Turning his eyes to* WALLY) Look at me, Wally . . . Wrath has become a poisoned gastric juice in the intestine. One does not *smite* evil any more: one holds one's gut, thus—and takes a pill. (*As he rises suddenly to full Jovian stance*) Oh, but to take up the sword of the Maccabees again! (*He closes down from the mighty gesture and sets down the "sword," then turns and lamely takes his pill and water*) L'chaim!

*Quick fadeout*

*Curtain*

*Time: Election night. Early fall.*

*In the darkness, the sounds of a not-too-far-distant vic-
tory celebration are heard: shouting, cheers and jubilation,
the indistinct electronic mumble of a loudspeaker, and "The
Wally O'Hara Campaign Song"—not sung this time by a
few, but taken over by the whole crowd. Now and then a
distinct shout "Wally!" or "O'Hara" can be heard to cut
through.*

*At rise:* SIDNEY *enters, in this spirit, and fumbles for his
key in the entrance. The phone rings within. He leaves the
door ajar as he crosses to the phone, snatching up glass and
bottle en route. The sound dims somewhat but continues
under.*

SIDNEY (*Sheer exhilaration; he is heady with victory, not
drink*) Oh—waaal, hello, dere, Mr. Dafoe! (*Fumbling
with phone and bottle*) Oh, I'm right here. Right here!
. . . Yes, yes . . . well, as I'm sure you can understand,
we're in no mood to backtrack on anything today, Mr.
Dafoe . . . Yes, by God, I am being smug, Mr. Dafoe!
Wouldn't you be . . . Don't you realize what happened?
Of all the crazy, impossible, illogical . . . Well, it *did*
happen. We dead have in fact awakened, Mr. Dafoe! All
right then, I will speak to you when I am sober. (*He
hangs up and takes the first drink.* ALTON *has entered
during the above and has stood quietly with his back to
the door waiting for* SIDNEY *to finish.* SIDNEY *sees him—
but not his expression*) Alton, old baby, do you know
the main trouble with us believers in this world? *We
don't believe!* I didn't believe that what happened today
could happen in a million years. That we would win.

That little old ladies and big tough truck drivers and little skinny Madison Avenue ad men would all get up today and go out and wipe out the Big Boss in one fell stroke! Can you believe it? (*He sits and savors the wonder, shaking his head back and forth, then drinks again*) You know what? We don't know anything about the human race, that's what. Not a damn thing when you come down to it. (*Suddenly thinking of a good taunt victim*) Where's that David? (*Gets up and goes outside. The cheers and sound come up*) Where is that sad-eyed little bastard today? Twenty years of political history overturned and he goes into hiding. (*Shouting up*) Hey, Strindberg! Where are you? What are you avoiding the partisans for today, huh?

ALTON (*Dully*) Leave him alone.

SIDNEY Leave him alone? I am going to make that sophomoric little elf eat his nineteenth-century profundities with a spoon! Do you know what we proved today, Alton? Do you *realize* what we proved? We proved that what the people need, what they want, is alternatives. Give them alternatives and all the dull stupid negative old shibboleths go up in smoke. *Poof!* (ALTON *is out of it; standing forlornly in a concentration of his own, not listening, not hearing*) Look, Alt, do you know how *old* the world is? Not very damn old. Why, the whole frigging planetary system is only five billion years old. By eternity's measure—perhaps one day and one night! Do you get me? . . . And, look, it was only twenty-five million years ago that primitive apes were strolling around at a half stoop, you know what I mean, Alt. And they were apes, *not men,* apes. Just apes. (*Just a touch of liquor's fire as well as his own*) By God, this is beautiful! Lucidity is positively flowing over me like the sweet oils of Persia! Apes! And between them and us came all the sub boys: Java, Peking, Neanderthal

Man and then finally, a long, long time after, finally:
Cro Magnon Man. A mere, a lousy, a nothing of a teensy
little thirty thousand years ago. Alton, *he's a baby!* He's
an infant!

ALTON (*Lifting bleary eyes wearily*)   Who, Sidney?

SIDNEY   *Man! The human race!* Yesterday he made a
wheel, and fire, so today we're all demanding to know
why he hasn't made universal beauty and wisdom and
truth too! (*Slumping down, spent*) A few thousand lousy
years he's had to figure out a calendar, and how to make
the corn grow; a few lousy years to figure out—*everything.* And we give 'im hell. (*Lifting his eyes with plaintive joy*) All he needs is a little more time . . . and he'll
be all right, doncha think, Alt? Time and alternatives,
like today? Maybe—maybe we could get through the
whole thing then. You think? (*Noting the other's face
finally, which is just staring at him*) Were you pulling
for the other side or something? (*Then rising and laughing and, lifting up his glass, singing Higgins' song from
My Fair Lady*) "I said to him we did it, we did it!"
(*Then*) What the hell is the matter with you?

ALTON (*His eyes trained on* SIDNEY)   Is it true, Sid?

SIDNEY (*Knowing at once*)   Is what true—?

ALTON (*Rising*)   We've hung out together a long time;
don't crap around. Is it true? Is it true she's a hooker?
And you were going to let me marry her? (SIDNEY *says
nothing; he sits, exhaling a great troubled sigh*) Why
didn't you tell me?

SIDNEY (*Staring at the floor*)   It wasn't my place to do so.
It was for Gloria to tell you. People change. She'll
change. She needs someone. Just don't make me sick
today, Alton. Just don't act like a fraternity boy meeting
his own girl under the lamppost.

ALTON    How would you act? (*They stare at one another*)
When you go into the mines, Sid, you get coal in your
skin; if you're a fisherman, you reek of fish! . . . She
doesn't *know* how to love any more, it's all a performance. It has to be.

SIDNEY (*Avoiding a direct reply*)    If you could understand
it, there is a great compliment to you in how I treated
this, Alt. The compliment that I thought you would be
man enough to absorb, and help Gloria like you wanted
to help the rest of the world once. (ALTON *just laughs*)

ALTON    Talk to me man to man today, Sidney: Would you
marry her?

SIDNEY    Alton, for Christ's sake! You were a revolutionary! Doesn't that stand for anything any more? It is one
thing to take bread to the Bowery and another to eat it
with them!

ALTON    *Would you marry her?*

SIDNEY    If I loved her . . . I don't know how to say it to
you except that if I loved her . . .

ALTON (*Screaming*)    Don't you know some of the things
these girls have to do?

SIDNEY    All right, I know. You are afire with all the
images; every faceless man in the universe has become—

ALTON    Someone who has coupled with my love . . . used
her like . . . an . . . inanimate object . . . a thing, an
instrument . . . a commodity . . .

SIDNEY (*With supreme compassion for all*)    In an effort
to assuage something of his own pathetic needs, Alton . . .

ALTON    A commodity! (*Looking up at* SIDNEY) Don't you
understand, Sidney? (*Rubbing his head*) Man, like I
am spawned from commodities . . . and their purchasers.

Don't you *know* this? I am running from being a commodity. How do you think I got the color I am, Sidney? Haven't you ever thought about it? I got this color from my grandmother being used as a commodity, man. The buying and the selling in this country began with *me*. Jesus, help me.

SIDNEY  All right.

ALTON  You don't understand . . . My father, you know, he was a railroad porter . . . who wiped up spit and semen, carried drinks and white man's secrets for thirty years . . . When the bell rang in the night he put on that white coat and his smile and went shuffling through the corridors with his tray and his whisk broom . . . his paper bags and his smile to wherever the white men were ringing . . . for thirty years. And my mother . . . she was a domestic. She always had, Mama did . . . bits of this and bits of that from the pantry of "Miss Lady," you know . . . some given, some stolen . . . And she would always bring this booty home and sit it all out on the kitchen table . . . So's we could all look at it . . . And my father . . . all the time he would stand there and look at it and walk away. And then one night, he had some kind of fit, and he just reached out and knocked all that stuff, the jelly, and the piece of ham; the broken lamp and the sweater for me and the two little vases . . . He just knocked it all on the floor and stood there screaming with the tears running down his face . . . "I ain't going to have the white man's leavings in my house, no mo'! I ain't going to have his *throw-away* . . . no mo'! . . ." And Mama, she just stood there with her lips pursed together and when he went to bed she just picked it all up, whatever hadn't been ruined or smashed, and washed it off and brushed it off and put it in the closet . . . and we *ate* it and *used* it . . . because we had to *survive,* and she didn't have room for my father's pride . . . I don't want white man's leavings, Sidney. I couldn't *marry* her. (*Getting up, and taking out a piece of paper*) I wrote her a note.

SIDNEY  Aren't you even going to see her? (ALTON *drops his head*) And if she was a black woman? (*It hangs*) That's racism, Alt.

ALTON  I know it—(*Touching his head*) here!

SIDNEY (*Sadly, looking at him*)    But— "A star has risen over Africa—"

ALTON (*Looking back at him*)  Yes.

SIDNEY  Over Harlem . . . over the South Side . . .

ALTON  Yes.

SIDNEY  The new Zionism is raging . . . (ALTON *hands him the note, turns*) Aren't you even going to see her?

ALTON (*From the door, in anguish*)  No. I don't ever want to see her.
  (*He runs off.* SIDNEY *follows him out*)

SIDNEY  You are afraid that you would forgive her! And you don't want to do that, do you?
  (*Stands looking after him as the sounds of the victory celebration—not the song now, but the loudspeaker and crowd—envelop him. Presently* MAVIS *enters*)

MAVIS  Sidney Brustein!
  (*Arms outstretched, coming to him fast, sincerely impressed and overwhelmed. She steers him into the apartment, the closing door shuts out the sound*)

MAVIS  Who'd of ever thought it! First thing when Fred saw the paper this afternoon, he called me from the office and said, "Mav, that brother-in-law of yours is some kind of political genius!" He's so excited. Why, he said that everybody is talking about you and the paper and Wally O'Hara. He said that it even went out on the national news. (*She has hugged and kissed him through most of this*) Let's have a drink together, Sidney. I don't know how to tell you how proud I am. I just thought it was another one of those things that you are always doing—like with the night club—(*Correcting herself*) I know, it wasn't a night club—and all. Where is everyone? . . . I thought this place would be—you know—

SIDNEY (*Fixing her a drink*)  —"jumping." I wasn't the candidate, Mav. Iris hasn't come in yet. Sometimes she stops off for the groceries . . .

MAVIS  Groceries! Aren't you kids going out and celebrate? Honest to God, you're so strange— You don't even look happy.

SIDNEY  Oh, I'm happy . . . It's kind of freakish though, you know, that we won. We never dreamed we would. (*To himself, with wonder*) We never dreamed we would.

MAVIS (*Takes a check out of her bag and puts it in* SIDNEY'*s shirt pocket*)  Here's a little present, for the paper. (*Noting his astonishment*) From *Fred,* let's say. No, don't talk about it. Don't say a word. There it is. That's all.

SIDNEY (*Looking at it*)  This is a *lot* of money, honey.

MAVIS (*Drinking*)  I said let's not mention it and I mean it. When I—that is when *Fred*—decided that he would give it to you we agreed that we didn't want any chance whatsoever to feel good and gooey and Real Big about it. So—put it away.

SIDNEY (*Looking at her, touched*)  Well, thank—you—
(*With great ostentation, this error*) Oh, I mean, *Fred*
for it.

MAVIS (*Warmly*)  Shut up. (*Looking at him, the liquor
warming and freeing her*) I'm glad to have a chance to
talk with you, Sidney. Alone. We've never really talked
—I know that you don't like me—

SIDNEY (*Because that remark must embarrass anyone*)
Mavis—

MAVIS  No, it's all right. I know it. You know it. When
you come down to it, what is there to like? Isn't it funny
how different sisters can be?

SIDNEY  Yes, different. All of us. Everything.

MAVIS  Yeeeess, don't I know it. I was trying to explain
that to Fred the other day. (*A little laugh*) I don't mean
I was trying to "explain" it . . . That sounds so funny:
Fred isn't a stupid man, as we all know—but sometimes.
Sometimes I get to thinking that certain kind of way.
The way, you know, that *you* do—(*With her hands,
a circle, and aptly, the universe*) of a whole—

SIDNEY  In abstractions.

MAVIS  That's right. You won't believe it—but—I enjoy
it when a person can say something so that it embraces
a lot, so that it's in—in—

SIDNEY (*Staring at her*)  Concepts.

MAVIS  Yes. I enjoy it. I've enjoyed the conversations
I've heard down here. And, Sidney, I've understood
some of them.
> (*There is a curious, believable and quite charming
> defiance in this announcement*)

SIDNEY  Good for you, Mavis. Good for you.

MAVIS (*Oddly*)  But we get stuck, you know.

SIDNEY  Hmmm?

MAVIS  Some of us, we get stuck, in—(*Stiltedly*) the original stimuli. Some of us never have a chance, you know—

SIDNEY (*Nodding wearily, not wishing to hear this saga again*)  I know—

MAVIS  Like Papa—he was such a dreamer. You know, sort of backwoods poet, kind of a cross between Willy Loman and Daniel Boone. He loved just sitting and thinking—

SIDNEY (*Looking at her, stunned*)  Didn't you and Iris have the same father?

MAVIS  Of course we had the same father! What do you think I'm talking about?

SIDNEY  *Rashomon*—what else?

MAVIS  He was a very wonderful man, very wonderful. And that's the joke on me—I thought, I thought I was marrying someone like Papa when I married Fred. Can you imagine—*Fred!*

SIDNEY  You mean you *wanted* him to be like your father?

MAVIS  Yes . . . and that's the way I thought Fred was, in those days. He *seemed* poetic—when he was young. Do you know that Fred used to drive in forty miles from Ellensville to see me when we were courting? Forty miles and then back forty, and in the world's worst car. That's what he was like then. Like Papa. (*A little high*) Papa used to read the classics to us, you know, Greek tragedy. Sometimes in Greek.

SIDNEY (*Wide-eyed*)  You are pulling my leg.

MAVIS (*Surprised*)  Why? Oh, he didn't really know *classical* Greek, Sidney. Just everyday Greek from his folks, but that made it interesting . . . we used to do little productions in our living room. He would always let me be Medea, because he said I was strong—(*She rises and bellows forth in robust, dramatic and effective Greek the following, enriching it with not badly conceived if stagey classical stance and gesture*) Ὁ πόνος μέ περικυκλώνει ἀπό ὅλες τίς μεριές καί ποιός μπορεῖ νά τό ἀμφισβητήσῃ. Ἀλλά δέν χάθηκαν ἀκόμα ὅλα. Νομίζω ὅχι. (*Then in English, the first line or so, rather rattled off*) "On all sides sorrow pens me in. Who can gainsay this? But all is not yet lost! Think *not* so. Still there are troubles in store for the new bride and for her bridegroom—" Well, *he* thought I was good.

SIDNEY  Mavis, I don't know you.

MAVIS  The ham part, I know. (*A little laugh*) I know all the parts—and all the strophes. Sure, Papa was something! He was a man of great, great imagination. That's why he changed our name. It was plain old everyday Parodopoulos, you know—

SIDNEY  No, I didn't know.

MAVIS  But Papa wanted something, you know, *symbolic*. So he changed it to Parodus. You know what the parodus is in the development of Greek tragedy.

SIDNEY  Ah . . . no.

MAVIS (*Proudly*)  Sidney! Shame on you! The parodus is the chorus! And you know—no matter what is happening in the main action of the play—the chorus is always there, commenting, watching. He said that we were like that, the family, at the edge of life—not changing anything. Just watching and being.

SIDNEY (*Struck*)     I see.

MAVIS     That was Papa, dramatic as hell. (*Drinking her drink*) I loved him very much. (*A beat*) And Fred's no Papa.

SIDNEY     It's been one big disappointment, your marriage?

MAVIS (*Dully*)     Not for a minute. I knew by the time that Fred and I got married that he wasn't the Fred he seemed to be. I knew what I was marrying and I was right. Solid as a rock. Hah! (*Abruptly*) We haven't touched each other more than twice since little Harry was born and that's . . . oh, six years now, isn't it? Harry will be six next month.

SIDNEY     Ah—by whose—

MAVIS     —design? Who knows? It just happens. (*Waving her hand*) He doesn't suffer. He's got a girl.

SIDNEY (*Gutturally*)     Fred?

MAVIS (*Looking at him*)     Fred. (*Shaking her head*) Sometimes I think you kids down here believe your own notions of what the rest of the human race is like. There are no squares, Sidney. Believe me when I tell you, everybody is his own hipster. Sure, for years now. Same girl, I'll say that for old Fred. I've met her.

SIDNEY (*He would genuinely like to seem blasé but he can't; he is truly astonished*)     You have—?

MAVIS (*All with bitter restraint*)     Oh sure. I went there. He has her all set up. Nothing fancy; Fred's strictly a family man, he puts the main money in the main place, our Fred. But decent, you know, respectable building, family people—a nice place for a single girl—(*The ultimate bitterness*) with a kid. (*He absorbs this with a silent start but knows to say nothing*) He's just a year younger than Harry. I saw him too. (*Now she is crying;* SIDNEY *is helpless in the face of this*) You do find out. And I did the usual: I hired a sordid little man to find out for sure. He did. And so, one day, I did what a woman has to do: I went to see. Not the spooky thing, I didn't want to come in on them together or any of that junk. I know what a man and a woman do; I just wanted to meet her. So I got in a cab, got out, rang a bell and there she was. Nothing like expected! Not a chorine or something as you always think, even with Fred—in my mind I had decided it would be some cheap mess; but no, there's this sandy-haired kid standing in pedal pushers and an apron, pregnant as all get-out. So I said I rang the wrong bell. And I went back, once, several months later—to see the baby. In the park. I had to see the baby. I didn't tell Fred about my knowing until after I saw the baby. And then, after that we went through the usual waltz . . . Divorce talk, all of it, you know.

SIDNEY   And then you decided against it.

MAVIS   Of course I decided against it. A divorce? For what? Because a marriage was violated? Ha! We've got three boys and their father is devoted to them; I guess he's devoted to all four of his boys. And what would I do? There was no rush years ago at home to marry Mavis Parodus; there was *just* Fred *then*. In this world there are two kinds of loneliness and it is given to each of us to pick. I picked. And, let's face it, *I* cannot type.

SIDNEY   (*Quietly shaking his head*)   But you want only simple people and simple problems in literature . . .

MAVIS   Sure, isn't life enough?

SIDNEY   Does Iris know any of this?

MAVIS   What would I tell her for? Listen, we all play our roles. (*Long beat*) Well, one thing is sure. I do not need another drop to drink. (*Fixing herself, compact in hand*) So how is my cream-colored brother-in-law-to-be?

SIDNEY    He's not going to be.

MAVIS    Well, thank God for something. She broke it off, huh?

SIDNEY (*Looking up, absorbing the assumption*) Yes . . . I guess so.

MAVIS (*Blithe ignorance again*)    It had to be. Look, the world's not ready. It just isn't. He seemed like a nice boy and all that, but it's just not possible. I mean in this world, you know. You have to think about children, you know. I knew Gloria would snap out of it. Why would she want to get into something like that? I mean he's very light, but—(*Halting*) I'm not fooling you, am I?

SIDNEY    No.

MAVIS    I can't help it, Sid. It's the way I feel. You can't expect people to change that fast.
    (*She gets up to go*)

SIDNEY (*Gently, more with wonder than assertion*)    Mavis, the world is about to crack right down the middle. We've gotta change—or fall in the crack.

MAVIS (*Not angrily*)    Well, I think we are back to ourselves and you are probably starting to insult me again. I knew I was going to tell you about it though, Sid—one of these days. I always knew that. Since I first saw you I knew those eyes could find a place for anybody's tale. Don't talk to Iris about it . . . . I know I don't have to ask it of you, but all the same. Don't, huh? She's a kid, Sidney. She doesn't know what she's all about yet. She will, she'll get herself together one of these days. (*Patting his cheek*) And so will you. (*Looking at him*) Gee, we're proud of you, Sid. I told Fred, "Say what you will, but the Jews have get-up!"

SIDNEY (*In that kind of mood*)   Say what you will.

MAVIS   Now, there was nothing wrong with that, was there?

SIDNEY (*Smiling*)   Well, let's say there isn't. Today. (*A beat. She opens the door and we hear again the sounds of the rally*) Mavis, what do you do . . . I mean . . . ?

MAVIS   To make up for Fred, you mean? (*As he follows her out, by the stairs*) I take care of my boys. I shop and I worry about my sisters. It's a life.

SIDNEY (*A beat. Gently, lifting his fists to the gods above; it is for their ears only*)   "Witness you ever-burning lights above!" (*Then to her*) You're tough, Mavis Parodus.

> (*Kisses her—and, because she does have depth,* MAVIS *says nothing at all as she walks off.* SIDNEY *goes back in, pours a drink and stands looking out his window at the celebration. After a while* IRIS *enters. She looks completely different: she has been costumed somewhere in those precincts of the city where expressions of the couturier's need for yearly change of radical fashion are most evident. Her hair has been cut and teased to a stiff sculpture and tinted an entirely unnatural metallic yellow. She carries two shopping bags.* SIDNEY *is at the window and does not immediately see her*)

IRIS   Well, congratulations, Sid.

SIDNEY   Your sister was here.

IRIS   Oh? Which one?

SIDNEY   What do you mean, which one?

IRIS  Gloria is due. I didn't get a chance to tell you, but she is in town and she's coming by tonight.
(IRIS *goes into the bedroom*)

SIDNEY  Oh, my God, that's all I need.

IRIS  Since when aren't you glad to see Gloria?

SIDNEY  I'm always glad to see Gloria . . . Oh, never mind.

IRIS  (*Emerges with a traveling case*)  What did Mavis want?

SIDNEY  Nothing. Just to talk. We talked.
(*He turns and rather freezes at the change in her but not for comedy*)

IRIS  I know. It looks pretty different. I won't ask if you like it. (*He is speechless and says nothing at all, merely stares as if he never really has seen her before. Brazening it out*) I got the job. Just like that—(*A snap*) they send you out to get fixed. (*She is putting on a new pair of shoes*) Everything but the shoes. They say it's gauche to walk out of a store in a pair of shoes you've just bought. At least that's what poor people say. I guess nothing is gauche if you're rich enough. (*Wise afterthought*) *Long* enough. Please don't stare at me like that, Sid. And let's don't discuss it.

SIDNEY  (*With thoughtfulness*)  Why did you always tell me all those stories about your father, Iris?

IRIS  (*Looking up*)  You and Mavis had yourselves a real little old heart-to-heart, didn't you? What's the world coming to?

SIDNEY  Why did you make him out to be some kind of dull-witted nothing? What was the point of it?

IRIS  (*Irritably, swiftly, falsely*)  Oh, why do you believe Mavis? She has some kind of transference about Papa.

It's very complicated. When she talks about Papa she's really talking about this uncle of ours who—

SIDNEY (*Knowing that she is going into a long involved lie*) Never mind, Iris. It doesn't matter.

IRIS (*Sincerely*) I guess—I just tried to live up to your fantasy about me. All of it. People do that—

SIDNEY Let's not talk about that—

IRIS You did a terrific job on the election. You must feel good.

SIDNEY (*Vaguely*) Yes, I feel good. (*A beat*) Mavis said she thought we'd be going out to celebrate. You haven't told her anything then?

IRIS No . . . who wants to hear all the wailing?

SIDNEY (*Looking at her, slowly, with emphasis*) I have a feeling she'd survive it.

IRIS Mavis' idea of marriage is something you do at twenty—and it stays that way—*no matter what*. Everything else shocks.

SIDNEY Sure. Dullsville. (*Several beats; as he studies her and the things she has brought in*) What do you do? On the—(*Gestures "television"*) thing. I don't even know what the hell it is that you're actually—(*He holds this word for a fraction longer than ordinary meaning would dictate. She has not missed this and so signifies by a lift of brow without, however, comment*) selling.

IRIS Home permanents.

SIDNEY (*Random gesture, not entirely innocent, circular waving of the hand*) Is that what—uh—they've used on you?

IRIS (*Determined not to let him provoke her*) Don't be

funny. This head has been in and out of all the booths in Mr. Lionel's for the last two and one half hours.

SIDNEY But that's not what you are going to tell the people, is it? I mean you're not going to tell them that you got your—(*He reads from the label of a large, golden, elegantly lettered box*) Golden Girl Curl by sitting in Mr. Lionel's for several hours, are you?

IRIS No, Sid, that certainly is not what I am going to tell them. I am going—(*Getting up and advancing on the Golden Curl sample*) to tell all the little housewifies that I just rolled it up on Golden Girl Curl . . . (*Before us, she assumes the manner of TV mannequins, holding up the box, with the slightest edge of hysteria just beneath the surface of her kidding*) and rollers, using my magic Golden Girl Curl Box to hold everything just so . . . which you understand, is one of the main features of Golden Girl Curl Home Permanent.

SIDNEY The box it comes in.

IRIS (*With genuine loathing for the whole nonsense, enunciating with contempt*) Yes! the box it comes in! (*She opens it—the bottom falls out and so do the rollers. Hurling it to the floor*) Which also does not work! (*Wheeling, crying, shrieking*) It's a job, Sidney! They do not pay you one hundred dollars an hour for hauling hamburgers at Hamlines. They do pay it for pretending that there is some difference between Golden Girl Curl and Wonder Curl, or between Wonder Curl and Home Perma Pearl, so what the hell do you want from me!

SIDNEY It doesn't work . . .

IRIS (*Precisely now in the manner of a defensive child*) It *does* work. It does work enough to justify it. They just send you to the hairdressers to play safe. They have to have everything just so when they tape things for television, Sidney. You don't realize how expensive it is to tape something. All those lights and cameras and technicians . . . they can't have your hair falling down from some . . . (*Swiping at Golden Girl Curl again*) crappy old home permanent just when they're ready to shoot . . .

SIDNEY (*Getting up and going to her and taking her in his arms*)  What's the matter, baby, what's happening to you? What's it all about—? What is it you're going after now? What is it that's got you all turned around? Where do you think it's heading you?

IRIS (*In his arms entirely, sobbing out rapidly and incoherently virtually all of the irrelevant parts of her problem*)  Nothing . . . will put a curl in your hair . . . like this but . . . heat . . . But it works *some,* Sid, I did try it . . . Do you think the FTC would let them just put anything . . . on the air . . . like that . . . ?

SIDNEY  Baby—

IRIS (*Shrieking—as the old comforting relationship threatens again*) I DON'T WANT TO PLAY APPALACHIAN ANY MORE!

SIDNEY  All right, honey, but there's no reason to get all tied up in new games . . . Iris . . .

IRIS (*Shaking her head violently*)  You don't understand, you still don't understand. I am not the same . . . I am different . . .

SIDNEY (*Laughing, with wonder*)  Dear, sweet God . . . I've been living with a little girl . . . Iris, you really *are* a child.

IRIS (*Raising her face at that*)  Sidney . . . *One* of us here is a child and it's not me . . . I've found out plenty about the world in the last few weeks, and it's nothing like you—or Papa—want it to be . . . It's not! It's not . . . There are things talked about . . . laughed about while you stand there framed by that sign . . . that make me wonder how I ever thought you knew anything about this world at all . . . *This* world, Sidney! It's so dirty.

SIDNEY (*Rising now and crossing to her again*)   And what I am trying to tell you, little girl, is that you are learning the cynicism bit at the wrong time in our lives . . . (*He is gesturing toward the sign in the window. The crowd outside is heard again, muffled cheers and the Campaign Song*) We *won* something today, Iris. Not too much . . . just a little tiny part of the world turned right side up . . . Just listen . . .

IRIS (*The final outpouring*)   Sidney! Stop it! I can't stand it! You haven't won anything, Sid, they're all the same people! (*The revelation does not penetrate*) Don't you hear me? I tried to tell you . . . They *own* Wally . . . The people you've been fighting . . . Own him completely: the house he lives in, the clothes on his back, the toothpaste he uses. *They own* him, utterly, completely, entirely . . . (*Dragging him to the window*) There it is, Sid, the real world! Do you hear it? The world you say was just turned right side up!

(*A helpless hysterical gesture of flinging it at him*)

SIDNEY (*Frantically, shaking his head "no"—but his eyes saying "yes"*)   What kind of psychotic filth is this?

IRIS   It is filth. You don't know what filth, you can't *imagine* what filth! But it's not psychotic. Oh, Jesus, it's not even obscure . . . I have met people who didn't *believe* that you didn't know this . . . Jesus, Sid! I tried to tell you. Look, you can count on it, in a few months he'll be having press conferences to explain how the pinkos and the bohemians duped him in the first place and how he has found his way back to the "tried and true leadership" of the . . . "mother party"! (*She starts out, walking very much like the dead, picking up her bags. As she opens the door, the triumphant sounds of the crowd fill the room*) I would stay with you awhile now . . . if it would help anything. But it wouldn't. (*Turning, weeping freely*) I'll send for my things some time this week. Tell Gloria I'll phone her later. (*Then, suddenly*) For God's sake, Sidney, take down that sign! *It's like spit in your face!*

> (*She exits. He reaches up and clutches the sign for a long moment, the tension mounting within him—but then releases it. Very much like a blind man, he moves to the drawing board, where his hand takes up the yardstick—the "sword of his ancestors"—which he holds aloft before him, saluting a foe that cannot be cut down . . . then lets it slip through his fingers. The sign pulses with a life of its own; the roar of the crowd grows louder; SIDNEY snaps the yardstick in half*)

*Curtain*

# ACT III

*Time: Several hours later.*

*At rise: There is darkened gloom and quiet in the room and the place is a mess.* SIDNEY *is stretched out under the coffee table, in considerable pain; one hand clutches at a center spot in his lower chest. An open whiskey bottle and glass are near. In rough spasms, he harshly hums an old Yiddish melody, "Rozhankis Mit Mandlen."*

*Presently, his sister-in-law* GLORIA *appears at the door, carrying a small valise. She is about 26, as lovely as we have heard, but with surprising, fresh-faced, wholesome, "all-American" looks. She has a gleaming, casual, almost collegiate long bob, and the clothes are of that kind of lively smartness rather than dark elegance. With her valise she reminds one of a coed home for the weekend and no other thing. She knocks at the door; finally tries it and comes in.*

GLORIA (*Quizzically looking about in the shadows*) Sidney? Sidney?
　　　(*She turns on a lamp*)

SIDNEY (*Roaring drunk, as it were*)  Stop it . . . Let there be darkness!  . . . Let the tides of night fall upon us and envelop us and protect us from the light . . . Shut it out, shut out the light . . . How do you like *them* apples, Goethe, old baby? Let there be darkness, I say! Out, I say! (*Then, recognizing her*) Gloria!

GLORIA (*Laughing*)  You're a nut!

SIDNEY  Gloria! (*She picks him up—drags him to couch*)

GLORIA  Where's Iris?

SIDNEY (*Singing "The Fireship" in reply: it is a song about a prostitute*)
> "She had a bright and roving eye-eye!
> And her hair hung down in ring-el-ets!"
(*He folds over and rather gags with pain*)
> "A nice girl, a proper girl, but one
> of the roving kind!"

GLORIA  You're having an attack—aren't you?
(*Thinks of it, then crosses to the refrigerator and gets a container of milk*)

SIDNEY  I'm all right!
(*Sings from the prone position*)
> "Her hair hung down in ring-el-ets!"
(*Sitting up suddenly*)
No, that's not the one.
(*Lifts his head like a howling dog and sings starkly "Come All Ye Fair and Tender Ladies"*)
> "If I'da known before I started
> I never would have courted none
> I'da locked my heart in a box of golden
> and fastened it up with a silver pin."

GLORIA (*Offering the milk*)  Come on, Sidney, you're not all that drunk. C'mon, drink this.

SIDNEY (*Drinks, expecting liquor—spits out the milk*)

"Oh don't you remember the days of our courtin'
When your head lay upon my breast—"

GLORIA　What's going on, Sidney?

SIDNEY (*Opening his eyes*)　Can it be that the fall of man
has entirely escaped even *your* notice?

GLORIA　What do you mean?

SIDNEY　All—all that sweat; all that up-all-night; all that,
you should excuse the allusion—(*Hissing out the word*)
*Passion*. All for a mere flunky of Power. (*Gaily*) Who
cares anyhow? The world likes itself just fine the way it
is, so don't pick at it. That's all you gotta know about
anything: Don't pick at it! (*He has crossed on these lines
to the door; he opens it and bellows up*) Hey, Orpheus,
come on down: I'm ready to cross over the Styx. (*He
turns around and mugs heavily at* GLORIA) Get it: I'm
just going to hell with myself!

(*He slaps his thigh burlesquing that kind of humor
thickly*)

GLORIA　You need looking after. Where *is* Iris?

SIDNEY　Who? Oh, Iris. My wife. Who the hell knows.
(*Wandering around*) She was one of the lesser goddesses
anyhow. A kind of "girl Friday for Zeus," as they put
it in *Time* magazine. (*Posing*) Lookit me, who am I?
(*Stands on the couch—in Zeus pose;* GLORIA *can only
laugh now*) Come on, who am I? I'll give you a hint: I'm
not Apollo. In fact, I am not a god. (*As Jimmy Durante
would say it*) Ignore my stately bearing for the time
being and look in my eyes, and you will see there un-
mistakable—mortality. (*Collapses again*) Here I am,
Modern Man: flat on my back with an oozing intestine,
a bit of a tear frozen in the corner of my eye, a glass
of booze which will saturate without alleviating . . . and
not the dimmest notion of what it is all about. (*He

*drinks and sits up*) And my wife has run off to capture lightning bolts for Zeus. On account of he pays well and you get to meet all the up and coming young gods and things.

DAVID (*Entering, coolly*)   Well, I see I have entered in a large moment.

SIDNEY   David, my boy! (*Throws the bottle*) The only man I happen to know personally who is unafraid of the dark. Have a drink.

DAVID   You're drunk and silly and I have a guest. (*He starts out*)

SIDNEY   Well, bring her—excuse me—*him* down and we'll have a happening or something.

DAVID   We're already having one, thank you.

SIDNEY (*Grabbing hold of him*)   All that motion, all that urgency . . . for nothing. That's the whole show, isn't it? A great plain where neither the wind blows, nor the rain falls, nor anything else happens. *Really happens,* I mean. Besides our arriving there and one day leaving again . . . That's what your plays are about, aren't they?

DAVID   Yes, I suppose so.

SIDNEY   Billy said it better than you though: ". . . a tale told by an idiot, full of sound and fury, signifying nothing." Billy said everything better.

DAVID   I won't argue. What's happened?

SIDNEY   Nothing . . . everything . . . And I won't argue with you any more either, David. You're right about everything.

DAVID   Well, at least you are learning.

SIDNEY   Oh yes, and to laugh! Finally. At the colossal absurdity. It's the only refuge, the only cove of endurance. To accept it all and offer back only a cold . . . shadowless stream of laughter. (*Does a vaudeville turn and strikes another especially ludicrous pose. Sings*)

"Oh, we're lost—out here in the stars!"

(*Turning, as if seeing her for the first time*) Gloria!

(*He holds out his arms to her. She goes to him and they embrace; there is a quite genuine affection between these two. He holds her rather desperately and, inadvertently, hurts her*)

SIDNEY   What's the matter?

GLORIA (*Covering quickly*)   Some bruises. It's all right. Are *you* all right?

(SIDNEY *grabs his mouth; starts for the bathroom with great dignity which he cannot sustain; he breaks and runs in, closing door behind him. She notes* DAVID *fully for the first time*)

GLORIA   And you must be—

DAVID   David Ragin. Hi.

GLORIA (*With recognition*)   From upstairs. Hi. I'm—

DAVID   Gloria. The sister who—"travels a lot." (*As she clearly reacts to his emphasis*) Oh, it's all right. I practically live here and it's, like, all in the family, no secrets. I do naughty things with boys only—so relax.

GLORIA   You're very free with personal information.

DAVID (*Blithely*)   Isn't it the great tradition for writers and whores to share the world's truths?

GLORIA (*Spinning with astonishment and fury*)   Listen, I don't like your language—or you.

DAVID   I'm sorry. I didn't know it would upset you.

GLORIA  Weren't you leaving?

DAVID  I said I was sorry. And I almost never apologize to anyone. I apologized to you—because I respect you.

GLORIA  I said, weren't you leaving?

DAVID  Look—it's okay with me. Relax. I'm writing about a—girl—like you. I cut away all the hypoc—

GLORIA  Look, little boy—(*Sudden strong, throaty tones*) I've never met you before, but I have met them like you a hundred times and I know everything you are about to say; because it's been asked and written four thousand times . . . anything I would tell you, you would believe it and put it down and feel like you'd been close to something old and deep and wise. Any bunch of lies I would make up. Well, these are not office hours. Now get the hell out of here!
   (*Rising, she winces and catches her side*)

DAVID  What's hurting you?

GLORIA  (*In apparent physical pain*)  Please be some kind of gentleman if you—think you can *swing* it and go away.

DAVID  (*Looking at her hard*)  You really don't like your life?!

GLORIA  (*Her head back, her eyes closed*)  The things people think in this world—!

DAVID  Can I get you something?

GLORIA  Just go away!
   (*He exits.* SIDNEY *re-enters, his head—and shirt—doused with water, affecting sobriety to little avail. He looks a state, crosses to* GLORIA *at the bar, carrying one shoe*)

SIDNEY  (*At the bottle*)  Want a drink? Oh, I always forget —about you and your face, the tissues and all.

GLORIA   It's all right—I'm learning to like it. (*Slapping playfully at the underchin and cheeks*) Let the damn tissues fall! (*Looking up at him, softly*) I've quit, Sid. *Really* quit.

SIDNEY (*Changing the subject*)   How did you—hurt yourself?

GLORIA   I didn't. That's the result of an evening spent with six and one half feet of psycho. I happen to have a predi —What do you call it?

SIDNEY   Predilection?

GLORIA   Predilection for psychos and vice cops, it's quite amazing! To the point where some of the girls tease me about it. This last one . . . I think he was trying to kill me. It was his thing . . . you know, violence. (*Looking around*) When's Iris coming? She must be working hard, this place is a wreck!

SIDNEY   She'll be along.

GLORIA (*Grinning*)   Hey—Sid, lookit me! (*Holding up the glass triumphantly*) Whiskey. I've joined the human race. No more goofball pills—I'm kicking everything. (*She makes a comic face and their glasses clink*) *I* did the whole gooey farewell bit with some of the kids. Adios, Muchachas! I'm going to marry him. Yes, I mean *after* we talk about it. I wouldn't unless I told him. I know girls who've done that. Doesn't work out. Never works out. You run into people. They make up all kinds of nutty things, but it doesn't work out. I'm going to sit down and say—(*A swinging recitation brimming over with confidence to conceal terror below: rehearsed too many times to perfection because she knows it won't work. The voice is bright with an assurance the eyes deny*) "I was a nineteen-year-old package of fluff from Trenersville, Nowhere, and I met this nothing who took one look at this baby face of mine and said, 'Honey, there's a whole special market for you. Slink is on the way out; all-American wholesomeness is the rage. You've got it made! You'll be part of the aristocracy of the profession!' Which is true. Only it's the profession they don't exactly describe. After that you develop your own rationales to make it all right to yourself: a) It's old as time anyhow; (*They clink glasses loudly and laugh*) b) (*Hand on heart—for God and country*) It's a service to society; (*They clink again*) and c) The *real* prostitutes are everybody else; especially housewives and career girls. (*Again they howl*) We trade those gems back and forth for hours. Nobody believes it, but it helps on the bad days. And, sweetie, there are a lot of bad days.

SIDNEY  Gloria—no matter what happens, honey, you've got to stick to that.

GLORIA  (*Glass poised in midair, she lowers it slowly*) Okay, Sid, what is it—a letter or a phonograph record with violins?

SIDNEY  Gloria—

GLORIA (*Supreme effort at self-control: to both steel herself for—and hold off—the inevitable*)  I was on this date once, Sid. He had a book of reproductions by Goya. And there was this one—an etching, I think. Have you ever seen it? There's this woman, a Spanish peasant woman and she's standing like this—reaching out. And what she's reaching for are the teeth of a dead man. A man who'd been hanged. And she is rigid with—revulsion, but she wants his teeth, because it said in the book that in those days people thought that the teeth of the dead were good luck. Can you imagine that? The things people think they have to do? To *survive?* Some day I'm going to buy that print. It's all about my life . . .

SIDNEY  He loves you, honey. He loves you terribly . . .

GLORIA  (*Tough, hoarse urgency: she is ready for it now*) Come on, Sidney! (SIDNEY *hands her the letter. There is presently in the silence only the single hurt outcry of any small creature of the forest, mortally struck. She crumples the letter in her hand. He crosses to her swiftly, tries to comfort her in his arms; she throws back a girlish head and emits now a cry deep, guttural and as primeval as the forest*) Men! Oh God, men!

SIDNEY  (*Pouring a drink fast and trying to push it on her*) Come on—drink this for me—

GLORIA  Get that trash out of my face, Sidney. Get it away—(*She knocks it away and rises; he tries to block this, but the inner sense of futility makes it a half-hearted effort*) Where's my handbag! Get out of my way, Sidney. Come on, who needs this world the way it is! (*Pulling free with a mighty jerk*) Let go! (*She gets the bag and downs the pills, calming long before the effect, simply because she knows that they are inside*) You see, no fuss, no muss . . . Drugs are the coming thing, Sid. Do you keep up with all the writings on mescalin and all? I find it fascinating . . . (*She lies down on the sofa. Her reversion is progressive; she is pushing hard for it; not letting the pills do it. Now she is drinking also*) Ha—you want to hear something! I was going to marry that vanilla dinge! Do you know what some of the other girls do—they go off and they sleep with a colored boy—and I mean *any* colored boy so long as he is black—because they figure that is the one bastard who can't look down on them five seconds after it's over! And I was going to *marry* one!

SIDNEY  (*Crossing to* GLORIA) Maybe he'll change his mind. He was sort of in a state of shock about it. I mean, try to understand, it's very complicated about Alton—

GLORIA  Oh, so *he's* in a state of shock! Oh Jesus, that yellow-faced bastard! *He's* shocked. Look, Sid, I'll bet you two to one that at this instant he is lying dead drunk in the arms of the blondest or blackest two-bit hooker in town. *Nursing* his shock! Telling his tale of woe! *His* tale! She'll be telling it somewhere by morning to the girls and roaring with laughter . . . Like I'm doing. Aw, what the hell am I carrying on for—it wouldn't have worked. And besides, the life beats the hell out of that nine-to-five jazz. (*Suddenly a violent sob*) Sidney! *What happened to my life!* (*He tries to go to her; she holds out a hand to stay him*) I'll be twenty-six this winter and I have tried to kill myself three times since I was twenty-three . . . I was always awkward . . . But I'll make it. Or maybe a looney trick will be thorough some night. (*Sitting up*) Well . . . that's enough gloom and doom, everybody! Come on, Sidney brother, cheer up. (*She rumples his hair, nuzzles playfully in a desperate effort at gaiety and release*) After all, how many things could a nice normal healthy American girl kick all at one time—the racket and the pills? And take on integration, too? Tch! Tch! (*Weaving toward the phonograph*) Let's have some music. And none of that creepy stuff my creepy father used to play. (*She puts on a record—some very modern jazz; it throbs low and warm and intense*) Yeah . . . that's good. I have to have music . . . it helps to close things out. It envelops you. (*She beckons and* SIDNEY *moves into her arms; they begin to dance in a tight embrace, he in a bemused and delicious half-stupor; she as if, in the mere physical body contact, she were clinging to life. Now the denaturalization of these moments begins to heighten as per their state. A light, deathly blue, of great transparency, settles slowly and as imperceptibly as possible; it gives way to a hot and sensual fuchsia. The music follows suit—the more familiar jazz sounds going even beyond their own defini-*

*tions. When each speaks it is stiffly and unnaturally, in-toned with a heightened, fragmented delivery beyond sense or sequence, as if lucidity no longer required logic. An absurdist orgy is being created in front of us—a dis-integration of reality to parallel the disintegration in* SIDNEY's *world.*)

GLORIA (*As in a trance*)    Things as they are are as they are and have been and will be that way because they got that way because things were as they were in the first place.

(DAVID *re-enters and slowly descends the stairs, glancing behind him several times. He stops half-way down to light a cigarette and stands—in sil-houette—thoughtfully smoking, while the dialogue continues*)

SIDNEY    "Society is based on complicity in the common crime . . ." (DAVID *continues down and stands just in-side the door, watching* GLORIA *and* SIDNEY *as the sensual heat mounts between them*) ". . . We all suffer from the murder of the primal father who kept all the females for himself and drove the sons away. So we murdered him and, cannibals that we are, ate him."

DAVID    Sidney, you've finally joined the human race! Wel-come to the club.

SIDNEY (*To* DAVID)    We are all guilty.

DAVID (*Approaching them*)    Therefore all guilt is equal.

GLORIA    Therefore none are innocent.

SIDNEY, DAVID and GLORIA (*Together*)    Therefore—

SIDNEY (*Inspired*)    None are guilty. (*He breaks from* GLORIA. *Facing audience, assumes his own parodied ver-sion of classic Hindu dance pose: standing on one foot, knee bent, the other up at right angles, toes turned out;*

*one hand to chest in lotus position, the other at top of head, fingers pointing to sky; head moving from side to side. Deadpan*)  Any two of anything is totalitarian.

(*The beat picks up, he turns back and the three dance their own versions of the Frug, Watusi, Twist, etc.* GLORIA *weaves from one to the other, but they do not dance* together: *they face each other, but each is locked in the vacant isolation of a separate world, from which he speaks*)

GLORIA  It is right and natural for the individual to be primarily concerned with himself.

DAVID  He must be dedicated to his own interests.

SIDNEY  There is a revolution in this idea.

SIDNEY, DAVID, GLORIA (*Together*)  Therefore—

SIDNEY  I shall make myself a magazine and build it like a brothel. The bricks will be old-fashioned: lovely bodies made dirty by the way I present them.

DAVID  But the mortar will be new: made of Great Names.

SIDNEY  So I will offer Rosemarie and Maryanne simply doing the splits—

DAVID  But leavened with Socrates on Punishment and William L. Shirer on the Blitz.

GLORIA  Oh, you'll show the boys Lucy Jones upside down—

SIDNEY  But only when she's back to back with a treatise on the excavation of an Etruscan town!

DAVID  It'll be a hell of a clever switch—

SIDNEY  But I'll prove I'm right—by growing rich!

SIDNEY, DAVID, GLORIA (*They sing in unison*)
"Ohhhhhhhhh—
This is the way the cheese will rot!

The cheese will rot! The cheese will rot!
Oh this is the way the cheese will rot!
All on a Sunday morning!
(SIDNEY *moves away to lie down on the couch as*
DAVID *melts into* GLORIA's *beckoning arms and they*
*dance as did she and* SIDNEY *earlier*)

GLORIA    Whaddaya do if your own father calls you a tramp
. . . on his deathbed . . . huh? Whaddaya do?

SIDNEY (*On his back, rousing, with a flourish*)    You only
*think* that flowers are fragrant. 'Tis an illusion!

DAVID    Trying to live with your father's values can kill you.
Ask me, I know.

GLORIA    No, Sweetie, living *without* your father's values
can kill you. Ask *me, I* know.

SIDNEY (*Sits up, cross-legged, Zen Buddhist fashion. Pan-*
*tomimes*)    Take a needle thus (*from lapel. Large ges-*
*ture*), peer through the eye. As much as you can see
will be a part of the world. But it will be a true part, will
it not? Therefore, set down what you have seen and call
it the truth; if anyone argues with you, explain to the
fool that it is harder to look *through* a needle than to
look around one. (*He flops back*)

DAVID    Any profession of concern with decency is the most
indecent of all human affectations.

SIDNEY (*Sits bolt upright. Declaiming*)    To be or not
to be! (*A great pause, he sears us with his eyes—and*
*falls back*)    Well, better leave *that* one alone!

SIDNEY, GLORIA and DAVID (*Singing in disjointed unison*)
"Oh, who's afraid of Absurdity! Absurdity! Ab-
surdity!
Who's afraid of Absurdity!

Not we, not we, not we!"
(*As* SIDNEY *dozes off on the sofa,* GLORIA *stops* DAVID *with a long wet kiss, then steps back.* DAVID *is a little shaken. The music comes to an abrupt halt.*)

GLORIA   Where's the music . . . ? What happened to the music?

DAVID   Don't let's stop! . . . It was mah-velous. We were so completely outside of ourselves.

GLORIA   (*Crossing to the phonograph as the surreal fuchsia light fades back to white moonlight. Drinking*)   Sure, baby, a drunk, a hophead and a sick little boy could conjure up the Last Supper if they wanted. (*She turns it on and crosses to the bar. Sits and drinks. The music throbs softly*)

DAVID   (*Following her. As much disengaged from her as she is from him. With wistful melancholy*)   No, listen. All your life you want certain things and when you try to trace them back with the finger of your mind to where you believe you first started to want them, there is nothing but a haze . . . I was seven. So was Nelson. We were both exactly seven. We used to make a great deal out of that. We used to play all day in my yard. He had fine golden hair and a thin delicate profile—(*He traces her mouth with the fingers of one hand, touches her hair*) and Mother always said: "Nelson is a real aristocrat." Then, just like that, one summer his family moved to Florence, Italy. Because that is the sort of thing that aristocrats do when they feel like it. And I never saw him again.

GLORIA   (*Nodding up and down drunkenly*)   And you've been looking for him ever since.

DAVID   He never came back.

GLORIA   And now . . .

DAVID   There is a beautiful burnished golden boy very much like Nelson sitting on a chair upstairs. He is from one of the oldest, finest families in New England. He is exquisite. But great damage has been done to him—

GLORIA   (*For this girl there are no surprises left*)   He requires . . . the presence of a woman . . . Not just any girl, but someone young enough, fresh enough, in certain light, to make him think it is somebody of his own class—

DAVID   Yes. But—there is nothing to do. Apparently—it is merely a matter of—watching.

GLORIA   (*Raising her eyes pathetically*)   And you're a friend of Sidney's . . .

DAVID   It's not for me. Perhaps you can understand: If he asked for the snows of the Himalayas tonight, I would try to get it for him. I thought—you might know of such things.

GLORIA   (*Agonized*)   Oh . . . I know of such things!

DAVID   Will you come up—?

GLORIA   (*A beat. Not really to him*)   Sure . . . why not?

DAVID   It's apartment three-F.
(*He goes out and up.* GLORIA *stands for a long moment, looking after him, then crosses quickly to the phonograph, which she turns up louder, as if to drown out some voice that speaks only to her, till the persistent lonely chaos of the music fills the room. She tries to dance a little, that doesn't work; she downs more goofball pills with liquor. Then, snapping her fingers and undulating a little to the*

*rhythms in the room, with a fixed smile, she goes out. But as she mounts the third step, she freezes in the grip of a physical revulsion she can no longer contain—then suddenly whirls*)

GLORIA (*Her words are a single guttural cry of pain*)  Sick people belong in hospitals!!! (*For a long moment her eyes dart frantically and she whimpers, trapped, seeking refuge. There is none. At last she looks at the bottle of pills in her hand, walks slowly back and stands, spent, in the doorway. Then, resolutely:*) Papa—I am better than this! Now will you forgive me—?

(*She crosses to the bathroom, clutching the bottle, halts, terrified at the unseen presence there, turns away; but then, with a final lift of her head, she enters and closes the door. The phone begins to ring as the lights slowly dim.* SIDNEY *sleeps on*)

*Dimout*

## Scene Two

*Time: Early the next morning.*

*At rise: There is now a stark, businesslike and cold atmosphere in the apartment, as opposed to the tone of the last scene. It is just after dawn; in the course of this scene the blue-gray of the hour slowly lifts, until, at the end, the sun breaks full. A* DETECTIVE, *with pad, routinely questions* IRIS, *who sits in the rocker facing front; slumped, in her coat, hands in pockets, eyes red and staring off at nothing in particular. For its part, the sign seems more naked now, more assertive, more dominating and, for all of its unnoticed presence, necessary. The bathroom door stands ajar.*

DETECTIVE   Age of the deceased?

IRIS   Twenty-six.

DETECTIVE   Your relationship?

IRIS   My sister.

DETECTIVE   Occupation? (SIDNEY *enters, in his coat, stands in the door for a moment, as if the mere fact of the apartment oppresses him.* IRIS *says nothing. The* DETECTIVE *coughs, tries again, anxious to get it over)* Occupation of the deceased?

SIDNEY   Like, she was a member of the chorus.

DETECTIVE   Chorus girl—
        (*He starts to write that;* IRIS *looks up but says nothing*)

SIDNEY   No—no, she was a model.

334

DETECTIVE (*Putting his book away*)  All right. You know there's gonna be an inquest.

> (IRIS *offers no response.* SIDNEY *finally nods. The* DETECTIVE *exits*)

SIDNEY  I got them a cab. When they got home, Fred said, he'd call the doctor and have Mavis sedated. (*Paces agitatedly. Halting and looking at her*) You should let it come, honey . . . Cry. It's worse if you do what you're doing . . . (*He spots* GLORIA's *headband on the floor, where she had dropped it; he picks it up, stands looking at the bathroom, then turns away—with a face contorted —to face his wife. A long beat. Then helplessly*) You want a cup of tea or something? (IRIS *gives a quick, tight, little shake of her head "no."* WALLY *appears at the door, knocks, though it is ajar. He comes in, hat in hand, face cut with concern.* SIDNEY *just looks at him. A beat. Then grandly*) I see, Wally: the drama has come of age! The deus ex machina no longer comes floating in with its heavenly resolution—or dissolution—it merely comes walking through the door—*like a man.*

WALLY (*To* IRIS)  I heard about—your sister. (*Awkwardly, sincerely*) There's never anything to say, is there? But if there's anything I can do. (IRIS *does not respond in any way. To* SIDNEY *softly*) She's in bad shape, Sidney. Why don't you call a doctor?

SIDNEY (*With an effort at restraint*)  What do you want here, Wally?

WALLY  I know, Sidney, you think I'm the prince of all the bastards—

SIDNEY  No, as a matter of fact, it's been my opinion for some time now that the merely ambitious have enjoyed too much stature through the centuries: I think you're a rather rank-and-file bastard.

WALLY (*With a half smile*)   It feels good, doesn't it, Sid? It must feel good: to be able to judge! One good betrayal vindicates all our own crimes, doesn't it? Well, I'm going to tell you something I learned a long time ago—

SIDNEY (*Swiftly, angrily, as if by rote*)   "If you want to survive you've got to swing the way the world swings!"

WALLY   It's true. You either negotiate or get out of the race. Face up, Sid—or is that too hard for you?—that I'm the same man I was a year ago. Two months ago. Last week. And I still believe I am making my contribution to changing things—but I happen to know that in order to get anything done, anything at all in this world, baby, you've got to know where the power is. That's the way it's always been and that's the way it always will be.

SIDNEY   How do you know?

WALLY (*As if there is no end to the innocence in this house*)   Baby—I am *of* this world; it's something you know.

SIDNEY (*Fingering* GLORIA's *purse; a private irony*)   And besides—(*Softly*) "all the *real* prostitutes are everybody else."

WALLY (*Ready for him*)   Name calling is the last refuge of ineffectuals. You rage and I function. Study that sometimes, Sid. (*Crossing to the window*) Look, you know that stop sign that the housewives have been trying to get at Macklin and Warren Streets? With the baby-carriage demonstrations and the petitions and all? Well, they'll get their stop sign now. *I'll* get it for them. But not as some wide-eyed reformer. And better garbage collection and the new playground and a lot of other things too.

SIDNEY (*Half smile*) And the narcotic traffic? What about that?

WALLY (*A quick hand-waving*) That's more complicated. There's more involved. You don't go jumping into things.

SIDNEY (*Instinctively, swiftly*) I see: We can go on stepping over the bodies of the junkies—but the trains will run on time!
> (*He clicks his heels and throws off the Fascist salute smartly*)

WALLY (*Throwing his head back, just a little*) As a matter of fact, I knew it would be like this. That you would be standing there with that exact expression on your face, smoking a cigarette . . . filled with all the simple self-righteousness of bleeding innocence again betrayed. Well, I've only got this to say about it, Sid—

SIDNEY (*Suddenly, without warning—the confrontation. The real one*) They're after my paper now, aren't they, Wally?

WALLY (*Thrown; he would have preferred this on his own ground*) You don't understand. They don't want anything . . . Look, I told them not to expect to buy you, Sid. (*The latter smiles and nods his head throughout*) I've made them understand that . . . Nothing changes. You go on exactly as before, that's all.

SIDNEY Ah! I see: you mean covering the art shows, doing charming little photographic essays of the snow on our quaint little streets.

WALLY Yes!

SIDNEY And leave the world—to you?

WALLY I didn't do you in, Sid. You did yourself in and there ought to be a lesson in it for you: stay up in the mountains with your banjos and your books where you belong.

SIDNEY    But should I persist?

WALLY    Sidney, I am talking to you as a friend . . .

SIDNEY    *Should I persist?*

WALLY    (*Had not wanted to say it like this*)    Then the paper won't last six months.

SIDNEY    (*With wonder—genuine wonder*)    Wally, don't you know what kind of a house you've walked into? Didn't it hit you in the face? Didn't death breathe on you as you came through the door? What's the matter with you, man? While I lay stoned on that couch, a girl who tried to accept everything that you stand for died in that bathroom today. Do you think I haven't learned anything in the last few hours? The slogans of capitulation can *kill!* Every time we say "live and let live"—death triumphs!

WALLY    Sidney, what is it that you're trying to say?

SIDNEY    That I am going to fight you, Wally. That you have forced me to take a position. Finally—the one thing I never wanted to do. Just not being *for* you is not enough. Since that girl died—(*To* IRIS) I'm sorry, honey, but I have to—since that girl died—I have been forced to learn I have to be *against* you. And, Wally, I'm against you—I swear it to you—and your machine. And what you have to worry about is the fact that some of us will be back out in those streets today. Only this time— thanks to you—we shall be more seasoned, more cynical, tougher, harder to fool—and therefore, less likely to quit.

WALLY    (*The genuine passion of the compromised*)    Sidney, you reek of innocence!

IRIS (*Suddenly, turning*)  The question is, Wally, what is it *you* reek of?

SIDNEY (*To* WALLY, *but the words are intended for* IRIS) I'll tell you what he reeks of: He reeks of accommodation. He reeks of collusion. He reeks of collaboration— with Power and the tools of Power . . . (*To* WALLY) Don't you understand, man? Too much has happened to me! I love my wife—I want her back. I loved my sister-in-law. I want to see her alive. I—I love you—I should like to see you redeemed. But in the context in which we presently stand here I doubt any of this is possible. That which warped and distorted all of us is— (*Suddenly lifting his hands as if this were literally true*) all around; it is in this very air! *This world*—this swirling, seething madness—which you ask us to accept, to help maintain—has done this . . . maimed my friends . . . emptied these rooms and my very bed. And now it has taken my sister. *This* world! Therefore, to live, to breathe —I shall *have* to fight it!

WALLY (*Picking up his hat—shaking his head*)  That's asking for it, Sidney . . .

SIDNEY  Then that should be the first thing I tell my readers—while I still can.

WALLY (*Gesturing incredulously to* IRIS, *as if to an ally*) Am I really supposed to believe this—? (IRIS *slowly nods "yes"—then shrugs with innocence: What can she do with* SIDNEY? WALLY *turns back with genuine wonder*) You really are a fool.

SIDNEY  Always have been. (*His eyes find his wife's*) A fool who believes that death is waste and love is sweet and that the earth turns and men change every day and that rivers run and that people wanna be better than they are and that flowers smell good and that I hurt terribly

today, and that hurt is desperation and desperation is——
—energy and energy can *move* things . . .

WALLY (*Looking from one to the other; pronounced exasperation with "children"*)   Let me know the time
and place of the funeral, won't you? I'd like to send
flowers.

> (*He starts out, adjusts his hat, notes the sign, gazes
> at them and then wanders off.* IRIS *rises*)

IRIS   For a long time now I've been wanting something.
For a long time. I think it was for you to be all of yourself. I want to come home, Sidney. I want to come home
but . . .

SIDNEY   We'll talk about it.

> (*With a supreme mustering of will, and her whole
> body, she pushes shut the bathroom door, as if on
> the Past—and yet for a moment longer stands trans-
> fixed by it—then turns and crosses to* SIDNEY *on
> the couch*)

IRIS (*Holding her hands before her and turning them
slowly*)   When she was little . . . she had fat, pudgy
hands . . . and I used to have to scrub them . . . because
she couldn't get them clean. And so I would pretend that
they were fish and I was the Fish Lady cleaning these
little fish to sell them . . . That always tickled her so, and
she would laugh and laugh and . . .

> (*She gags on the first great sob, he folds her into
> his arms and, in the desperateness of this contact
> without words, the tears come freely now*)

SIDNEY   Yes . . . weep now, darling, weep. Let us both
weep. That is the first thing: to let ourselves feel again
. . . Then, tomorrow, we shall make something strong
of this sorrow . . . (*They sit spent, almost physically
drained and motionless . . . as the clear light of morning
gradually fills the room*)

*Curtain*

# About the Contributors

ROBERT NEMIROFF, Lorraine Hansberry's literary executor, shared a working relationship with the playwright from the time of their marriage in 1953. Originally an editor, music publisher, and award–winning songwriter, he produced Ms. Hansberry's second play, *The Sign in Sidney Brustein's Window*. Mr. Nemiroff's own play, *Postmark Zero*, was presented on Broadway in 1965, in London, and on national television. Since then his adaptations of Ms. Hansberry's works, *To Be Young, Gifted and Black* and *Les Blancs*, have been hailed by both the critics and the public. In 1974 he won the Tony Award ("Best Musical of the Year") for *Raisin* (based on Ms. Hansberry's play), which he produced and coauthored.

FRANK RICH is a former principal drama critic of *The New York Times*. Currently, he is a *Times* editorial columnist.

AMIRI BARAKA (LeRoi Jones) is a poet, activist, and teacher. Among his published works are *Preface to a Twenty-Volume Suicide Note, Blues People, Dutchman and the Slave, The Dead Lecturer, The System of Dante's Hell, The Baptism and The Toilet, Black Art, Black Music*, and *Arm Yourself or Harm Youself*. Among his recent publications are *Eulogies*, a book of eulogies he has given over the last twenty years; *Why's/Wise*, poetry; and *Jesse Jackson and Black People*, a book of essays about Jackson and the Afro-American Peoples struggle for democracy and self-determination. He is co-director, with his wife, Amina Baraka, of Kimako's Blues People, the art space of the couple in Newark. In 1993, when named Newark Artist-in-Residence, he presented two new works, *Meeting Lillie*, a one act play, and *Black History Music*, a history of black music and black people in poetry and music with Blue Ark, his performance group. In 1993, the University of Connecticut presented him with the Wallace Stevens Prize for Poetry and the North Carolina Black Drama Festival with "The Living Legend Award."

JEWELL HANDY GRESHAM NEMIROFF was married to Robert Nemiroff from 1967 to his death in 1991. She is a former English professor, now social and literary critic and writer.